Essay Strategies for Canadian Students

Reading

Writing

Second Edition

Essay Strategies for Canadian Students

Reading *Writing*

Second Edition

Geri Dasgupta
Centennial College

Jon Redfern
Centennial College

I(T)P Nelson

an International Thomson Publishing company

Toronto • Albany • Bonn • Boston • Cincinnati • Detroit • London • Madrid • Melbourne
Mexico City • New York • Pacific Grove • Paris • San Francisco • Singapore • Tokyo • Washington

I(T)P® International Thomson Publishing
The ITP logo is a trademark under licence
www.thomson.com

Published in 1998 by
I(T)P® Nelson

A division of Thomson Canada Limited
1120 Birchmount Road
Scarborough, Ontario M1K 5G4
www.nelson.com

Canadian Cataloguing in Publication Data
Dasgupta, Geri, 1949–
    Reading Writing

2nd ed.
Includes index.
ISBN 0-17-607331-0

1. Essay – Authorship. 2. English language – Rhetoric.
3. Readers – Essays. I. Redfern, Jon, 1946– II. Title.

PEI408.D234 1998   808.84   C97–932053-4

Publisher and Team Leader	Michael Young
Acquisitions Editor	Nicole Gnutzman
Project Editor	Jenny Anttila
Production Editor	Jim Gifford
Production Coordinator	Brad Horning
Art Director	Sylvia Vander Schee
Cover Design	Kevin Connolly
Senior Composition Analyst	Alicja Jamorski

Printed and bound in Canada

1 2 3 4 (WC) 01 00 99 98

Contents

Unit Four

Unit Five

Unit Six

Reading and Writing from Sources: The Research Paper **183**

Appendix A

Reading Your Writing **215**

Appendix B

Short Stories **231**

Alternate Contents: Readings by Theme

Cultural Issues

Historical Perspectives

Language and Learning

Personal Relationships

Self-Awareness

Social and Political Contexts

Preface

The book begins by concentrating on reading skills—skimming, scanning, reading from context—and their use in constructing writing strategies. When we chose rhetorical models, we divided them into two categories: informative and affective discourse. We admit that such a division can be interpreted as an arbitrary distinction, because informative writing ultimately attempts to affect readers whereas affective writing seeks to educate. In addition, descriptive and narrative prose (as separate from fiction) is often a component or subcategory of other rhetorical modes, and argument and persuasion subsume all other rhetorical modes. For these reasons, we separated narration, description, and argumentation/persuasion from the more clearly delineated expository patterns of organization, such as classification and cause and effect, found in Unit Four. For the second edition, we have added a component on writing an essay on a piece of literature. Additional short stories are also included in Appendix B.

Unit Six, on the research paper, shows how composing the research essay uses reading *for* writing. Our reading selections were based on three criteria: brevity, depth, and student interest; all selections have been used in classroom teaching.

Appendix A offers an editorial checklist for essays. For this edition, it has been expanded to teach the essentials of grammar and should be used along with the suggestions for revisions of essay writing found in Unit Three. The additional readings (Appendices B and C) have no follow-up exercises, leaving teachers and students free to utilize them as they wish. We have often included these readings as parts of unit studies or as subjects for seminar discussions and oral reports. Terms that appear in bold in the index are explained further where they first appear in the text.

Acknowledgments

We wish to thank all of our students for their inspiration. We'd also like to acknowledge the patience and generosity of our teaching colleagues, in particular Diane Fagel, Robin Potter, Carole Short, Wendy Struthers, David O'Rourke, Gary Lipschutz, and Tom Hartley. Special thanks to Jack David for guidance and excellent advice. We are grateful also for the comments and suggestions on the first edition that were provided by several of our peers: Cynthia Brouse, George Brown College; Harriet Duer, Dawson College; John F. Green, Durham College; John Lucas, Dawson College; Roger Mann, Mohawk College; Elaine R. Mullen, Mount Royal College; Karen Pancer, Humber College; and Pat Rogin, Durham College. For this edition, we thank Kim Dugan, Fanshawe College; Renate Scheelar, Red Deer College; and Rita Terron, Fanshawe College. Finally, we would like to thank ITP Nelson, especially Nicole Gnutzman, Jenny Anttila, and Jim Gifford, for their efforts.

Reading the Writing:

Skimming, Scanning, Reading from Context, Active Reading

> *"I do not understand; I pause; I examine."* (Montaigne)

Canadian and American: Is There a Difference?

Mayra Perea

Introductory paragraph: A comparison of U.S.A. & Canada introduced.

1 Back in my country, people would refer to Canadians as Americans. I always thought that was wrong. "But they are all the same," people would say, even when I pointed out they were mistaken. Having lived in both Canada and the U.S., I felt there were differences, even though at first glance the two countries seemed very much alike. Had I known, as I do now, the results of *Maclean's* "Decima Two-Nations Poll," I would have been able to argue with something objective and not just a feeling. <u>The poll showed there are fundamental differences in how Canadians and Americans view and react to a broad range of topics, such as the environment, the economy, and social issues.</u>

Thesis statement: limited <u>subject</u> + key ideas:
1) Environment
2) Economy
3) Social issues

Topic sentence for key idea #1.

2 <u>For Canadians, the most important problem is the environment</u>. The Americans rank it much lower as an issue of concern. Canadians have confidence in the air and water quality of their country and are willing to sacrifice personal comfort and convenience to benefit all citizens. The *Maclean's* poll shows, for example, that fifty percent of Canadians feel that driving an automobile should, and can be, restricted further to reduce congestion, as opposed to only thirty-four percent of Americans willing to do the same. The poll also indicates that Canadians would prefer to shut down a major company that pollutes, regardless of the loss of jobs, while the Americans would be less inclined to do so. In general the poll shows that in comparison to Canadians, the Americans put materialistic considerations first, favouring the economy over the environment.

1st body paragraph with supporting details that explain the topic sentence.

Supporting, details for Key idea # 1.

Good transition to next key idea.

3 Economically, the U.S. is a world leader that doesn't depend on international trade as much as Canada does, which means that Americans have a

Supporting details for key idea #2.

Topic sentence for key idea #2. Notice that you can place this sentence mid-paragraph.

Topic sentence for key idea #3.

A good transition from one key idea to the next is achieved by comparing the two major sources of anxiety.

This key idea is divided into two paragraphs because the writer has more supporting details to emphasize her point.

Summary of discussion.

Restatement of thesis.

Personal views.

relatively stable economic base. In spite of its status as the world's largest debtor nation, the U.S. feels secure. When global inflation rises, the <u>Americans tend to be less preoccupied by their economic situation than Canadians are</u>. Although the U.S. is not immune to economic hardships, Canada seems to suffer more anxiety over its economy caused in part by a combination of the current recession, the free trade agreement, the GST, and the ever-increasing national debt.

4   <u>American anxiety is most evident, as the poll shows, in areas where the U.S. is weakest and most troubled. The biggest of these concerns social issues.</u> Social services in America are notoriously underfunded, underdeveloped, and in need of improvement. By comparison, Canada is regarded as a model for social services, as seen in its superb medicare system. In the U.S., each state has its own version of a private medicare system that is often expensive, restrictive, and in some cases inadequate. Canada's medicare system, on the other hand, is a national government policy offering free and uniformly efficient access to basic health care.

5   As social problems in the U.S. grow and seem to be untreatable, fear of the future in that country mounts. One problem area of great concern is the increasing abuse of drugs and alcohol. This abuse affects all facets of American society, from the economy to politics, from life in big cities to life in small towns. The *Maclean's* poll clearly shows that such issues are very much on Americans' minds, and in fact rank number one as their most difficult problem. Canadians, in comparison, seem relatively untouched by the same anxiety although they are aware such social issues are a growing aspect of Canadian life.

6   It is evident, then, that Canadians are conscious of and value highly facets of society that are not as much appreciated by Americans. Conversely, Americans worry about things Canadians view as less important. Americans and Canadians may look alike, sometimes talk alike, and even share the same continent, but they see the world through very different eyes. <u>The environment, the economy and social issues are just three indications of how they are not the same.</u> The *Maclean's* poll reaffirms what I've felt for a long time: Canadians and Americans are truly different.

RESPONDING TO THE READING

Mayra Perea, a student at Centennial College, wrote the above essay in her first-year English course. The poll referred to in her essay was first published in the Canadian magazine *Maclean's*.

"Canadian and American: Is There a Difference?" is an example of a comparison-and-contrast essay. Based on your reading of the essay and the comments in its margins, write a definition of each of the following:

1. an introductory paragraph
2. a thesis statement
3. a topic sentence

4. a body paragraph
5. a transition
6. a supporting detail

Knowing these terms can help you as a reader to understand how information in an essay may be organized. Mayra Perea used reasons and examples to present her observations on Canada and the United States. Reasons explain why an idea is true, while examples illustrate an idea with specific details. Mayra also compared and contrasted her subjects by pointing out how they were alike and how they were different. Other patterns of information that writers use can include classification or process analysis—formats that will be covered later on in this textbook.

Good writing depends on careful reading. One of the best ways to learn how to write effective essays like Mayra Perea's is to read what other writers have written. Careful reading helps you develop vocabulary, introduces you to sentence style, and makes formats such as comparison and contrast familiar. There are *kinds* of reading, each with its own useful purpose: skimming, scanning, reading from context, and active reading.

Skimming

Skimming means reading a text rapidly in order to get a general understanding of its content. It can be used to introduce yourself to the style of a piece of writing, to its format and its key ideas. Skimming is also very useful as a technique for reviewing familiar material.

Skimming begins with reading the title of a piece of writing (such as the title of Mayra Perea's essay or that of a textbook chapter). A title gives a general idea of a piece's content or states one important aspect of the author's point of view. In Mayra Perea's case the title poses a question that the essay answers. Once you've read the title, run your eyes quickly over the paragraphs in order to find any sub-titles or headings (these are printed like titles, above the text) that may further indicate the scope of a piece's content. Following this read-through, the next step to skimming entails a deliberately slower reading of all the sentences in both the introductory and concluding paragraphs. By reading only those specific paragraphs, you can locate the **thesis statement**, if there is one (some essays imply rather than state a thesis), and get a summary of important ideas and supporting facts that are frequently gathered in a final paragraph.

Finally, to complete your skimming, read the **topic sentences** of each of the **body paragraphs** as they state the key ideas. Skimming should be a fast process, a speedy reading or "overview" reading of content, for you want only a glance at the more obvious features of a piece of writing, a partial understanding of the shape and extent of its content.

Skim the following essay. It is written by the American writer Kurt Vonnegut, the author of such novels as *Slaughterhouse-Five, Jailbird,* and *Cat's Cradle.*

How to Write with Style

Kurt Vonnegut

1   Newspaper reporters and technical writers are trained to reveal almost nothing about themselves in their writings. This makes them freaks in the world of writers, since almost all of the other ink-stained wretches in that world reveal a lot about themselves to readers. We call these revelations, accidental and intentional, elements of style.

2   These revelations tell us as readers what sort of person it is with whom we are spending time. Does the writer sound ignorant or informed, stupid or bright, crooked or honest, humorless or playful—? And on and on.

3   Why should you examine your writing style with the idea of improving it? Do so as a mark of respect for your readers, whatever you're writing. If you scribble your thoughts any which way, your readers will surely feel that you care nothing about them. They will mark you down as an egomaniac or a chowderhead—or, worse, they will stop reading you.

4   The most damning revelation you can make about yourself is that you do not know what is interesting and what is not. Don't you yourself like or dislike writers mainly for what they choose to show you or make you think about? Did you ever admire an empty-headed writer for his or her mastery of the language? No.

5   So your own winning style must begin with ideas in your head.

1. Find a Subject You Care About

6   Find a subject you care about and which you in your heart feel others should care about. It is this genuine caring, and not your games with language, which will be the most compelling and seductive element in your style.

7   I am not urging you to write a novel, by the way—although I would not be sorry if you wrote one, provided you genuinely cared about something. A petition to the mayor about a pothole in front of your house or a love letter to the girl next door will do.

2. Do Not Ramble, Though

8   I won't ramble on about that.

3. Keep It Simple

9   As for your use of language: Remember that two great masters of language, William Shakespeare and James Joyce, wrote sentences which were almost child-like when their subjects were most profound. "To be or not to be?" asks Shakespeare's Hamlet. The longest word is three letters long. Joyce, when he was frisky, could put together a sentence as intricate and as glittering as a necklace for Cleopatra, but my favorite sentence in his short story "Eveline" is this one: "She was tired." At that point in the story, no other words could break the heart of a reader as those three words do.

10   Simplicity of language is not only reputable, but perhaps even sacred. The Bible opens with a sentence well within the writing skills of a lively fourteen-year-old: "In the beginning God created the heaven and the earth."

4. Have the Guts to Cut

11   It may be that you, too, are capable of making necklaces for Cleopatra, so to speak. But your eloquence should be the servant of the ideas in your head. Your rule might be this: If a sentence, no matter how excellent, does not illuminate your subject in some new and useful way, scratch it out.

5. Sound Like Yourself

12   The writing style which is most natural for you is bound to echo the speech you heard when a child. English was the novelist Joseph Conrad's third language, and much that seems piquant in his use of English was no doubt colored by his first language, which was Polish. And lucky indeed is the writer who has grown up in Ireland, for the English spoken there is so amusing and musical. I myself grew up in Indianapolis, where common speech sounds like a band saw cutting galvanized tin, and employs a vocabulary as unornamental as a monkey wrench.

13   In some of the more remote hollows of Appalachia, children still grow up hearing songs and locutions of Elizabethan times. Yes, and many Americans grow up hearing a language other than English, or an English dialect a majority of Americans cannot understand.

14   All these varieties of speech are beautiful, just as the varieties of butterflies are beautiful. No matter what your first language, you should treasure it all your life. If it happens not to be standard English, and if it shows itself when you write standard English, the result is usually delightful, like a very pretty girl with one eye that is green and one that is blue.

15   I myself find that I trust my own writing most, and others seem to trust it most, too, when I sound most like a person from Indianapolis, which is what I am. What alternatives do I have? The one most vehemently recommended by teachers has no doubt been pressed on you, as well: to write like cultivated Englishmen of a century or more ago.

6. Say What You Mean to Say

16   I used to be exasperated by such teachers, but am no more. I understand now that all those antique essays and stories with which I was to compare my own work were not magnificent for their datedness or foreignness, but for saying precisely what their authors meant them to say. My teachers wished me to write accurately, always selecting the most effective words, and relating the words to one another unambiguously, rigidly, like parts of a machine. The teachers did not want to turn me into an Englishman after all. They hoped that I would become understand-able—and therefore understood. And there went my dream of doing with words what Pablo Picasso did with paint or what any number of jazz idols did with music. If I broke all the rules of punctuation, had words mean whatever I wanted them to mean, and strung them together higgledy-piggledy, I would simply not be under-stood. So you, too, had better avoid Picasso-style or jazz-style writing, if you have something worth saying and wish to be understood.

17   Readers want our pages to look very much like pages they have seen before. Why? This is because they themselves have a tough job to do, and they need all the help they can get from us.

7. Pity the Readers

18 They have to identify thousands of little marks on paper, and make sense of them immediately. They have to *read,* an art so difficult that most people don't really master it even after having studied it all through grade school and high school—twelve long years.

19 So this discussion must finally acknowledge that our stylistic options as writers are neither numerous nor glamorous, since our readers are bound to be such imperfect artists. Our audience requires us to be sympathetic and patient teachers, ever willing to simplify and clarify—whereas we would rather soar high above the crowd, singing like nightingales.

20 That is the bad news. The good news is that we Americans are governed under a unique Constitution, which allows us to write whatever we please without fear of punishment. So the most meaningful aspect of our styles, which is what we choose to write about, is utterly unlimited.

8. For Really Detailed Advice

21 For a discussion of literary style in a narrower sense, in a more technical sense, I commend to your attention *The Elements of Style,* by William Strunk, Jr., and E.B. White (Macmillan, 1979). E.B. White is, of course, one of the most admirable literary stylists this country has so far produced.

22 You should realize, too, that no one would care how well or badly Mr. White expressed himself, if he did not have perfectly enchanting things to say.

RESPONDING TO THE READING

How much of Vonnegut's essay were you able to grasp by skimming? Test yourself by answering the following questions. Do not reread the essay before you start.

1. List the main pieces of advice on writing well that Vonnegut gives.
2. Why, according to Vonnegut, should we try to improve our writing style?
3. Write a sentence of your own (using your own words) stating what Vonnegut's essay is about.

Now, reread the essay. Go more slowly than when you were skimming. Notice how Vonnegut included numbered subheadings (e.g., 2. Do not ramble, though; 3. Keep it simple) and how they served as topic sentences for his body paragraphs. Notice, too, how he uses examples and definitions and how, like Mayra Perea, he states his personal views. You may also find names and references that will need some research (who was Cleopatra, for instance, or Picasso?). Looking up new words and references is more a function of close reading than of skimming.

Making skimming a regular part of your reading of *any* piece of writing will increase your reading efficiency and prepare you for the close reading or in-depth reading that careful readers must develop.

— should be communicating in writing

Scanning

Scanning, like skimming, is selective reading, but unlike skimming it is a much slower activity. It is a deliberate searching for a detail or fact, and its purpose is to locate a specified item of information. For instance, how do you use the telephone book? You do not sit down for an hour to study its names and numbers. Instead, like most people, you run your eyes over the columns on the pages to find one single name or number. Reading the telephone book is a form of scanning.

Scanning begins with the "something" you must locate. You know what you want, you just have to find it. As a reading skill, scanning is useful for finding a key fact or name while doing research or looking up a quick reference. It is also helpful in studying when you need to locate a formula in a textbook chapter or look up a specific name in an essay. To help make scanning a more efficient reading exercise, it is helpful to ask yourself how the material you are reading is organized. Are you searching through a list, like the telephone directory, or an essay, a report, a series of step-by-step instructions, a manual? Understanding the structure of a piece of information can save time in your search.

Reports, for instance, often list statistics in a separate section. If you were looking for a specified number or percentage, it would help you to know where the statistics are placed. Often the thesis statement in a long essay will define the sections of information to be discussed. Again, if you needed to locate a man's name or a description of an event, knowing how the essay is set up would help you to locate the data you are looking for faster.

To try your hand at scanning, go back to Kurt Vonnegut's essay in this chapter and locate the following:

1. James Joyce
2. With how many words does James Joyce "break the heart of the reader"?
3. When should a writer cut out a sentence in a piece of writing?
4. What should your attitude be toward your readers? Why?

Reading from Context

Reading from context is a third useful reading skill. When you were skimming Vonnegut's essay, did you notice a number of difficult words? Did you see any new words? You may have done so quite often, but like most readers you read on because you gained the general meaning of the content without actually knowing the exact definition of those particular words. Careful readers can guess or give a temporary meaning to new or difficult words as they read because the other words nearby supply enough information to make the ideas reasonably clear. In doing this, careful readers are *reading from context*.

In one way, reading from context is a kind of single-word skimming. You grasp a general meaning from a quick guess. Nevertheless, it is important that new words be properly defined. You will need to consult a dictionary. Once you have identified new or difficult words, you must go and look up their meaning. Here, reading from context can guide you as to which meaning in the dictionary is the correct one. Many words in English have more than one meaning. The author who has written the piece you are reading has chosen his words carefully, so you must be sure the context of his ideas helps you find the correct meaning of the word in the dictionary.

You will face a more difficult task in reading from context when you come across an **idiomatic expression.** Such groups of words cannot be read (or defined) literally—that is, just as they are written down on the page. Consequently, the meaning of an idiom must be understood from the context.

To test your ability to read from context, look at some of the idiomatic expressions Kurt Vonnegut uses. Once you have read over these expressions in the context of their sentences, try to explain the meaning of each in your own words.

1. If you scribble your thoughts *any which way*, your readers will surely feel that you care nothing about them.
2. They will *mark you down* as an egomaniac or a chowderhead—or, worse, they will stop reading you.
3. I won't *ramble on* about that.
4. At that point in the story, no other words could *break the heart* of a reader as those three words do.
5. *Have the guts* to cut.
6. It may be that you, too, are capable of making necklaces for Cleopatra, *so to speak.*
7. English was the novelist Joseph Conrad's third language, and much that seems piquant in his use of English was no doubt *colored by* his first language, which was Polish.
8. The one most vehemently recommended by teachers has no doubt *been pressed on you*, as well.
9. Our audience requires us to be sympathetic and patient teachers, ever willing to simplify and clarify—whereas we would rather *soar high above the crowd*, singing like nightingales.
10. A love letter to the girl next door *will do.*

In the following brief summary of the Vonnegut essay, write in the missing words. Do not use the same words the author wrote; instead, use **synonyms**—words that are different but convey the same meaning.

Kurt Vonnegut provides eight _____ to improve your writing style so that readers will not only _____ but also _____ you. First, find a _____ that you _____ but keep your discussion short. Make your language _____ and direct and be willing to _____ unnecessary words. Try to write so that you sound natural; however, you must follow the rules of _____ English to communicate effectively. A good writer is aware of the _____ readers often have. For more _____ advice, Vonnegut suggests consulting *The Elements of Style.*

Comprehension

Answer each question in your own words. According to Kurt Vonnegut:

1. How should you choose the subject you write about?
2. What kind of language should you use when you write?
3. What is the best way to say what you mean?
4. What approach to your readers should you take?
5. Why is it important to edit your work?

Analysis

1. Find some examples of Vonnegut's sense of humour. What is the effect of his humour on the reader?
2. Find some examples of references Vonnegut makes to other writers. In what ways are these references supposed to influence the reader?
3. Who is the intended reader of this essay? How can you tell?
4. In what ways does the order of Vonnegut's suggestions help a writer write more effectively? Could the order be changed? Why or why not?

Discussion

Did you notice how much a good writer like Vonnegut considers his readers? He presents his ideas with detailed examples, references, and definitions. As readers, we also learn about Vonnegut's approach to writing through his sense of humour, which both delights and instructs. Learning biographical information about Vonnegut would be another way of discovering how he, as a writer, thinks and reacts. Searching out background facts of this kind is an important facet of careful reading. Finding out about a writer through research helps readers understand not only a writer's bias but also his values and his way of looking at the world.

Does the fact that you know Vonnegut is a famous and respected novelist (both humour and science fiction) affect your attitude toward the advice he gives in his essay? His argument can stand alone since it is logical and well expressed, but are you more apt to believe him than you would an unknown professional? Famous people are often experts in their chosen fields. The reputation of such a person has a wide-reaching influence. When this essay first appeared, it was as an advertisement sponsored by a paper company that claimed in a sidebar to "believe in the power of the printed word." The ad was accompanied by Vonnegut's signature and by a number of whimsical photographs of the author. How might the presence of these visual elements affect the reader's impression of the text?

What I Have Lived For

Bertrand Russell

1   Three passions, simple but overwhelmingly strong, have governed my life: the longing for love, the search for knowledge, and unbearable pity for the suffering

of mankind. These passions, like great winds, have blown me hither and thither, in a wayward course, over a deep ocean of anguish, reaching to the very verge of despair.

2   I have sought love, first, because it brings ecstasy—ecstasy so great that I would often have sacrificed all the rest of life for a few hours of this joy. I have sought it, next, because it relieves loneliness—that terrible loneliness in which one shivering consciousness looks over the rim of the world into the cold unfathomable lifeless abyss. I have sought it, finally, because in the union of love I have seen, in a mystic miniature, the prefiguring vision of the heaven that saints and poets have imagined. This is what I sought, and though it might seem too good for human life, this is what—at last—I have found.

3   With equal passion I have sought knowledge. I have wished to understand the hearts of men. I have wished to know why the stars shine. And I have tried to apprehend the Pythagorean power by which number holds sway above the flux. A little of this, but not much, I have achieved.

4   Love and knowledge, so far as they were possible, led upward toward the heavens. But always pity brought me back to earth. Echoes of cries of pain reverberate in my heart. Children in famine, victims tortured by oppressors, helpless old people a hated burden to their sons, and the whole world of loneliness, poverty, and pain make a mockery of what human life should be. I long to alleviate the evil, but I cannot, and I too suffer.

5   This has been my life. I have found it worth living, and would gladly live it again if the chance were offered me.

RESPONDING TO THE READING

Simply looking up words in the dictionary cannot always convey the full meaning of language as poetic as that found in this essay by Bertrand Russell, an English philosopher and mathematician. The power of Russell's last sentence in paragraph one arises from his use of a **metaphor**, a literary device that compares one thing to another. Russell compares the force and motivation of his passions to the winds of an ocean blowing a ship. Like a ship, Russell was occasionally pushed to an extreme, an emotional edge: five hundred years ago on the Atlantic sailors believed that storms could push them and their boats off the edge of the known world.

Read over the following selection of quotations from Russell's essay and try to rephrase them in more ordinary language:

- "[O]ne shivering consciousness looks over the rim of the world into the cold unfathomable lifeless abyss."
- "Love and knowledge, so far as they were possible, led upward toward the heavens."
- "Echoes of cries of pain reverberate in my heart."

Russell's remarkable vocabulary astonishes most readers because his simple words are made to express deep feelings and complex ideas. He wrote the essay to address readers with a similar philosophical background, yet a person not familiar with his background could readily grasp his profound thoughts.

Read these quotations from Russell's essay and answer the questions that follow each.

1. "Three passions … have governed my life." What part of speech is *passion?* What is the adjective form of the word? Write a sentence using the adjective form.

2. One of Russell's governing passions is his "unbearable pity for the suffering of mankind." *Pity* here is used as a noun, but it can also be a verb and it has adjective forms. Write two sentences using *pity* as a verb and an adjective.

3. The author's passions have pushed him "to the very verge of despair." Use *despair* as a verb in a sentence.

4. "[L]ove … brings ecstasy." What is the adjective form of *ecstasy?* Is there a verb form for *ecstasy?*

5. Love gives Russell a consciousness of relationships. The verb form of *consciousness* is *to be conscious of.* Use this verb form in a sentence.

6. "[I]n the union of love I have seen, in mystic miniature, the prefiguring vision of the heaven that saints and poets have imagined." Write a sentence using the word *miniature* as an adjective.

7. Russell tried to apprehend mathematics, the power of numbers, spoken of by the philosopher Pythagoras. There is a noun form for *apprehend.* Write a sentence using it as a noun. There is also an adjective form. Use it in a sentence.

8. *Reverberate* is used as a verb by Russell. Change it to a noun form and write the noun in a sentence.

9. Pain makes a mockery of human life. Use the verb form of *mockery* in a sentence. What is the adjective form of *mockery?* What is a synonym for mockery?

10. "I long to alleviate the evil." Here, *alleviate* is a verb. Use the noun form in a sentence. What is a synonym of *alleviate?* Use it in a sentence.

11. Write in the missing words but do not use the same ones that are in the Russell essay. Instead, find synonyms.

Three _____ that have _____ Bertrand Russell are the _____ for love and _____ and the resulting _____ for all life. The desire for _____ brings him much _____ and gives him a sense of his own special place in the world. The _____ for _____ helps him _____ the physical universe and human beings. Finally, _____ allows him to care deeply for _____. His _____ to achieve this adds to his own suffering.

Discussion

What lifts Russell's writing above the average is the power and intensity of his imagery, some of which you studied in the vocabulary section of this chapter. Russell was an English philosopher who became famous for his writings on mathematics and physics in the first sixty years of the 20th century. In his later life, he devoted his time to world peace and often spoke at conferences and rallies for the elimination of nuclear weapons and the greater distribution of food to starving nations. His interest in both science and human affairs affected his writing style, for he wished to communicate with as many people as possible through a direct use of everyday language rather than through the heightened formal style more often favoured by scientists and academics. In fact, he became famous for his ability to relate complex ideas in a simple but eloquent manner. "What I Have Lived For" is a part of his autobiography, a book that influenced many people to take a more active part in world affairs.

Comprehension

1. What is the thesis statement of Russell's essay? Could you rewrite it using different words?
2. What reasons does Russell give for pity's bringing him back to earth?
3. Who was Pythagoras? Why is he important to Russell?
4. How does the concluding paragraph relate to Russell's thesis statement?
5. What three reasons does Russell give for seeking love?

Analysis

1. What does Russell mean by his title, "What I Have Lived For"?
2. For Russell, in what way is pity different from love and knowledge?
3. What do you think Russell means when he claims he was driven to the *verge of despair* by his passions?

Writing Suggestions

1. What has made your life worth living? Start by identifying the three most important things in your life and then, using reasons and examples, show readers in a paragraph why *one* of them is important.
2. Would you, like Russell, choose to live your life again? Why or why not? Explain your answer, using reasons and references to actual experiences in your life.
3. Compare your life as you have chosen to live it with the life of someone else you know well. How are you alike in your values, your passions, and your fears? Write this in the form of a letter to a best friend.
4. Discuss in what ways Russell's essay has influenced your thoughts about your own life. Write this either as a paragraph or as a letter to one of your parents. Be sure to keep in mind the expectations of your reader.

Active Reading

Active reading goes beyond skimming, scanning, and reading from context. A slower process based on rereading, it enables you to come to a deeper understanding of a text. As an active reader you notice how words and ideas are used and placed for effect; you become aware of the author's purpose, point-of-view, and audience. Active reading involves thinking about and questioning the information and ideas in the text.

When you worked through the Comprehension, Analysis, and Discussion sections following the articles by Kurt Vonnegut and Bertrand Russell, you were, in fact, engaged in active reading. For example, you had to think about Vonnegut's sense of humour and its effect on the reader. You were also asked to evaluate the order of his suggestions. To understand Russell more clearly, you had to explore his use of language and to think about the ways in which your life is significant to you.

Essentially, active reading is a process by which you draw conclusions by asking yourself *critical questions* about the text. Critical questions include distinguishing between fact and opinion, and considering how a writer supports his or her ideas through vocabulary and organization of details. Drawing conclusions is based on your responses to the critical questions.

Read the following passage from *Hard Times* by Charles Dickens and answer the critical questions that follow.

Murdering the Innocents

Charles Dickens

1 Thomas Gradgrind, sir. A man of realities. A man of facts and calculations. A man who proceeds upon principal that two and two are four, and nothing over, and who is not to be talked into allowing for anything over. Thomas Gradgrind, sir—peremptorily Thomas—Thomas Gradgrind. With a rule and a pair of scales, and the multiplication table always in his pocket, sir, ready to weigh and measure any parcel of human nature, and tell you exactly what it comes to. It is a mere question of figures, a case of simple arithmetic. You might hope to get some nonsensical belief into the head of George Gradgrind, or Augustus Gradgrind, or John Gradgrind, or Joseph Gradgrind (all suppositions, non-existent persons), but into the head of Thomas Gradgrind—no, sir!

2 In such terms Mr. Gradgrind always mentally introduced himself, whether to his private circle of acquaintance, or to the public in general. In such terms, no doubt, substituting the words "boys and girls" for "Sir" Thomas Gradgrind now presented Thomas Gradgrind to the little pitchers before him, who were to be filled so full of facts.

3 Indeed, as he eagerly sparkled at them from the cellarage before mentioned, he seemed a kind of cannon loaded to the muzzle with facts, and prepared to blow them clean out of the regions of childhood at one discharge. He seemed a

galvanizing apparatus, too, charged with a grim mechanical substitute for the tender young imaginations that were to be stormed away.

4   "Girl number twenty," said Mr. Gradgrind, squarely pointing with his square forefinger, "I don't know that girl. Who is that girl?"

5   "Sissy Jupe, sir," explained number twenty, blushing, standing up, and curtseying.

6   "Sissy is not a name," said Mr. Gradgrind. "Don't call yourself Sissy. Call yourself Cecilia."

7   "It's father as calls me Sissy, sir," returned the young girl in a trembling voice, and with another curtsey.

8   "Then he has no business to do it," said Mr. Gradgrind. "Tell him he musn't. Cecilia Jupe. Let me see. What is your father?"

9   "He belongs to the horse-riding, if you please sir."

10   Mr. Gradgrind frowned, and waved off the objectionable calling with his hand.

11   "We don't want to know anything about that, here. You musn't tell us about that, here. Your father breaks horses, don't he?"

12   "If you please, sir, when they can get any to break, they do break horses in the ring, sir."

13   "You musn't tell us about the ring, here. Very well, then. Describe your father as a horsebreaker. He doctors sick horses, I dare say?"

14   "Oh yes, sir."

15   "Very well, then. He is a veterinary surgeon, a farrier, and horsebreaker. Give me your definition of a horse."

16   (Sissy Jupe thrown into the greatest alarm by this demand.)

17   "Girl number twenty unable to define a horse!" said Mr. Gradgrind, for the general behoof of all the little pitchers. "Girl number twenty possessed of no facts, in reference to one of the commonest of animals! Some boy's definition of a horse. Bitzer, yours."

18   The square finger, moving here and there, lighted suddenly on Bitzer, perhaps because he chanced to sit in the same ray of sunlight which, darting in at one of the bare windows of the intensely whitewashed room, irradiated Sissy. For the boys and girls sat on the face of the inclined plane in two compact bodies, divided up by the center by a narrow interval; and Sissy, being at the corner of a row on the sunny side, came in for the beginning of a sunbeam, of which Bitzer, being at the corner of a row on the other side, a few rows in advance, caught the end. But whereas the girl was so dark-eyed and dark-haired that she seemed to receive a deeper and more lustrous colour from the sun when it shone upon her, the boy was so light-eyed and light-haired that the selfsame rays appeared to draw out of him what little colour his eyes possessed. His cold eyes would hardly have been eyes but for the short ends of lashes which, by bringing them into immediate contrast with something paler than themselves, expressed their form. His short-cropped hair might have been a mere continuation of the sandy freckles on his forehead and face. His skin was so unwholesomely deficient in the natural tinge, that he looked as though, if he were cut, he would bleed white.

19   "Bitzer," said Thomas Gradgrind. "Your definition of a horse."

20   "Quadruped. Graminivorous. Forty teeth, namely, twenty-four grinders, four eye-teeth, and twelve incisive. Sheds coat in the spring; in marshy countries, sheds hoofs, too. Hoofs hard, but requiring to be shod with iron. Age known by marks in mouth." Thus (and much more) Bitzer.

21   "Now, girl number twenty," said Mr. Gradgrind. "you know what a horse is."
She curtseyed again, and would have blushed deeper if she could have blushed deeper than she had blushed all this time. Bitzer, after rapidly blinking at Thomas Gradgrind with both eyes at once, and so catching the light upon his quivering ends of lashes that they looked like the antennae of busy insects, put his knuckles to his freckled forehead and sat down again.

RESPONDING TO THE READING

Analysis

1. a. In a group, reread "Murdering the Innocents" and list details about Thomas Gradgrind. Using the information in your list, determine what sort of man he is. Is he a teacher whose class you would enjoy? Why or why not? In what way is his name reflective of his character?

   b. Does Charles Dickens approve of Thomas Gradgrind? How do you know?

   c. What details tell you how Thomas Gradgrind views boys and girls?

   d. What is meant by "He seemed a galvanizing apparatus, too, charged with a grim mechanical substitute for the tender young imaginations that were to be stormed away"?

2. a. Dickens wrote *Hard Times* in the middle of the 19th century. What details can you find in the passage that illustrate the differences between our system of education and that of Victorian England? List each detail separately.

   b. Would it surprise you to know that Dickens was a social reformer and educational activist? How is his interest in education reflected in this excerpt?

   c. What changes do you think Dickens would have wanted to see in Gradgrind's classroom?

3. There is enough information in this excerpt for you to be able to draw a floorplan of Gradgrind's classroom and to include with it such details as lighting and probable class size. Draw up a plan.

4. a. Look at the words Dickens uses to describe Bitzer and then those he uses for Sissy. What impression does Dickens give you of each child? What, for example, does each child's name suggest to you?

b. Is it clear to you with which of the two children Dickens sympathizes? What do you make of the fact that Thomas Gradgrind thoroughly approves of Bitzer and is dismissive of Sissy?

5. a. What does Bitzer's definition of a horse sound like to you?

b. Given that Sissy lives with horses (her father is a horse trainer in a circus), what do you think Dickens intended his reader to understand when Gradgrind says, "Now, girl number twenty ... you know what a horse is."

Writing Suggestions

1. Are there any aspects of Gradgrind's classroom that you think ought to be incorporated into today's education system? Why or why not?
2. Do you believe that education is more than being "filled so full of facts"? Why or why not

Writing from Readings:

Summary, Paraphrase, and Levels of Language

"Brevity is the soul of wit." (Shakespeare)

Summary

A summary is a shortened version of a piece of writing. It is reworded by the writer, but the information is given in the same order as in the original. Summary is not analysis. Also, in writing a summary you do not add to or change the author's facts or ideas, nor do you comment on or redesign his or her information. Its aim is to condense but not refashion an author's work: a summary always follows the pattern of information and development found in the original piece.

In the opening sentence of any summary, you must state the name of the author whose piece of writing you are summarizing, the title of the piece, and the source (i.e., the publication details of the copy you are using), so that you will not be accused of **plagiarism**. Summary writing can be time consuming. You may need to rewrite a number of times, changing unclear phrases, correcting verb tenses, combining sentences, and revising paragraphs.

There are three types of summaries:

1. A single-sentence summary. Although very short, this must explain the content and focus of the original passage. For example, if you had to write a single-sentence summary of a paragraph, you could simply reword the topic sentence. However, if you combined the reworded topic sentence with the major supporting details, your single-sentence summary would be more effective and comprehensive. In textbooks, and in business and technical reports, single-sentence summaries often function as headings. In effect, the thesis statement of an essay is its single-sentence summary.

2. A selective summary. This is a shortened version of specific information taken from the original passage. When writing a selective summary, you choose only the facts and ideas you need for your purposes. You scan for

the relevant information and record it in point form. These points are then reworded into your summary. A selective summary can be used in writing research papers, recording significant details from articles or textbooks, and preparing the texts for oral presentations.

3. Point-by-point summary. This is a shorter, reworded version of an entire passage. In this kind of summary, you identify main ideas and major supporting details, reword them, and then put them in the same order as in the original. This type of summary is used in year-end reports, minutes in meetings, outlines of technical data, and abstracts of formal company reports.

Read the following passage about memory and writing by Roberta Rees. Be sure to prepare yourself for summary writing by first skimming to get an overview of Rees's content.

Seven Plates

Roberta Rees

1   When I was born my father was a jockey and my mother could hit a home run out of any ballpark. They met at the Stampede Bar & Grill, where my mother who was almost sixteen served fries and gravy and burgers to jockeys from the track. My father who was almost seventeen was so shy the only eyes he could look directly into were a horse's, into the velvety cones deep inside. My mother could sling hash, balance seven plates up her arms, wipe a table in three fast swipes, but she could not bring her mother back, her tiny dark French mother who could not breathe when the horses came to town, whose heart one night spasmed, pulled away from her main aorta. My mother could not bring her mother back, could not bring back her oldest sister who died a year later, could not stop her father from drinking and beating her. But she could hit a home run, run away from home, could love the tiny dark jockey who sang to her in the dark, the tiny baby with eyes like her mother's. Her mother named after the patron saint of music.

2   This has everything to do with the way I write, the content of my writing, the reasons I write, the reasons I often cannot write. In the novel I am working on now a girl named Jessie sings R-a-g-g M-o-p-p Raggmopp, jitterbugs with her dead sister, brings her dead mother back. If I write one scene at a time, let Jessie speak the way she needs to, the novel unfolds. If I get too lofty in my intentions, too clever, too self-conscious, neither I nor the novel can move.

3   My first babysitter was a horse, a chestnut thoroughbred on the track. He loved children, bit adults. I would spend hours in his stall, walking under his belly, reaching up and rubbing, hugging a long leg. When my father reached over the stall door to pick me up, Next Case bit his arm.

4   Of course I had human babysitters before this, and I don't know how long I actually spent in Next Case's stall or how often. What I know is the softness of a horse's lip, a horse's rich scent, the smell and feel of the land from a horse's back.

I also know the tightening in my chest, pain deep in my lungs, hammering of my heart when I am near anything that's been near a horse.

5   This has everything to do with how I write, what I write, why I write. Why I sometimes cannot write.

6   It started with my eyes burning, swelling shut. Then my nose, my throat, my bronchial tubes. I was five, and the treatment I received was a shot of serum from a pregnant mare's urine, only one in a lifetime the doctor told my parents, it's so potent. My arm swelled twice its size. Horse blood from my father's side, generations of Welsh men breathing horse. Blood from my mother's, two generations of French women stopped breathing in their forties because of horses. Flowing together in my veins. Would I wake up a horse, I wondered, and if I did, would I be allergic to myself?

7   This has to do with my ambivalence about what and how and why I write. This has to do with my need to get beyond ambivalence, to let writing be the body where the heart can beat, lungs breathe; all the contradictory impulses beneath the thin tissue of the skin make that body dance.

8   I hear through the proverbial grapevine that someone in my community asks of my first book, *Eyes Like Pigeons*, a long poem exploring what it means to long for mothering. "Doesn't Roberta know where she ends and others begin?" All winter I hold this question inside, struggle with having exposed myself, exposed people I love. I try to imagine how I could have published this book. Women at readings come to me with their stories, thank me for voicing the sound and feel of our often painfully silent fear and longing and celebration. Yet I can't stop this trembling, this sense of guilt and shame.

9   A friend writes to me about the responsibility that writing out loud brings, how this responsibility can make us anxious because women aren't used to being so public. She mentions the danger in objectifying our own writing, our own selves. She says how important it is to listen to what our bodies tell us. Around the same time, I go to a talk by an Afro-American scholar, Barbara Christian, on Toni Morrison. She talks about Morrison's writing being an act of community healing.

10   When I start the next project, I vow to write out of fictional proposition. And I write prose poems about the difference between what I want to write and what I am moved to write, about the way my heartbeats echo when I watch my twin two-year-old nieces play and I see my sister in their jumping spinning baby bodies. I write a non-fiction piece about how my father and his brother and his sister and his sister's daughter come down with cancer and as a family we move together through tragedy, sometimes transform it. Sometimes not.

11   When I was a teenager, someone convinced my father to sing on stage. He had a drink to do it. But once he was up there, he loved it. He got a band together, started singing in clubs and bars. Then he started singing in large halls, cut a small record, had his own television show. Every week I watched him vomit before a performance, take a few drinks, transform himself into the most charming, confident, powerful performer everyone wanted to touch. Then he sabotaged his television show, his record contract. Sabotaged them royally. Then he lay on the couch every evening, wouldn't go out with my mother. Then he got cancer and died.

12 This was how I saw it. The same year that I rushed him into hospital where he was diagnosed with stage IV lymphoma was the same year I quit my full-time teaching job and started taking a creative writing class. By the end of two years of writing classes, two years of accompanying my father as close to death as I could, I decided that art kills you if you do it, kills you if you don't.

13 Fortunately for me, years later I told another wise friend what I'd learned, and she asked if my father had actually quit singing or had he simply quit performing. And I remember what I had left out of my version. I remember my father sitting in the kitchen, getting that faraway look in his eyes, getting up and going for his guitar, sitting away from the rest of us, holding it close and singing. Eyes closed, singing. I remember how he sang until he physically couldn't. How singing didn't stop him from dying, but helped keep him alive until he died.

14 This has to do with how I continue to write, how and why. This, and my mother's fingers combing my hair, "I wish you could have met my mom. You would have liked her."

RESPONDING TO THE READING

Comprehension

Answer each question in your own words.

1. What was Roberta Rees's mother's occupation?
2. What sort of babysitter did Rees have?
3. What remedy was Rees given for her allergy to horses?
4. Does Rees have any siblings?
5. What did her father die of?

Analysis

1. Why does Roberta Rees say more than once, "My mother could hit a home run"?
2. How would you describe the relationship between Rees's parents?
3. In what ways do her parents inspire Rees to write?
4. Rees makes a reference to Toni Morrison. Who is she? How would you find out about her? Why is she important to Rees?

Summary Exercises

1. Write a selective summary of the information Roberta Rees gives about her mother.
2. Write a selective summary on the symptoms of and cure for an allergy to horses.
3. Write a selective biographical summary about Rees's father.
4. Write a point-by-point summary of the entire passage.
5. Rees relates stories about her parents and her childhood in order to explain why she writes. She does not have a stated thesis, but her main idea is clear. Write a thesis statement (a single-sentence summary) for this passage.

Paraphrase

Here is a quotation from Roberta Rees's article.

This has to do with my need to go beyond ambivalence, to let writing be the body where the heart can beat, lungs breathe ...

A paraphrase of this quotation might be:

This is why I find it necessary to overcome vagueness and find truth, so that my words can truly come alive.

Or, more simply:

I have to put my true self into my writing and show what I feel and believe.

The purpose of paraphrase is to put something into your own words so that you can more easily understand its meaning. Paraphrase is useful when you have to explain or understand difficult or technical ideas or concepts, or when you have to simplify sophisticated vocabulary.

Babes in Toyland

Mark Kingwell

"Sailor Moon" is all the rage, but a butt-kicking Amazon named Xena is a **better role model** for your daughter

1   As someone with the upper-body strength of an eleven-year-old boy, it's not often I find myself feeling like Arnold Schwarzenegger. But just before Christmas I ventured into the toy section of a major department store and entered a crush of people who, like The Muscled One's character in the bad-idea holiday movie *Jingle All the Way*, had no higher purpose on earth than securing this year's toy of choice.

2   The object of our desire? A "Sailor Moon" action figure, spin-off merchandise from the hugely popular animated children's series that targets girls between six and eleven. If you don't know any children of that description, you may never have heard of the show. If you do, you probably find yourself even now humming its inane but catchy theme song—"Fighting evil by moonlight, winning love by daylight, never shrinking from a real fight, she's the one called Sailor Moon." Yes, she is, and the action figure comes in three sizes ranging in price from ten to thirty dollars.

3   Based on a hit comic book, "Sailor Moon" is a Japanese cartoon fantasy that has quickly become the most popular children's show in the world. Carried in Canada on the CanWest Global Network, YTV, and several private stations, it has a growing, passionately loyal audience, about sixty percent female. (On some cable services you can see it as many as four times a day, including, rather incongruously, late at night.) The show centres on a group of five schoolgirls, all of them Caucasian and well endowed with enormous eyes, slim legs, and manes of flowing hair, who live in a city that sports Japanese signs and cars but no visible adult

residents. The five are led by the blonde Serena, otherwise known as Sailor Moon, who spearheads their daily battles against the evil Queen Beryl and the wicked alien twins, Alan and Ann. Serena's pals Raye, Amy, Mina, and Lita round out the Sailor Scouts, living their double lives as, respectively, Sailors Mars, Mercury, Venus, and Jupiter.

4 According to its supporters, "Sailor Moon" is doing something unprecedented in children's television: providing a strong role model for pre-teen girls: "The issue of a girl being empowered is a wonderful theme you just don't see in America animation," says Andy Heyward, president of DIC Entertainment, the California-based company that adapted the show for North America. "There's very little, if anything, out there starring a girl."

5 And girls, it seems, are now ready to trade in Betty and Veronica, not to mention those alternatively frumpy or perky girls on "Scooby Doo," for genuine comic-book heroes. This isn't just Nancy Drew: it's Nancy Drew *with supernatural powers*, deadly rays and freeze guns, and exploding balls—the whole array of superhero armament. As the DIC press release concludes, with true comic-book hyperbole: "The combination of her cry 'MOON POWER' and the Hi-Tech powers from her secret locket will make SAILOR MOON the female force of the 90s!" So that's an *action figure*, not a *doll*, you can buy at Eaton's—and with lots more to come. Sales of "Sailor Moon" merchandise in Japan reached $1.5-billion (U.S.) between 1993 and 1995, outstripping both Teenage Mutant Ninja Turtles and Mighty Morphin Power Rangers. For Irwin toys, Canada's biggest toy company, it was the top-selling line this past Christmas.

6 The show itself is long on energy but short on coherence, with no explanation provided for its basic premise, no clues as to how Serena and her friends acquired their various superhero powers—or their supermodel bodies. In battle each of the girls transforms from a school-uniformed fourteen-year-old into a bizarre male fantasy of adolescent beauty. The knee-length pleated skirts of their sailor suits shrink to micromini size, their Buster Browns mutate into sexy boots or high heels. Their virginal Victorian-style blouses become form-fitting sleeveless tunics that emphasize pubescent breasts and collarbones, even as the Scouts arch their backs, preen, and knock their knees together in poses borrowed directly from the Victoria's Secret catalogue. I am not making any of this up.

7 Which explains the appeal of "Sailor Moon" for a certain kind of man, I suppose, possibly including the original producers. It also explains some of the controversy the show has generated. In December, my local CBC affiliate ran a news segment in which a professor of mass media at York University called it sexist and inappropriate, citing in particular all the primping the Sailor Scouts engage in before battle. George Irwin, president of Irwin Toys, defended the show by saying, rather unfortunately, that it is "reflective of the type of girls and what they do these days."

8 Obviously, parents aren't concerned. Some of them undoubtedly are happy that the show includes, at the end of each episode, a preachy "Sailor Says" segment in which Sailor Moon articulates an uplifting moral: "If you get angry with younger kids, talk to your parents or another adult about it," she chirps after one adventure involving a difficult baby. "Be patient with your little brothers and sisters — one day they might grow up to be a lot bigger than you!"

9   But girls find "Sailor Moon" compelling for other reasons: the idea of a secret life, for instance, or the prospect of fighting evil in close-knit groups, talking in tough-guy clichés. ("You're sushi!" Sailor Moon snarls to an enemy in one episode. I wonder if that was in the Japanese script.) They are also drawn to the small differences between the five Scouts, identifying one or another as a favourite. The doll boxes even offer little personality profiles to encourage this— Serena's listed hobby is shopping, for example, and Lita's cooking, but Raye is "into meditation" and "actively dislikes television." Evil Queen Beryl, by the way, who has narrow eye slits in place of the girls' insectoid globes, is listed as being "twenty-something," which I suppose is morbidly old if you're ten.

10   And while it's true that these gestures of individuation, as well as the larger theme of female empowerment, sit uneasily with the soft-porn visuals of the series, more disturbing is the basic arc of the narratives, which repeatedly show the Scouts stumbling into alien battles they really can't handle. At the decisive moment, just as they are about to be scorched by Beryl or Alan, a male figure called Moonlight Knight appears, throws down what looks like a carnation, and delivers a little sermon that bucks the girls up and turns the tide of battle. For some reason I have yet to fathom, Moonlight Knight is dressed in flowing desert robes and Laurence of Arabia headgear. The Scouts look at him with abject teenage love in their eyes; you can tell because their massive pupils are suddenly replaced by throbbing red hearts.

11   "Well done, Sailor Scouts," he tells the five after one narrowly averted disaster. "Keep a melody in your heart and a lilt in your voice. So long." The girls heave a collective sigh. "What a hunk-meister," Sailor Moon whispers, blushing madly.

12   There's a better answer out there to the lack of TV role models for girls, though it might seem an unlikely one at first. "Xena: Warrior Princess," shown on most of the same stations as "Sailor Moon," is a live-action fantasy show centring on a strong female character whose belief in justice is matched only by her ability to swing a sword, perform dexterous back flips, and land brutal roundhouse kicks.

13   A reformed mercenary, the beautiful Xena (Lucy Lawless) now uses her war-rior abilities for good rather than evil, slapping miscreants into shape and treating cruel rulers to her gleeful brand of Amazonian butt-kicking. The series is like a Marvel comic book brought to life, complete with wisecracking hero, adolescent cleverness, and background of garbled lore. In one episode, the mythological figure Sisyphus appears as an evil magician trying to get Xena to take over his eternal rock-rolling fate—an incident missing from my edition of Bulfinch.

14   On the other hand, who cares? "Xena" is good fun, and its cartoonish wit is drawing a fast-growing, enthusiastic teenage and young-adult audience, male and female, as well as the main target group of pre-teen girls. Its more loyal fans, who call themselves "Xenites," watch the show in groups while consuming Xena's favoured snack of nut bread. Inevitably, the show has spawned a number of sites on the World Wide Web, including one called *Whoosh!*, after the cheesy sound effect used in the series for everything from sword thrusts to Xena's back flips. The site boasts a complete episode guide, an "Encyclopedia Xenaica," and apparently serious articles on such subjects as "Visual Metaphor in Xena: Warrior Princess,"

and "Xena: Warrior Princess: A Native American Perspective." I'm not making this up either.

15   So maybe some grown-ups have way too much time on their hands. But for younger fans, "Xena," along with the equally silly "Hercules: The Legendary Journeys," from which it was spun off, is obviously striking some deep mythopoeic chord.

16   It also, in contrast to "Sailor Moon," makes the traditionally male superhero genre cool for girls without hollowing out the strong message. Yes, the blue-eyed, raven-haired Xena does cavort in revealing leather jerkins and thigh-high boots: an outfit that got *her* anatomically correct action figure included on an annual list of "warped Christmas playthings." And her moral pronunciamentos aren't much more sophisticated than Sailor Moon's—"It takes a lot more strength to resist violence than to surrender to it," she opines in one episode. But they are at least based on hard-won experience. And Xena never has to be rescued by a man; on the contrary, she does the rescuing herself.

17   You might think "Xena" is just comic-book cheesecake, the way Lynda Carter's *Playboy*-style "Wonder Woman" series was in the seventies. But don't underestimate Xena's ability to inspire self-reliance in young female fans, even a kind of new-style power feminism. In this age of explicit televisual disclosure of bodily attributes, when "Baywatch" is the worldwide standard of what's watchable, the warrior princess compellingly combines action with appearance. In an episode that found her transported into the equally luscious body of her arch-enemy, Callisto, Xena shut down one man's amorous approach by saying, "It's not my body that makes me who I am—it's my deeds." Then she punched him.

18   If only Sailor Moon would do that to Moonlight Knight once in a while.

RESPONDING TO THE READING

Paraphrase Exercises

The thesis statement for this article is its subheading: "Sailor Moon is all the rage but a butt-kicking Amazon named Xena is a better role model for your daughter." Now that you have read the article, paraphrase its thesis. Then paraphrase each of the sentences and passage below. Look up any words whose meanings you are unsure of. But if the dictionary gives more than one meaning for the word, make sure you choose the meaning that is appropriate to its context in the article.

1. If you do, you probably find yourself even now humming its inane but catchy theme song ...
2. On some cable services you can see it as many as four times a day, including, rather incongruously, late at night.
3. The five are led by the blonde Serena, otherwise known as Sailor Moon, who spearheads their daily battles against the evil Queen Beryl and the wicked alien twins, Alan and Ann.

4. The issue of a girl being empowered is a wonderful theme you just don't see in American animation.

5. And girls, it seems, are now ready to trade in Betty and Veronica, not to mention those alternatively frumpy or perky girls on "Scooby Doo," for genuine comic-book heroes.

6. The show itself is long on energy but short on coherence, with no explanation provided for its basic premise, no clues as to how Serena and her friends acquired their various superhero powers—or their supermodel bodies.

7. And while it's true that these gestures of individuation, as well as the larger theme of female empowerment, sit uneasily with the soft-porn visuals of the series, more disturbing is the basic arc of the narratives, which repeatedly show the Scouts stumbling into alien battles they really can't handle.

8. The series is like a Marvel comic book brought to life, complete with wisecracking hero, adolescent cleverness, and background of garbled lore.

9. But for younger fans, "Xena," along with the equally silly "Hercules: The Legendary Journeys," from which it was spun off, is obviously striking some deep mythopoeic chord.

10. In this age of explicit televisual disclosure or bodily attributes, when "Baywatch" is the worldwide standard of what's watchable, the warrior princess compellingly combines action with appearance.

Comprehension

I. Scan to find the following information on "Sailor Moon" in Mark Kingwell's article.

1. What do the Sailor Scouts look like? In what ways do they change from teenage girls to superheroes?
2. What is a typical storyline in a "Sailor Moon" episode?
3. What reasons does Kingwell give for young girls' attraction to "Sailor Moon"?
4. Supporters of "Sailor Moon" claim that it provides a "strong role model for pre-teen girls." What evidence shows that Kingwell disagrees with this statement?

II. Scan to find the following information on "Xena: Warrior Princess."

1. What is Xena's background and how does she prove she is a superhero?
2. How is the popularity of "Xena" described by Kingwell? What sorts of things do "Xena" fans do?
3. What are the main differences drawn between "Xena" and "Sailor Moon"?
4. Write a selective summary of the reasons why Kingwell says "Xena is good fun."
5. What distinction does Kingwell imply exists between a doll and an action figure? Why are the Sailor Scouts and Xena toys action figures and not dolls?

Analysis

1. What play on words is being used in the title, "Babes in Toyland"?
2. Why do you think Kingwell refers to Betty and Veronica, Scooby Doo, Nancy Drew, Ninja Turtles, and Power Rangers? What do these characters represent in our culture?
3. When he talks about Xena, Kingwell makes reference to myth. What do you understand a myth to be? How does Kingwell show that "Xena" uses myth?
4. Is Sailor Moon a popular myth in our culture? What does it represent?

Writing Suggestions

1. Based on Kingwell's reasons, write a paragraph of your own showing why Xena is a better role model for young girls than Sailor Moon.
2. Is there a popular TV show that you believe provides a positive role model for children? Describe the show and give reasons.

Levels of Language

English can be both formal and informal. Formal English is used in business, education, and government. It more often follows the strict rules of grammar and has an elevated, exact vocabulary.

The most informal level of language is slang. Slang frequently changes the dictionary definitions of words and originates within a specific social group: teenagers, for example, invent slang as a kind of private language separate from their parents'. Slang is used only in speech, unless you are writing a chatty letter to a personal friend. In some instances, slang is used in journalism articles to add liveliness to the writing, particularly when the articles talk about such things as movies or rock music. The problem with slang is that it quickly loses its meaning and vitality. The following article by Terry E. Johnson points this out.

Slang: Language That's Out of Date

Terry E. Johnson

1   Dave and Isobel Rosen considered themselves reasonably knowledgeable of contemporary slang until they ran into an old friend about a year and a half ago.

2   "We talked with him for about 15 minutes, and I only understood about three words he said," recalls Dave Rosen, a 30-year-old South Philadelphian. "And the guy's only about a half a year younger than I am.

3   "He told me that a friend of ours 'cracked up in a Z.' I thought he meant the guy overdosed on drugs. But I found out later that the guy was driving a Z car and got into an accident."

4   The problem is not that the Rosens are so out of touch with members of their own generation that they need an interpreter. The difficulty is that North American slang is so prolific and so ephemeral that it is almost impossible for anybody except the most astute students of the language to keep up with it.

5   "Slang is always going to be out of date," says Connie Eble, a University of North Carolina linguist who has written several articles on the subject. "By the time you and I (middle-aged adults) know about it, it's passé. When we know about it, that means it has left its control group and is into the mainstream."

6   The most widely accepted definition of slang is that it is those old or newly created words used consciously for a witty or satirical effect, says Stewart Flexner, a co-editor of the *Dictionary of American Slang,* currently considered the definitive book on the subject.

7   Thurayya Barry, 13, has never read the *Dictionary of American Slang,* but she can tell you that "decent" is the most frequently used slang word at St. Barbara's school in West Philadelphia, where she is in Grade 8.

8   "It means something really nice," she says. "Anything you like you would say it's decent. Like, if you saw a good movie, you would say it's decent."

9   Like decent, "awesome" is an old, established word with plenty of tradition behind it, but still it has been transformed into a slang word. While it once meant to inspire awe, "awesome" is now used vaguely to describe anything ranging from the beautiful to the grotesque.

10   "We can be watching the same thing on television and see something we both really like and I'll say it's 'baaad-to-the-bone' and my daughter will say that it's 'awesome,'" says Frank Morris, 42, of Philadelphia. Daughter Debbi is 14.

11   "I'd say my daughter's favorite word is "awesome"; my daughter thinks everything is 'awesome,'" says Morris, who still favors his 1960s vocabulary.

12   In the 1960s it was common to hear something good described as "bad," "neat" or "far out." And, primarily among those who identified with liberal social attitudes and various protest movements, almost everything important or profound was "deep," "real deep" or "heavy … very, very heavy."

13   While many words, including "bad" and "cool," have remained part of the slang vocabulary, the lengthy list of new entries includes "thorough," "fly," "kickin' it," "homey" or "home-boy" and "fresh."

14   For Jamie Cook, 19, getting dressed up is more than merely changing the clothes he wears to his job selling vegetables at a Philadelphia market. When Cook dresses up, he gets "thorough." "Say, for example, I had on a leather suit," says Cook. "I would be thorough."

15   Cook also says dressing up could be called getting "fly," "ragged" or "sharp."

16   "Doing it to death," a popular 1960s phrase that meant doing something to the point of excess, has been replaced in the 1980s by "kickin' it," which means doing something consistently or intensely. "If I were just doing something a lot I would be kickin' it," said Cook.

17   At school or on the subway, Philadelphia teenagers use the slang word "fresh" to describe something that is new or different. "Fresh" has already been used in the lyrics of several popular records, including Rockmaster Scott and

Dynamic Three's hit *Request Line,* in which a teenager calls a disc jockey and asks to "hear something fresh from the request line."

18   In an age when many distinctions are blurred, slang tends to highlight differences that range from generational to cultural to geographic. Detroit's "What's up, doe?" and Philadelphia's "What's up, homey?" might both be inquiring as to the state of things, but in Detroit, the "doe" is a dog, or exploited person, while in Philadelphia the "homey" is someone from the neighborhood.

19   The use of slang is often a ritualistic method of expressing a person's eagerness to become part of a group or opposition to it. It can be derogatory. It can reveal as well as conceal secrets.

20   Eble says slang is sometimes used because it is not polite and represents rebellion against the status quo. In other words, it reflects general social and economic trends. In the 1830s, for example, "workie" was a popular slang word for members of a political party with a strong labor following.

21   "Slang has certain secretive characteristics about it," says Eble. "Its use is a way of including and excluding. Slang also has the ability to polarize. It is very much peer-group controlled and is used as a means of maintaining solidarity. Those groups that use it the most are those that need to feel solidarity and are not in a position of power."

22   John Lighter says that slang—not to be confused with black dialect—is prevalent among "minorities, blacks and anybody who has lived in the inner city at any time. But it all depends on your perspective. In some cases, what is slang for one person is not necessarily slang for another. Part of the fun and appeal of using slang is that you know what it means, but people outside your group don't know what it means."

23   In its more mainstream role, slang gives language the ability to change and adapt to new concepts and technological advances, says Lighter, who teaches linguistics at the University of Texas at Austin.

24   "The computer revolution, the atomic age and all the new trends in American life help create new words," says Lighter. Technology has given us such phrases as "space cadet" (a person who is out of touch with reality), "giving static" (causing trouble) and "overexposure" (the act of being in the public eye too long), among countless others.

25   "When there are new attitudes expressed by young people, very frequently those attitudes crystallize around a new sense of an old word or sometimes a new word," Lighter says. "The expression 'cool' is a good example of that."

26   The word "cool," according to the *Dictionary of American Slang,* is associated with the cool or progressive jazz movement of the 1950s.

27   The cool attitude became popular among Beat poets and writers of the 1940s and '50s as a result of their association with black jazz musicians, poet Allen Ginsberg says. "We were the first group of power writers to incorporate black slang and musical slang into our everyday speech," he said.

RESPONDING TO THE READING

The above article, written in 1985, makes the point that slang expressions go out of date. Paraphrase the following slang expressions by writing them first in formal language and then in more current slang:

 a. workie
 b. It's bad to the bone.
 c. far out and real deep

What do the following slang expressions mean?

 a. off the wall
 b. chill out!
 c. wicked
 d. buff

Comprehension

1. Explain each of the following expressions:
   out of date
   getting dressed up
   something fresh
   to run into an old friend
2. What three key ideas are in the thesis statement (paragraph 4)?
3. Johnson gives a lot of reasons for the use of slang. What are they?

Analysis

1. Johnson begins the article with an anecdote (a story used as an illustration) about Dave and Isobel Rosen. What is its purpose?
2. Why do you think Johnson quotes so many average Americans in his essay?
3. Given Johnson's examples of its use, why do you think slang would be popular with teenagers?

Summary

Summarize the article by Johnson. Write out your first sentence with Johnson's name, the title of his essay, and his thesis statement from paragraph 4, reworded. Make your summary approximately 250 words.

Discussion

1. What current slang expressions do you use?
2. What are the major sources of your slang expressions?
3. If you were to reword them, how would you do so?
4. Johnson claims that slang can reveal as well as conceal secrets.

Which of *your* slang expressions do one or the other?

Joseph Epstein, who wrote the following essay, claims that when you define ambition "you instantly reveal a great deal about yourself."

The Virtues of Ambition

Joseph Epstein

1   It may seem an exaggeration to say that ambition is the linchpin of society, holding many of its disparate elements together, but it is not an exaggeration by much. Remove ambition and the essential elements of society seem to fly apart. Ambition, as opposed to mere fantasizing about desires, implies work and discipline to achieve goals, personal and social, of a kind society cannot survive without. Ambition is intimately connected with family, for men and women not only work partly for their families; husbands and wives are often ambitious for each other, but harbor some of their most ardent ambitions for their children. Yet to have a family nowadays—with birth control readily available, and inflation a good economic argument against having children—is nearly an expression of ambition in itself. Finally, though ambition was once the domain chiefly of monarchs and aristocrats, it has, in more recent times, increasingly become the domain of the middle classes. Ambition and futurity—a sense of building for tomorrow—are inextricable. Working, saving, planning—these, the daily aspects of ambition—have always been the distinguishing marks of a rising middle class. The attack against ambition is not incidentally an attack on the middle class and what it stands for. Like it or not, the middle class has done much of society's work in America; and it, the middle class, has from the beginning run on ambition.

2   It is not difficult to imagine a world shorn of ambition. It would probably be a kinder world: without demands, without abrasions, without disappointments. People would have time for reflection. Such work as they did would not be for themselves but for the collectivity. Competition would never enter in. Conflict would be eliminated, tension become a thing of the past. The stress of creation would be at an end. Art would no longer be troubling, but purely celebratory in its functions. The family would become superfluous as a social unit, with all its former power for bringing about neurosis drained away. Longevity would be increased, for fewer people would die of heart attack or stroke caused by tumultuous endeavor. Anxiety would be extinct. Time would stretch on and on, with ambition long departed from the human heart.

3   Ah, how unrelievedly boring life would be!

4   There is a strong view that holds that success is a myth, and ambition therefore a sham. Does this mean that success does not really exist? That achievement is at bottom empty? That the efforts of men and women are of no significance alongside the force of movements and events? Now not all success, obviously, is worth esteeming, nor all ambition worth cultivating. Which are and which are not is something one soon enough learns on one's own. But even the most cynical secretly admit that success exists; that achievement counts for a

great deal; and that the true myth is that the actions of men and women are use-less. To believe otherwise is to take on a point of view that is likely to be deranging. It is, in its implications, to remove all motive for competence, interest in attainment, and regard for posterity.

5   We do not choose to be born. We do not choose our parents. We do not choose our historical epoch, the country of our birth or the immediate circumstances of our upbringing. We do not, most of us, choose to die; nor do we choose the time or conditions of our death. But within all this realm of choicelessness, we do choose how we shall live: courageously or in cowardice, honorably or dishonorably, with purpose or in drift. We decide what is important and what is trivial in life. We decide that what makes us significant is either what we do or what we refuse to do. But no matter how indifferent the universe may be to our choices and decisions, these choices and decisions are ours to make. We decide. We choose. And as we decide and choose, so are our lives formed. In the end, forming our own destiny is what ambition is about.

RESPONDING TO THE READING

Vocabulary

1. Write your own formal definition of ambition as an introduction to a college-level essay on the topic.
2. Write an informal definition (you may use current slang) of ambition for an oral presentation in the classroom.
3. Are there other words you know of and could look up in a thesaurus that mean the same or almost the same as ambition?

Paraphrase

1. "[A]mbition is the linchpin of society, holding many of its disparate elements together."
2. "[A]mbition implies work and discipline to achieve goals."
3. "[H]usbands and wives ... harbor some of their most ardent ambitions for their children."
4. Using slang, paraphrase: "[A]mbition ... has, in more recent times, increasingly become the domain of the middle classes."

Comprehension

1. In paragraph 1, Epstein gives a number of examples to prove that ambition keeps society functioning. What are they?
2. In paragraph 2, Epstein imagines what life would be like without ambition. Why does he then say "how unrelievedly boring life would be without ambition"?

3. What do "success is a myth" and "ambition is a sham" mean? How does Epstein argue against the meaning of these two phrases in paragraph 4?
4. Epstein indicates that we choose few things in life. What are we able to choose?

Analysis

1. Do you agree with Epstein that "ambition is the linchpin of society"? Write a paragraph explaining why you do or do not agree. Use your own examples.
2. What do you think Epstein means in his concluding sentence?
3. Epstein talks about society and the individual. What does he think the relationship between them is? Do you agree or disagree? Explain your viewpoint in a short paragraph.

Summary

Summarize Epstein's article in 100–150 words. Remember to start your summary with a sentence stating the author's full name, the title, and a reworded thesis statement.

Writing Suggestions

1. All of the essays in this chapter have dealt with language in some way. Can you think of an occasion when your use of English created a difficult situation for you? Write a well-organized paragraph discussing this occasion. Use examples and reasons.
2. What are the effects in someone's life of being overly ambitious? Are they negative or positive effects? Using examples, write a paragraph that discusses either the positive or the negative effects.
3. Write a short formal paragraph stating your thoughts on your current career choice or on your current experiences in college. Afterward, write out the same information in a more informal manner (as if you were writing a letter to your best friend) using slang.
4. What motivates you to achieve something—for example, high marks or a goal in a sport? Is it something from your past, as it was with Roberta Rees and her memories of her parents? Or is it peer pressure as discussed by Mark Kingwell or pure ambition as defined by Joseph Epstein? Or, is it a combination of all three? Organize your ideas around this topic and show your reader in a well-structured paragraph why you do what you do.

3

Organized Writing:

Composing a Formula Essay

"True ease in writing comes from art, not chance." (Alexander Pope)

Learning to write a formula essay is essential because it enables you to select, order, and present information in a clear and logical fashion. Furthermore, the format of a formula essay can be adapted to all types of writing tasks, ranging from a course essay to a business letter, and from a research report to a project proposal. In Unit Four this formula is modified to suit the varied purposes of writers and patterns of essay development.

The formula essay has an introduction, a thesis statement, body paragraphs, and a conclusion. Expository writing is based on this formula. The purpose of expository writing is to share information as clearly and succinctly as possible. There are four steps to writing a formula essay:

1. generate information
2. order the information
3. write the information
4. edit the information

Generate Information

Brainstorm

First of all, an essay must have a **subject,** one idea worth writing about. For instance, a five-paragraph student essay may be about finding a job, describing a scientific procedure, or discussing why a war began. Sometimes you are not given a subject, so how do you come up with one? One way is to choose a topic you are interested in and know something about. To generate ideas and details you then **brainstorm,** which means thinking freely about ideas at random but recording only those related to your chosen subject. Set yourself a firm time frame—say, a maximum of ten minutes—and list everything you can think of. If you can't seem to put anything worthwhile down on paper, search for another topic. When you believe your subject has inspired you to produce plentiful material, you can move on to the next step.

For instance, if your subject is driving, something of interest to many of us, you might start by listing the things you like about driving. For example:

> sense of control
> freedom of movement
> showing off my car (Porsche, fully loaded)
> status
> convenience
> changing gears
> washing and grooming the car

For each item in such a list, you would then brainstorm to generate more specific details to support the precise focus you wish to wrtite about. For example, regarding convenience, you might list the following:

> come and go at any hour you wish
> no waiting at icy bus stops
> easy for shopping
> picking up friends
> getting to work or school on time (no waiting for a scheduled bus)
> getting away for a weekend whenever you want to

These lists could have been written as webs, as in the following example, in which the things you might hate about driving are shown:

Driving: I hate

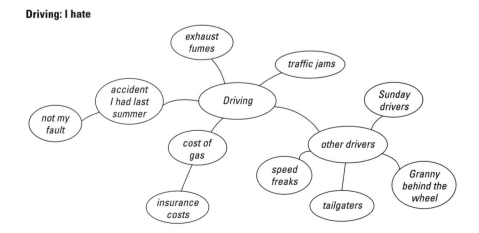

Question

Often student writers take on a subject that is too broad and therefore unmanageable. Their subject has so many angles to cover, it offers too much information to discuss in five paragraphs. With many details and ideas to choose from, student writers frequently find writing an essay a frustrating experience. It is necessary to narrow down or focus a subject.

The way to focus your subject is to ask questions: *who? what? when? where? why? how?*

These questions help you to sort out your ideas and details. There is much you could say about the costs of driving, the hazards, the joys, the frustrations. Asking questions such as the following may help you decide exactly what your essay on driving will be about: Who drives? What makes an effective driver? When should a person learn to drive? Where is the best place to drive? Where is the best place to learn to drive? Why drive at all? Why do people drive as they do? How can one improve driving methods? How does one learn to drive a car well?

How you answer any one of these questions will depend on what you know and how many facts you can come up with for a typical formula essay. You may find that one question will be enough to activate your imagination. However, once you have questioned and found what you consider to be satisfactory answers, which of the ideas and details can you use best to write the actual essay?

Order the Information

Select

Selecting your best information and details depends on two criteria:

1. A subject that you know will interest your readers.
2. A subject that you know will interest you as the writer.

A subject that interests you often falls into shape on its own. You must keep in mind, however, that the subject must be a worthwhile one for you as well as for your readers.

You must make sure a subject is valid:

1. Are there enough supporting details?
2. Are the details separate and unique?
3. Can the details be verified with reasons and examples?

This step can be difficult and must be thought through with care. Try labelling your details and ideas, sorting them into groups, to see if you have a sufficient number to write into paragraphs. Check to see that you haven't repeated yourself. Once you've completed checking, you can begin to organize your selection for your readers.

Below we look at how one student writer composed a five-paragraph formula essay on driving. After Marcelo Olenewa had decided to talk about driving, he asked himself these questions:

- How do we learn to drive?
- How did I become an effective driver?
- What are examples of effective driving?

By asking these questions and coming up with a series of responses, Olenewa wrote down the following focused subject:

"I learned to become an effective driver."

Organize

Readers appreciate clarity. As a writer, you must choose and order your details in a way that best suits the subject of your essay. There are four basic ways to arrange information:

1. *Climactic order.* Arrange your details from the least important to the most important. Save the most difficult, complex, or convincing ideas for the last.
2. *Chronological order.* Present details in a series of steps or events, following a logical time sequence.
3. *Logical order.* Show how one idea leads to another, or how one idea causes another to occur.
4. *Equivalent order.* Arrange details in any order, as each one is of equal importance.

Marcello Olenewa chose the *equivalent order* to organize his information on driving. Bertrand Russell, on the other hand, chose *climactic order,* as pity is more fundamentally important than the previous two passions he discussed. Mark Kingwell used *logical order* because he could only praise Xena, the character, after having discussed why he finds Sailor Moon, the character, unremarkable. Kurt Vonnegut, on the other hand, chose to present his information in a series of random suggestions.

Outline

An outline is a working plan for your essay, although not everybody needs to write one. You can write it in point form or draw a diagram. Its purpose is to give you a preliminary overview of the scope of your essay. It helps you to "see" the essay's structure and to define your audience. Write out your selected ideas and details in a brief format. You may use titles, abbreviated in point form, as in this model outline based on Bertrand Russell's essay in Unit One.

SUBJECT: What has made my own life worth living
AUDIENCE: The general reader

PATTERN—KEY IDEAS:

1. Love—need for, reasons why
2. Knowledge—desire for, reasons why
3. Pity—recognition of, reasons why
4. Conclusion

Notice how few specific details were included. The outline serves only as a foundation upon which you can build up details in a first draft. For a longer essay, such as the research paper, a fuller outline may be required. See Unit Six for two more model outlines.

Write the Information

The Thesis Statement

A **thesis statement** tells your readers what your essay is about. It acts as a brief guide to what will follow, and is valuable both for helping the writer remain aware of the organization of his or her details and guiding readers by letting them know from the start exactly what the essay is about.

Exploring the idea of effective driving, Marcelo Olenewa eventually developed his thesis statement:

Effective driving involves the mastery of vehicle management, interaction with the driving environment, and recognition of the need for courtesy.

Notice how Olenewa has three key ideas to write about:

- mastery of vehicle management
- interaction with the driving environment
- recognition of the need for courtesy.

Because Olenewa uses examples to develop his thesis, these three key ideas have been written in parallel grammatical structure. Each idea is written as a noun phrase. Each key idea is explained later in the essay, in a paragraph of its own.

Based on the brainstorming or questioning activities you have done, you have enough details for your essay. And through selection and organization, you know that each key idea has enough information to support it without needless repetition. Unnecessary repetition will give your readers the impression that you don't really know enough about your subject.

Effective Driving

By Marcelo Olenewa

1   When I was growing up, I had an absolute trust in my parents' driving ability. This trust was often translated by my prolonged day-dreams while my mother or father

slalomed through the congested city streets; they were in absolute control. The first time I drove my parents' car fear overcame me. I did not own the same sense of confidence I had in my parents' ability to manage the four-wheeled weapon I was now piloting. However, with practice, I learned to be confident. I learned to become an effective driver. Effective driving involves the mastery of vehicle management, interaction with the driving environment, and courtesy.

2   When I became a member of the driver's licence club, my choices were to take the bus or to learn how to drive a car with a manual transmission. Since I had been taking the bus for too many years already, the latter seemed like a better choice. After watching my friends drive manual transmission for years, I felt like a seasoned professional; however, all thoughts of my mastery of this form of driving quickly dissipated when I was told to put the car in first gear and roll away. First, the car began bucking like a wild stallion (due to the fact that I let the clutch out too fast); then forgetting that I was supposed to be the driver of the car, I tried to squeeze myself into the passenger seat. My poor father was not impressed. After all, I told him I could manage a manual transmission car with the greatest of ease. I eventually learned to master the fundamentals of driving a car with a manual transmission, everything from up-shifting to down-shifting, speeding up to slowing down; actual vehicle management became second nature to me. This, however, was only a part of the driving experience. Now I had to put my driving abilities to the test. It was time to move from empty parking lots to the open road.

3   Interacting with the driving environment seemed daunting at first but became easier with practice. The perspective of the pedestrian is quite different from that of the driver in terms of having to negotiate the road with other cars around you and, sometimes, ominous weather. Rain, sleet, and snow often spell chaos to many drivers and I was no different. It frightened me. In times of poor weather, extra caution needs to be exercised. I learned quickly not to follow too close, to signal my intentions to change lanes well in advance, and to begin slowing down a good distance from where I wanted to stop the car. What strikes me as crucial is how much I have to be aware of the position of my car in relation to other cars. This reminds me of the time I was on a slight incline and my car began to roll backwards, almost into a Rolls-Royce. After that incident I make sure always to check for other cars before making any sort of move. Interaction with the environment, however, goes beyond just being aware of traffic lights and weather; courtesy is the aspect of driving that is not taught in the classroom but is taught on the road.

4   Regardless of how a driver has mastered his vehicle and regardless of the skill with which he negotiates driving with other vehicles, effective driving has a philosophical dimension to it that transcends mechanical aptitude: courtesy. I learned that I must abide by the notion that driving is a privilege, not a right, and that every privilege has a responsibility that has to do with respect for the laws that lead to making road conditions as safe as possible for all drivers. Driving is more than mechanical skill. Driving is common sense (something most of us seem to lack when driving a car). How often have I been frustrated by the person who insists on being a road hog and not letting me change lanes? A lesson in the etiquette of driving was taught to me in a most horrifying incident. I was in the express lanes and

wanted to merge onto the collector lanes and another car was blocking the lane and I almost ended up as part of the guardrail.

5   There needs to be a greater appreciation for the skill required to be an effective driver. This skill is acquired only through many years of experience on the road. However, there are basic guidelines that can be followed. It is important to master the fundamentals—that is what makes an effective driver. The key is to be familiar with the car you are operating, be attentive while on the road, and always be kind to other drivers. My experiences throughout the years have allowed me to gain a true appreciation for what my parents were doing in the car while I was chasing rainbows or flying to the moon. Now I am the one who slaloms through the congested streets of the city.

The Paragraph

A **paragraph** is a series of related sentences that develop or explain one key idea. For this reason, the standard paragraph has a **topic sentence** and a **body.**

The topic sentence states *what* the key idea of the paragraph will be and indicates *how* and *why* the paragraph will develop.

The body is made up of supporting details. Each detail explains an aspect of the key idea (by using an example, say, or giving a reason). Details must be separate and unique, and they must explain what the topic sentence tells readers. The scope and variety of the supporting details develop the key idea. Because the topic sentence controls the paragraph body by indicating its content, it is most important to write one that is clear.

I learned to drive manual transmission.

This sentence appears to have a topic (manual transmission); however, while it states what a paragraph could be about, it doesn't direct the development of the supporting details by stating how and why. It could not be an effective topic sentence because it gives no direction for paragraph development.

Look at this potential topic sentence:

I began to drive on the roads.

Again, while we as readers know what the paragraph will be about, this sentence gives no indication as to why and how the topic will be developed.

Both of these examples of potential topic sentences simply state facts. Statements of fact do not require explanation. To become topic sentences in a paragraph, they have to be improved and give a paragraph a direction to follow. Notice the following revisions:

Learning to drive manual transmission was harder than I had thought it would be. (*what* and *how* and *why*)

When I began to drive on the roads, I found myself in a dangerous environment. (*what* and *how* and *why*)

Now, these revised sentences both have clear topics and a direction for development.

In the first body paragraph of Marcelo Olenewa's essay, the topic sentence appears after two opening sentences:

> After watching my friends drive manual transmission for years I felt like a seasoned professional; however, all thoughts of my mastery of this form of driving quickly dissipated when I was told to put the car in first gear and roll away.

This topic sentence presents Marcelo's first key idea: mastery of vehicle management. It also leads readers to expect supporting details that will show how difficult learning to drive a car with manual transmission was for Marcelo.

In the paragraph that follows this topic sentence, Olenewa makes references to such varied details as a wild stallion, his father's reaction, and methods of changing gears.

> First, the car began bucking like a wild stallion (due to the fact that I let the clutch out too fast); then forgetting that I was supposed to be the driver of the car, I tried to squeeze myself into the passenger seat. My poor father was not impressed. After all, I told him I could manage a manual transmission car with the greatest of ease. I eventually learned to master the fundamentals of driving a car with a manual transmission, everything from up-shifting to down-shifting, speeding up to slowing down; actual vehicle management became second nature to me. This, however, was only a part of the driving experience. Now I had to put my driving abilities to the test. It was time to move from empty parking lots to the open road.

Are Olenewa's supporting details relevant and logical? How many separate and unique supporting details does he include?

Now, let's look at his second topic sentence.

> Interacting with the driving environment seemed daunting at first but became easier with practice.

What sort of supporting details do you expect? Examples here might show how scary driving on the road can be initially. When you read his second body paragraph, notice how Marcelo Olenewa develops his topic and finishes it with many supporting details. His details range from the weather to an anecdote about a Rolls-Royce.

In his third topic sentence, Olenewa introduces courtesy, the third key idea of the thesis statement.

> Regardless of how a driver has mastered his vehicle and regardless of the skill with which he negotiates driving with other vehicles, effective driving has a philosophical dimension to it that transcends mechanical aptitude: courtesy.

Readers expect this paragraph to give examples of courteous or discourteous driving. They also expect the paragraph to show that a driver's attitude is an important component of effective driving. Does Olenewa actually do this?

> I learned that I must abide by the notion that driving is a privilege, not a right, and that every privilege has a responsibility that has to do with

respect for the laws that lend to making road conditions as safe as possible for all drivers. Driving is more than mechanical skill. Driving is common sense (something most of us seem to lack when driving a car). How often have I been frustrated by a person who insists on being a road hog and not letting me change lanes? A lesson in the etiquette of driving was taught to me in a most horrifying incident. I was in the express lanes and wanted to merge onto the collector lanes and another car was blocking the lane and I almost ended up as part of the guardrail.

Remember, the paragraph is a *single unit of thought*. It must have a clear beginning—in a topic sentence stating what, how, and why—and it must lead readers logically through a series of related, pertinent ideas and details that develop the topic sentence. Each *supporting detail* must be separate and unique, adding information or complementing other details that *expand* and *develop* the topic sentence. A paragraph that develops a single unit of thought must be complete and must end with a logical *conclusion*, a final detail or a summary of previous details or a *transition* statement leading toward the next paragraph. Paragraphs in an essay are linked to one other with *transitions* and their pertinence to the thesis statement.

To develop separate and unique details, you must select and question each one you have chosen to include to make sure it is pertinent. To develop a paragraph in a varied manner, you must use such devices as *examples, definitions, comparison, statistics, analogies, summary,* and *facts*. Unit Four of this text offers a number of paragraph-writing strategies that define specific writing methods. In particular, look at the section on the essay of example, where we discuss typical student problems in paragraph development and suggest solutions.

The final phase of writing a formula essay is actually the beginning: readers need an introduction.

The Introduction

The **introduction** is a paragraph, or in some cases a couple of sentences, that presents a general view of the subject of the essay. The introduction offers a preview of the focused subject leading to the thesis statement. The main purpose of an introduction is to catch readers' attention and interest. There are several ways of doing this: by telling an anecdote, by revealing a list of questions, and by relating a startling fact, to name just three. These techniques are used to attract readers and lead them, by reference, to the thesis statement and the essay itself. The introduction should not use details that belong in the essay's later paragraphs. The information used in the opening sentences should be separate and general in content.

Marcelo Olenewa starts his essay by relating his feelings about his parents' driving ability, which leads readers toward his thesis statement. By writing about his general feelings in this section of the essay, he has given readers a chance to relate to his subject and his point of view. Readers can relate to Olenewa's personal feelings. Thus, Olenewa has caught his readers' attention.

The Conclusion

The **conclusion** of an essay is essential. Readers need to have an ending that is not abrupt or disruptive. The conclusion commonly provides a short summary of the essay's key ideas, stated in different words. Often the thesis statement is presented in different terms, to reinforce the writer's focus on the subject. Writers use the conclusion to provide a closing to their discussion; however, they frequently add a statement to inspire readers to explore the subject further. As well, a conclusion can present one final detail or idea (both of which relate directly to the thesis statement) that may stimulate readers to think beyond the scope of the essay, or to reflect on it in a slightly different way. Compare the way Olenewa concludes his essay with the way Bertrand Russell concludes his.

Unity and Coherence

Just as the essay has to present a single, focused subject, each paragraph must do the same. In each of Olenewa's paragraphs the rules of **unity** and **coherence** were observed. When a paragraph has unity, all the sentences relate in content directly to the topic sentence. No sentence should contain an idea beyond the range introduced by the topic sentence. When a writer wanders "off topic" (adding unrelated information), the paragraph lacks unity. To achieve unity, a writer must check each detail and idea, making sure it relates, discusses, and refers to the topic sentence.

One method for checking is to start with the paragraph's final sentence and read each sentence before it back to the topic sentence, asking yourself if the details relate. *Coherence* means making sentences "stick together." Sentences should lead smoothly from one to the other. **Transition,** or linking, words and phrases are used for this purpose. Paragraphs in an essay should flow from one to the other as well, so connecting words and phrases or "pointing" words help readers move forward. To help you understand transitions, unity, and coherence, first read the list of transition words and phrases and then complete the exercises that follow.

Using Transitional Words and Phrases

1. **Adding a Point**

and	a second point	furthermore
also	besides	next
or	again	further
moreover	another	likewise
too	as well as	in addition
by comparison	in the same way	

2. **Showing Connections in Time**

before	next	when
previously	immediately	thereafter
formerly	lately	once
soon	eventually	then

now	in the future	ultimately
subsequently	presently	meanwhile
at this time	at present	nowadays
simultaneously	after	afterward

3. Emphasizing a Point

above all	in fact	especially
certainly	to be sure	chiefly
in particular	without doubt	to repeat
doubtless	unquestionably	indeed
primarily	obviously	undoubtedly
of course	truly	for sure

4. Showing Similarity

in like manner	in the same way	similarly
like	in comparison	likewise
also	to compare	

5. Showing Difference

but	nevertheless	yet
however	on the contrary	otherwise
on the other hand	despite	in contrast
unlike	contrary to	still
instead	although	whereas
conversely	nonetheless	in spite of

6. Introducing Examples or Details

for example	for instance	namely
as you can see	for one thing	in fact
in particular	to illustrate	that is

7. Restating a Point

in other words	to put it another way	that is
in effect	that is to say	similarly
in short		

8. Showing Cause and Effect

as	then	accordingly
because	therefore	hence
as a result	for	thus
consequently	for that reason	since
it follows that	so	thereby

9. Indicating Chronology or Sequence

| first (second, ...) | next | also |
| in the first place | then | |

10. Concluding

in brief	as a result	therefore
to sum up	on the whole	thus
consequently	to conclude	accordingly
finally	as we have seen	briefly

Coherence in Paragraph Writing

The following sentences are adapted from an essay titled "Unwritten Laws Which Rule Our Lives," by Bob Greene. All linking and transition words and phrases have been removed to illustrate how disjointed the paragraphs would be without any variation in sentence structure and punctuation.

After reading the disconnected sentences, you will read two more coherent versions of the same passage. We have written the passage in two different ways to demonstrate the variations that are available to you, as a writer, when you are writing your own paragraphs. Which version do you prefer?

Last week I was sitting in a restaurant with my husband.
A steady hum of conversation hung over the room.
The man sitting next to me started shouting at the top of his voice.
His face was red.
He yelled at the woman sitting opposite him for about 15 seconds.
In the crowded restaurant it seemed like an hour.
All other conversation in the room stopped.
He must have realized this.
As abruptly as he had started, he stopped.
He lowered his voice.
He finished whatever it was he had to say.
He spoke in a tone the rest of us could not hear.
It was startling.
This was precisely because it almost never happens.
There are no laws against such an outburst.
With the pressure of our modern world you would almost expect to run into such a thing on a regular basis.
You don't.
I had never thought about it before.
As a matter of fact it was the first time I had witnessed such a demonstration.
I have eaten many meals in restaurants.
I have never seen a person start screaming at the top of his lungs.

When you are eating among other people, you do not raise your voice.
This is just an example of the unwritten rules we live by.
I have been thinking about it.
These rules probably govern our lives on a more absolute basis than the ones we could find if we looked in the lawbooks.

There would be chaos without them.
Society is disintegrating in the 1990s.
For some reason we still obey these rules.

Version A

Last week I was eating dinner in a restaurant with my husband; a steady hum of conversation hung over the room. Suddenly, the man sitting next to me started shouting at the top of his voice. His face was red, and he yelled at the woman sitting opposite him for about 15 seconds. In the crowded restaurant, it seemed like an hour. All other conversation in the room stopped, and everyone looked at the man. He must have realized this, because as abruptly as he had started, he stopped; he lowered his voice and finished whatever it was he had to say in a tone the rest of us could not hear.

It was startling precisely because it almost never happens, there are no laws against such an outburst, and with the pressures of our modern world you would almost expect to run into such a thing on a regular basis. But you don't; as a matter of fact, when I thought about it, I realized that it was the first time in my life I had witnessed such a demonstration. In all the meals I have had in all the restaurants, I had never seen a person start screaming at the top of his lungs.

When you are eating among other people, you do not raise your voice; it is just an example of the unwritten rules we live by. When you consider it, you recognize that these rules probably govern our lives on a more absolute basis than the ones you could find if you looked in the lawbooks. The customs that govern us are what make a civilization; there would be chaos without them, and yet for some reason—even in the disintegrating society of the 1990s—we obey them.

Version B

Last week while I was sitting in a restaurant with my husband, a steady hum of conversation hung over the room. Abruptly, the man sitting next to me started shouting at the top of his voice; his face was red. He yelled at the woman sitting opposite him for about 15 seconds, although in the crowded restaurant it seemed like an hour. He must have realized this, for as abruptly as he had started he stopped. Lowering his voice, he finished whatever it was he had to say in a tone the rest of us could not hear.

It was startling precisely because it almost never happens, yet there are no laws against such an outburst. With the pressures of our modern world, you would almost expect to run into such a thing on a regular basis, but you don't. As a matter of fact, when I thought about it, I realized that it was the first time in my life I had witnessed such a demonstration. Even though I have eaten many meals in restaurants, I had never seen a person start screaming at the top of his lungs.

When you are eating among other people, you do not raise your voice. This is just an example of the unwritten rules we live by. When I think about it, these rules probably govern our lives on a more absolute basis than the ones you could find if you looked in the lawbooks; there would be chaos without them. Oddly, even though society is disintegrating in the 1990s, for some reason we still obey these rules.

Assignment

Rewrite the following passage of disconnected sentences into more coherent paragraphs. Vary your sentence structure using **complex sentences** (an independent clause plus a subordinate clause) as well as **compound sentences** (two independent clauses joined by coordinate conjunctions).

1. In restaurants and coffee shops, people pay their bills.
   This is a simple enough concept.
   Yet it would be remarkably easy to wander away from a meal without paying at the end.
   In these difficult economic times, you might expect that to become a common form of cheating.
   It doesn't happen very often. Whatever the unwritten rules of human conduct are, people automatically pay for their meals.
   They would no sooner walk out on a bill than start screaming.

2. Rest rooms are marked "Men" and "Women."
   Often there are long lines at one or another of them.
   Males wait to enter their own washrooms.
   Women enter theirs.
   This is an era of sexual equality.
   You would expect impatient people to violate this rule on occasion.
   There are private stalls inside.
   It would be less inconvenient to use them than to wait.
   It just isn't done.
   People obey these signs.

3. I know a man.
   When he pulls his car up to a parking meter, he will put change in the meter.
   He does this even if there is time left on it.
   He regards this as the right thing to do.
   He says he is not doing it just to extend the time remaining.
   Even if there is sufficient time on the meter to cover whichever task he has to perform at the location, he will pay his own way.
   He believes that you are supposed to purchase your own time.
   The fellow before him purchased only his.

Edit the Information

Once you've written a draft or two of your essay, you need to read it over carefully one last time before you hand it in. **Editing,** or **revision,** is the final step in composing an essay.

To edit or revise means to rewrite, clarify, and polish. Revision includes restructuring sentences, moving them around in your paragraphs if clarity is to be achieved, checking facts, and adding and deleting information. Revision is difficult because most writers are protective of their writing and feel it is complete in itself simply because it exists on the page.

How do you revise an essay effectively? There are many methods, but here are a few suggestions:

1. Write your essay in final draft, leave it for a day or two, then reread it. Ask yourself: Have I written what I truly *wanted* to write? You may or may not be able to be objective. Have a friend read your essay out loud to you and *listen* to your own words. Do they make sense? Read your essay aloud to yourself, pretending it was written by a colleague. Is it clear?

2. You should read your essay at least twice in the revision stage. Read from the conclusion back to the thesis. Does it hold together as a coherent collection of data? Does the thesis relate to the body paragraphs? If you find your essay lacks coherence or clarity, you will have to rewrite it, rephrase sentences, or change or add facts.

3. Once you feel that the facts and the format are sufficiently polished, check the grammar, mechanics, and spelling. This can be done by referring to your dictionary or the spell-check on your computer. You can also read over the points in the following Proofreading Checklist:

Proofreading Checklist

Structure

1. Is there a clear thesis statement written in correct parallel form?
2. Does each paragraph have a topic sentence that contains *one* idea and that relates to the *key ideas* expressed in the thesis statement?
3. Do the supporting details in the paragraphs develop the single ideas expressed in the topic sentences?
4. Does each paragraph have unity and coherence? (See pages 36–41.)
5. Are transition words used correctly? (See pages 36–38)
6. Is there a proper introduction and conclusion? (See pages 35–36.)

Sentences

1. Does each sentence have a subject and a verb? Are the tenses used in the sentences correct and consistent?
2. Are there any fragments, or run-ons?
3. Is word order—**syntax**—correct and readable?
4. Do verbs agree with subjects?
5. Do pronouns agree with antecedents? (Note: watch out for the use of *their* when referring to a single subject.)
6. Are words in the sentence appropriate to the idea in the sentence?
7. Is sentence length appropriate?

8. Are there any dangling modifiers? Incomplete dependent clauses? Misuse of *which* or *that*? Do all clauses have correct verb forms?
9. Are there any shifts in person (from first to second)? Is the second person *you* overused?

Words

1. Are all verbs correctly spelled (with the appropriate *s* or *ed* endings)?
2. Are apostrophes used correctly for possessives and contractions? (Be careful with the *its/it's* confusion.)
3. Is there any jargon or unclear use of terms? Is there incorrect usage of words, or inappropriate "big" words?
4. Are there any errors in "mismatched" words that sound alike but are spelled differently, or that are similar in spelling (e.g., *there* vs. *their* vs. *they're,* or *then* vs. *than*)?
5. Are all nouns and adjectives correctly spelled? Are adverbs used correctly? (Be careful with the *real/really* confusion.)

Punctuation

1. Does every complete sentence end with a period or semicolon?
2. Are commas used to separate list items, introductory dependent clauses, short phrases, and interjections?
3. Is the semicolon confused with the comma?
4. Is the colon used correctly to introduce a series? Make sure the colon is *not* used after any form of the verb *to be.*
5. Is capitalization complete? Are first words of sentences and all proper nouns in capitals?
6. Are quotation marks placed correctly? (See Units Five and Six for use of quotations in essays and research papers.)
7. Do all questions end with question marks?

Presentation

1. If there is a title page, and is it accurate? Is the teacher's name spelled correctly? Are the numbers for sections and courses correct?
2. Are pages numbered clearly and consecutively?
3. In a research paper, is the use of the MLA or APA style correct and consistent? (See Unit Six)
4. If an essay or research paper is keyed or typed, are there any errors in the typing?
5. Is the essay or research paper double-spaced?
6. If an essay is handwritten, is it clear of mark-outs and cross-outs? Is the handwriting readable?
7. If an essay is handprinted, is it in upper- and lower-case letters?

Marcelo Olenewa's essay about driving is based upon a series of examples that illustrate and explain his ideas about effective driving. Because he had three main points in his thesis statement, Olenewa wrote a five-paragraph formula essay. This next essay, by J.B. Priestley, is a classification essay with a three-part thesis statement. In its structure, it follows the format discussed above, but Priestley changes the format—lengthening it—to suit his needs.

Priestley writes about the ideas or beliefs that influence our behaviour, which he calls "isms." He divides or classifies political ideology into three distinct types. Notice that each type is stated in the thesis statement and that each is then discussed in a series of paragraphs. Also, there are more than five paragraphs in this essay, but Priestley does not go off topic: his examples and reasons explain only the three main points of his thesis statement.

Wrong Ism

J.B. Priestley

1   There are three isms that we ought to consider very carefully—regionalism, nationalism, internationalism. Of these three the one there is most fuss about, the one that starts men shouting and marching and shooting, the one that seems to have all the depth and thrust and fire, is of course nationalism. Nine people out of ten, I fancy, would say that of this trio it is the one that really counts, the big boss. Regionalism and internationalism, they would add, are comparatively small, shadowy, rather cranky. And I believe all this to be quite wrong. Like many another big boss, nationalism is largely bogus. It is like a bunch of flowers made of plastic.

2   The real flowers belong to regionalism. The mass of people everywhere may never have used the term. They are probably regionalists without knowing it. Because they have been brought up in a certain part of the world, they have formed perhaps quite unconsciously a deep attachment to its landscape and speech, its traditional customs, its food and drink, its songs and jokes. (There are of course always the rebels, often intellectuals and writers, but they are not the mass of people.) They are rooted in their region. Indeed, without this attachment a man can have no roots.

3   So much of people's lives, from earliest childhood onwards, is deeply intertwined with the common life of the region, they cannot help feeling strongly about it. A threat to it is a knife pointing at the heart. How can life ever be the same if bullying strangers come to change everything? The form and colour, the very taste and smell of dear familiar things will be different, alien, life-destroying. It would be better to die fighting. And it is precisely this, the nourishing life of the region, for which common men have so often fought and died.

4   This attachment to the region exists on a level far deeper than that of any political hocus-pocus. When a man says "my country" with real feeling, he is thinking about his region, all that has made up his life, and not about that political entity, the nation. There can be some confusion here simply because some countries are so small—and ours is one of them—and so old, again like ours, that much

of what is national is also regional. Down the centuries, the nation, itself, so comparatively small, has been able to attach to itself the feeling really created by the region. (Even so there is something left over, as most people in Yorkshire or Devon, for example, would tell you.) This probably explains the fervent patriotism developed early in small countries. The English were announcing that they were English in the Middle Ages, before nationalism had arrived elsewhere.

5   If we deduct from nationalism all that it has borrowed or stolen from regionalism, what remains is mostly rubbish. The nation, as distinct from the region, is largely the creation of power-men and political manipulators. Almost all nationalist movements are led by ambitious frustrated men determined to hold office. I am not blaming them. I would do the same if I were in their place and wanted power so badly. But nearly always they make use of the rich warm regional feeling, the emotional dynamo of the movement, while being almost untouched by it themselves. This is because they are not as a rule deeply loyal to any region themselves. Ambition and a love of power can eat like acid into the tissues of regional loyalty. It is hard, if not impossible, to retain a natural piety and yet be forever playing both ends against the middle.

6   Being itself a power structure, devised by men of power, the nation tends to think and act in terms of power. What would benefit the real life of the region, where men, women and children actually live, is soon sacrificed for the power and prestige of the nation. (And the personal vanity of presidents and ministers themselves, which historians too often disregard.) Among the new nations of our time innumerable peasants and labourers must have found themselves being cut down from five square meals a week to three in order to provide unnecessary airlines, military forces that can only be used against them and nobody else, great conference halls and official yachts and the rest. The last traces of imperialism and colonialism may have to be removed from Asia and Africa, where men can no longer endure being condemned to a permanent inferiority by the colour of their skins; but even so, the modern world, the real world of our time, does not want and would be far better without more and more nations, busy creating for themselves the very paraphernalia that western Europe is now trying to abolish. You are compelled to answer more questions when trying to spend half a day in Cambodia than you are now travelling from the Hook of Holland to Syracuse.

7   This brings me to internationalism. I dislike this term, which I use only to complete the isms. It suggests financiers and dubious promoters living nowhere but in luxury hotels; a shallow world of entrepreneurs and impresarios. (Was it Sacha Guitry who said that impresarios were men who spoke many languages but all with a foreign accent?) The internationalism I have in mind here is best described as world civilisation. It is life considered on a global scale. Most of our communications and transport already exist on this high wide level. So do many other things from medicine to meteorology. Our astronomers and physicists (except where they have allowed themselves to be hush-hushed) work here. The UN special agencies, about which we hear far too little, have contributed more and more to this world civilisation. All the arts, when they are arts and not chunks of nationalist propaganda, naturally take their place in it. And it grows, widens, deepens, in spite of the fact that for every dollar, ruble, pound or franc spent in explaining and praising it, a thousand are spent by the nations explaining and praising themselves.

8   This world civilisation and regionalism can get along together, especially if we keep ourselves sharply aware of their quite different but equally important values and rewards. A man can make his contribution to world civilisation and yet remain strongly regional in feeling: I know several men of this sort. There is of course the danger—it is with us now—of the global style flattening out the regional, taking local form, colour, flavour, away forever, disinheriting future generations, threatening them with sensuous poverty and a huge boredom. But to understand and appreciate regionalism is to be on guard against this danger. And we must therefore make a clear distinction between regionalism and nationalism.

9   It is nationalism that tries to check the growth of world civilisation. And nationalism, when taken on a global scale, is more aggressive and demanding now than it has ever been before. This in the giant powers is largely disguised by the endless fuss in public about rival ideologies, now a largely unreal quarrel. What is intensely real is the glaring nationalism. Even the desire to police the world is nationalistic in origin. (Only the world can police the world.) Moreover, the nation-states of today are for the most part far narrower in their outlook, far more inclined to allow prejudice against the foreigner to impoverish their own style of living, than the old imperial states were. It should be part of world civilisation that men with particular skills, perhaps the product of the very regionalism they are rebelling against, should be able to move easily from country to country, to exercise those skills, in anything from teaching the violin to running a new type of factory to managing an old hotel. But nationalism, especially of the newer sort, would rather see everything done badly than allow a few non-nationals to get to work. And people face a barrage of passports, visas, immigration controls, labour permits; and in this respect are worse off than they were in 1900. But even so, in spite of all that nationalism can do—so long as it keeps its nuclear bombs to itself—the internationalism I have in mind, slowly creating a world civilisation, cannot be checked.

10   Nevertheless, we are still backing the wrong ism. Almost all our money goes on the middle one, nationalism, the rotten meat between the two healthy slices of bread. We need regionalism to give us roots and that very depth of feeling which nationalism unjustly and greedily claims for itself. We need internationalism to save the world and to broaden and heighten our civilisation. While regional man enriches the lives that international man is already working to keep secure and healthy, national man, drunk with power, demands our loyalty, money and applause, and poisons the very air with his dangerous nonsense.

RESPONDING TO THE READING

Comprehension

1. Paraphrase in one or two sentences what Priestley means by:
   a. regionalism
   b. nationalism
   c. internationalism

2. Explain what is meant by each of the following words or expressions. You may use a dictionary but will have to rely on context to aid your choice of definition:
   a. big boss
   b. rather cranky
   c. they are rooted in their region
   d. hocus-pocus
   e. emotional dynamo
   f. to play both ends against the middle
   g. paraphernalia
   h. entrepreneurs and impresarios
   i. hush-hushed
   j. nationalist propaganda
3. Answer the following in full sentences:
   a. Why does Priestley compare nationalism to a bunch of plastic flowers?
   b. Priestley says that regionalism nourishes people. What examples prove this?
   c. Why does Priestley say nationalism is "mostly rubbish"?
   d. Explain what Priestley means when he says: "You are compelled to answer more questions when trying to spend half a day in Cambodia than you are now travelling from the Hook of Holland to Syracuse."
   e. What is the relationship between the United Nations and Priestley's idea of "internationalism"?

Analysis

1. In the last sentence of paragraph 8, Priestley changes the form of his essay. In making a "clear distinction between regionalism and nationalism," he begins to compare these two "isms." Why does he do this? What is the argument he is making here?
2. Does this comparison change the focus or thesis of his essay, or can you find evidence in the introduction to show that he intended this comparison from the start?
3. How does he bring the idea of "internationalism" back into the essay discussion in paragraph 9?

Discussion

1. Priestley relates nationalism to a desire for power. Do you think he is right?
2. Given current events, do you think Priestley is right when he says: "Even the desire to police the world is nationalistic in origin"?
3. How optimistic are you about the political future of the world? How accurate do you think Priestley was in his analysis of political states given world events now?

Writing Suggestions

Write a five-paragraph formula essay with a three-point thesis statement on one of the following topics. When you compose your thesis, you may choose to write in a single sentence. If you do, write each of the main points in the same format. If you choose to write each as a noun, make sure you use three nouns. Do not mix up nouns and phrases. Here is an example:

PARALLEL: I have three delights in my life: movies, parties, and skiing.

NOT PARALLEL: I have three delights in my life: movies, parties, and going to the ski hill. (The last five words make up a phrase. To be parallel, they should be written as one word—the noun, *skiing*.)

Essay Topics

1. What are three main concerns facing students graduating from colleges and universities in a recession?
2. In what important ways has television educated young people in the past ten years?
3. What are the three worst effects of racism on an individual?

The following essay was written by Canadian novelist and teacher Edward McCourt, who has taught at the University of Saskatchewan in Saskatoon and written a number of travel books, one of them about the north of Canada called *The Yukon and the Northwest,* from which the following essay is taken. He begins "The Little Things" with a personal definition of travel and states his point of view on his focused subject in a three-point thesis statement. McCourt develops his key ideas in the paragraphs that follow, using examples, definitions, and personal reminiscence.

The Little Things

Edward McCourt

1   The pleasures of travel are rarely confined to scenery and contacts with people. Indeed I would go so far as to say that the chief pleasure of travel is the sum of little things that happen or are seen and heard along the way—little things that linger in the memory long after the impact of big things like a twenty-thousand-foot mountain or a meeting with a great man has weakened almost to extinction.

2   In Watson Lake, for instance, I came across a peculiar treasure—a brochure advertising the merits of a motel association in prose that belongs to the ages. Grading of the member units began with "excellent"—nothing lower—and progressed upwards through "exceptional" to "extraordinary." And the description of the attractions of one western member of the association is something I'm sure I will cherish all the days of my life: "Air conditioning and double soundproof walls, plus a welcome as big as the surrounding Cariboo country—vast and rugged—and

hospitality as western as any cowboy ballad ... Elizabethan decor ..." It seems superfluous to add that this motel rates "extraordinary."

3   And what of the attraction, indeed the awful fascination, of the word spoken but uncomprehended, the phrase snatched from a vagrant breeze, the sentence isolated from its fellows that brands itself upon the brain for no other reason than the sure knowledge that being in transit you will never know what went before or came after. Thus, strolling down the main street of Watson Lake I saw approaching me through the dust-haze the two mini-skirted Alaska-bound California girls in the company of a handsome white-haired elderly gentleman wearing a flaming red shirt. The girls had been our road companions for several days now and I bared my teeth in anticipation of a brisk exchange of social pleasantries, but they never so much as glanced my way. All their attention was fixed on the white-haired gentleman. "And then," I heard him say as we drew abreast, "I was bitten by a seal. At thirteen thousand feet."

4   And that was all. They went their way, the girls playing duplicate Desdemonas to the white-haired gentleman's Othello ("They loved me for the dangers I had pass'd"), and I went mine: they no doubt light-hearted, not a care in the world, and I with a phrase snatched out of a passing stranger's mouth that assured me many a sleepless tortured hour. How in God's name could a man be bitten by a seal at thirteen thousand feet? Of course there was Richthofen's World War I Flying Circus but I don't think any seals belonged.

5   The little things. Printed words. Spoken words. And tangible objects which in ordinary circumstances would not arouse the faintest curiosity but in the extraordinary circumstances under which I so often find them in the course of my wanderings serve to oppress me with the awful burden of the unsolved riddles of existence.

6   For instance, the false teeth.

7   We found them in a deserted cabin which stood on the bank of a nearly dry Klondike creek. They sat in the middle of the cabin floor and grinned up at us. They were surrounded by dust and debris and they posed the fearful question—*where was the rest of the man?* Was he the dust in which they sat? Had he, being a careful man not wishing to destroy an expensive set, removed the plates before putting the muzzle of the gun into his mouth and blowing his head off? I will never know.

8   The teeth are just one more addition to the sum of unanswered questions that hurried journeys pose. Like Ulysses, but for different reasons, I cannot rest from travel. Particularly around 4 a.m. when I'm home and in bed and a seal starts biting me with his false teeth.

RESPONDING TO THE READING

Comprehension

1. Where is the thesis statement in McCourt's first paragraph? How are his topic sentences used to relate information to the thesis statement?

2. Do the paragraphs follow the format discussed in this chapter? How do they achieve unity and coherence? How are they different from the way Jeff Haas (Unit Four) organizes his information?

3. Who is Othello? What are "duplicate Desdemonas"? How does McCourt explain his references to these names?

4. In what way do the details in the conclusion relate to the introduction and thesis statement?

Analysis

1. Why is McCourt's thesis statement perfect for an essay of example?

2. In what ways is the brochure described in McCourt's second paragraph so unusual? What would be the more common language of such a brochure?

3. Why does McCourt describe the scene with the old man and the two girls in the miniskirts? How does it relate to his focused subject and his thesis statement?

4. Why do the "little things" oppress McCourt with "the awful burden of the unsolved riddles of existence"? (paragraph 5)

5. Who was Ulysses and why does McCourt refer to him?

When a writer makes a reference to another piece of writing or an event, he or she is making an **allusion**. An allusion gives readers a chance to compare what they are reading with their own background knowledge. An allusion may also expand readers' ideas. McCourt alludes to two heroes from literature: Othello and Ulysses.

Dan Zollmann's prize-winning essay appeared in *Contest: Essays*, a collection of student essays written in 1991. This essay is based on the formula essay as taught in this unit and states its thesis at the end of the first paragraph.

Illiterate Like Me

Dan Zollmann

1   Most Canadians believe that something should be done to help the illiterate. Yet other social issues often take precedence when it comes to distributing tax dollars. If illiteracy were simply an inconvenience suffered by a handful of Canadians, then the low priority we accord to dealing with it would be justified because time and money are finite, and we must allocate these scarce resources on the basis of importance. However, illiteracy is not merely an inconvenience, nor does it afflict only a few Canadians. Instead, it is nothing less than political, economic, and social alienation of a large number of individuals from their society. As such, it is urgent as any other social problem we face.

2   What is it really like to be illiterate? I do not know, nor will I ever be capable of knowing, any more than I could know what it would be like to be blind, or to be a paraplegic. Four years ago, however, I moved to Quebec City to study French at Laval University, an experience that provided me with some insight into the reality

of illiteracy. As someone who had learned to speak French by ear, I knew the alphabet, could recognize a few words, but had almost no practical experience reading and writing French. In other words, at age twenty I joined the ranks of the illiterate.

3 How does an illiterate survive in a situation requiring a higher level of literacy than most jobs in Canada require, namely, as a university student? With great difficulty. Although in high school I had participated a great deal in class discussion, in university I stopped offering my opinions because I had no confidence in my understanding of the texts under discussion. Always a good writer in high school, I now found myself incapable of finishing an essay exam question within the time limit, never mind producing logical, concise answers. Even the basics of dealing with the university's administration became a struggle: calendars, course changes, registration forms, regulations, all were a complete mystery to me. Sometimes the results were disastrous: for example, I accidentally signed a form that forced me to spend hours the following year trying to get re-admitted to the university. Moreover, I had no idea how services such as guidance, tutoring, or the ombudsman could help me deal with these problems since I was incapable of fully comprehending my student handbook.

4 Not only was attending university difficult, but many problems that literate people daily overcome suddenly became insurmountable. I opened a bank account without even attempting to understand the form I had to sign. My furnace broke down several times in the winter, yet I had no idea to whom I should complain. Moreover, I was incapable of writing a letter of complaint even if I had known where to send it. Although I had some idea of the basics of written French, using it every day was extraordinarily difficult because I knew that when I wrote in French I made mistakes in grammar that most people stopped making after grade three. This embarrassed me to the point that I was afraid to put up an advertisement on the bulletin board to sell last term's textbooks, or to fill out a job application, or to leave a note for someone on my apartment door, or even to write down a phone message for a roommate. I became paralyzed with fear when faced with the most trivial of daily tasks.

5 My inability to read or write also had a profound effect on the way I related to my community. I constantly saw things around me that aroused my anger, yet I was powerless to change them. For example, I wanted to write a letter of complaint to the owners of the pulp mill that filled my lungs with sulphur dioxide gas every time I passed by on the way to the university, yet I knew that any letter I wrote would first be laughed at, and then ignored. Since we tend to judge a person's intelligence by his or her ability to write, how could I expect the owners of the pulp mill, or the editors of a newspaper, to take seriously the complaint of someone who appeared to be too ignorant to write beyond the primary school level?

6 Gradually, I became divorced from the world in which I lived. I voted in the provincial elections, but I did not understand the brochures delivered to my apartment by the candidates. I occasionally bought *Le Devoir* with the intention of reading it cover to cover, yet found myself incapable of following any article longer than a few paragraphs. Unable to read newspapers, I had to accept the second-hand

reports of literate people around me. Unable to understand political debate, I judged on the basis of appearance, rather than issues. Incapable of communicating with my own community, I renounced all personal responsibility, hoping that others would write letters, circulate the petitions, and lobby local officials. In short, I gave up, resigning myself to the frustrated yet passive existence of the alienated.

7 The comparison between my experiences in Quebec City and those of someone who is truly illiterate, however, can go only so far. After all, I was already literate in one language and was in Quebec by choice, not necessity. In contrast, the millions of Canadians who can neither read nor write either official language cannot simply pack their bags and return to their home province when they grow tired of their alienation. Moreover, it is quite possible that most of these people are not even aware of the extent to which they are isolated from society because they know no other existence, no other way of living. This, in turn, highlights the ultimate tragedy of illiteracy, namely that those who suffer from it are powerless to exert the political pressure necessary to change their situation.

8 Illiteracy is, therefore, more than merely a minor inconvenience. In Canada, and in all other Western societies, an inability to read and write means alienation from one's community and from one's country. At a political level, illiteracy makes a mockery of the democratic process by creating an oligarchy composed of an educated elite. At a personal level, illiteracy means subjection to an economic and political marginalization; in short, the exploitation of one of the most vulnerable groups in society.

RESPONDING TO THE READING

Comprehension

1. What are the three key ideas around which Zollmann develops his essay?
2. What does Zollmann do to catch readers' interest in his subject? Why does he believe illiteracy should receive more attention and literacy movements be better funded than they currently are?
3. What is the effect of beginning paragraphs 2 and 3 with a question?
4. What problems are presented as examples of how difficult it is to be illiterate?
5. In paragraph 4, Zollmann develops his topic sentence by using two distinct techniques: examples and cause and effect. Identify the two and explain how they illustrate the key idea in the topic sentence.
6. Explain the examples Zollmann presents to prove how powerless he became as a functional illiterate in Quebec.
7. Paraphrase "the ultimate tragedy of illiteracy."
8. How does the concluding paragraph relate to the thesis statement and the essay as a whole?
9. Using context clues, define the word "oligarchy," which appears in paragraph 8.

Analysis

1. Why does Zollmann give his essay the title "Illiterate Like Me"? After all, Zollmann is not illiterate. What is the impact of this title?
2. In what ways do you believe an illiterate could be like a paraplegic?
3. Writers often use **hyperbole**. That is, they overstate an idea or a case to achieve a dramatic effect. Does Zollmann indulge in hyperbole when he says "I became paralyzed with fear when faced with the most trivial of daily tasks"? What evidence in other paragraphs suggests that similar statements are fact and not hyperbole?
4. Is it true that as a society "we tend to judge a person's intelligence by his or her ability to write"?
5. What parallels with Zollmann's examples can you see at your college?

Writing Suggestions

1. Is there an issue about which you have felt strongly and that moved you to act or complain in public? What were the results of your actions?
2. Define an issue and then voice your concerns using examples and reasons.
3. Dan Zollmann empathizes with the illiterate. Is there a group or cause for which you feel great empathy? (Be careful to distinguish between empathy and sympathy.)
4. Write a five-paragraph formula essay with a three-point thesis statement on one of the following:
   a. the pleasures of travelling to an unknown place
   b. the problems of travelling with a friend
   c. the effects of staying in one place too long
   d. the results of learning about new people while travelling
   e. the changes occurring in an individual after a great trip to a foreign city or country

4

Patterns in Reading and Writing:

Example, Process, Comparison/Contrast, Analogy,

Classification, Cause and Effect

"The pen is the tongue of the mind." (Cervantes)

The reading techniques you've practised so far in this textbook are the basis of all good reading. However, the ability to recognize and follow a writer's pattern of thought, the structure chosen by the writer to express ideas, will help you understand what you read more efficiently. This unit will help you recognize an author's organizational format, and offer rhetorical models to structure your own writing.

Remember, the purpose of any writing is to share information or ideas. Organizing your writing into distinct patterns enables you to express yourself more clearly and allows your readers to follow more easily.

Patterns of Organization

EXAMPLE: Explains through illustrations or specific instances

PROCESS: Illustrates how to do something or how something happened

COMPARISON/CONTRAST: Draws similarities and differences between two subjects

ANALOGY: Describes one subject in terms of another

CLASSIFICATION: Sorts subjects into categories based on an organizing principle

CAUSE AND EFFECT: Shows how subjects can be related through conditions and consequences

I. Essay of Example

An **example** is a verbal snapshot. An example, or set of examples, works like a photograph in a magazine or a diagram in a textbook. It helps readers see and feel and sometimes taste an idea. An example is an explanatory group of words (in one or more sentences) that makes an idea "come alive" by using concrete details.

The Common Stone

Jeff Haas

Thesis statement

Introductory paragraph

1   The common stone, despite its simplicity, has guided the design and use of many tools and institutions in technology, science and politics from ancestral times to the present. The simple stone has actually provided us with many things, without which our modern complicated lives would not be possible.

Key example #1

2   Technology is tool making, and tools are a human construction used to make living easier. While the stone age hammer has been replaced by ones of steel, their general design does not differ. Basic similarities can be found among many tools. The stone chisel is much the same as its modern counterpart. But even though the stone chisel is inferior, it helped create the pyramids and the statues of Easter Island, feats which are still wondered at. While the stone drill, powered by a wooden bow, has been replaced in workshops by electric powered steel drills, it's not uncommon to find stone drills and cutters in the modern world. Diamond-studded drills are used to cut through rock to get at oil, the staple of modern technology.

Key example #2

3   Stone, while not normally considered a part of science, has actually played a major role in scientific development. Ancient humans, without knowing it, discovered many important scientific facts. They learned trajectories from throwing rocks and spears at animals. They learned kinetic energy from observing what the rock did to the target. They learned stress factors and gravity from standing too close to the edge of a cliff. Modern science has developed geology to study how the earth developed. Stones have taught us of the shifts in the magnetic poles, and where to look for oil and metals. Thus the simple stone with its aspects of metallurgy is not so simple after all.

Key example #3

4   The influence of the stone has shown itself in many odd places, such as politics. Was it not common to settle the first disputes by bashing in the head of the opposition? Since that time little has changed except the method of delivery and the composition of that which is delivered. Stone arrow-heads were in use in Europe long after the introduction of bronze or steel. This is because stone was sharper and cheaper; obsidian, for example, can be made into knives sharper than

surgical steel. The common hand-thrown stone, settler of ancient disputes, has become the hand-grenade, settler of modern disputes. Where we once made catapults to hurl boulders at opponents' castles, we now make rockets and artillery to fire on the cities of our enemies. Thus the lowly stone has helped create our most frightening achievement: war.

<table>
<tr><td>Restatement of
the thesis</td><td>5</td></tr>
</table>

Restatement of
the thesis

Concluding
paragraph

5   <u>The common stone, still as simple as ever, continues in its service to humankind in technology, science and politics.</u> In fact the stone has yet to leave the arsenal. Its deployment can still be seen alongside modern weapons in Korea, Ireland and the U.S.A. where it is being thrown at the police or any other likely target.

RESPONDING TO THE READING

Reading Strategy

Jeff Haas's essay, "The Common Stone," shows mastery of the essay formula. From the marginal notes accompanying this essay, you can see that Haas begins with an *introductory paragraph,* the purpose of which is to introduce the subject of the essay while at the same time catch the reader's attention. It is also written to state clearly the essay's *thesis statement.*

In an **essay of example** the thesis statement is usually a single sentence that consists of:

a. the focused subject to be discussed
b. the *key* examples, which illustrate the subject in the order they will be discussed
c. the writer's approach to the subject, which presents the essay's distinguishing point of view

Haas chose to introduce his essay directly with his thesis statement—the first sentence of the essay. This statement can be broken down into a number of components:

- The *common stone* is the focused subject to be discussed.
- *Technology, science,* and *politics* are the three key examples placed in the order Haas will discuss them in the body paragraphs.
- The words *despite its simplicity, has guided the design and use … from ancestral times to the present* link the focused subject to the key examples, but they also tell readers what Haas's approach to the subject is—his particular point of view—on the uses of the humble stone. Readers can thus expect Haas to develop a series of examples from past and present illustrating the impact of the stone on our lives.

The sentence following Haas's thesis statement is transitional. It links the sentences in the introductory paragraph to the first body paragraph by using emphasis: it briefly points out the influence of the stone in modern times.

Jeff Haas wrote this essay when he was a student at Centennial College. He wrote it in a first-year English composition course and followed the steps outlined in this unit on writing the essay of example. As you read his essay again, notice that Haas writes shorter paragraphs than Marcelo Olenewa (whose student essay on driving is in Unit Three). Notice, too, that Haas's essay places the thesis statement right at the start, as the opening sentence to the reader. The general description of the subject—usually written as an introduction—follows the thesis statement as a transition sentence. Haas decided to reverse the order of his information for a reason: he wanted to make an unusual claim about the ordinary stone. By doing so, he allowed the essay to begin with a startling fact. Haas's thesis statement is complex in another way. Readers can expect not only a discussion on the use of the common stone in three areas (technology, science, politics) but also a comparison between the stone's use in the past and in the present.

Next, notice the structure of the three body paragraphs. Each of the key examples stated in the thesis statement is discussed and developed in its own separate paragraph. Haas uses definition and a series of supplementary examples to illustrate each key example clearly stated in each paragraph's topic sentence.

The fiffth paragraph is the concluding paragraph. Notice it begins with the same words as the thesis statement. As you read essays, notice how unity is created by the use of repetition or parallel structure. Haas repeats another device: the startling fact. His final words to his readers claim that the simple stone is still a part of modern guerilla warfare. This fact, witheld by Haas until the end of his essay, is used to reinforce his point of view and to secure his readers' interest in the subject of the essay.

Comprehension

1. Using paragraph 2 as a model, show how Jeff Haas compares examples from ancestral times to the present.
2. How does Haas explain the meaning of the following terms from paragraph 3: trajectories, kinetic energy, gravity?
3. How many separate supporting details are there in paragraph 4?
4. How does Haas keep the comparison of the stone's uses in the past and present going in his concluding paragraph?
5. In what other parts of the essay does Haas use repetition as a device? Haas uses the startling statement, definition, repetition, and comparison as devices. How many of each does he use with his examples? Does he use other techniques: analogy? cause and effect? If so, locate the examples that show these techniques.

Analysis

1. Why did Haas title his essay "The Common Stone"?
2. This essay received an A grade. Why?

3. Why does Haas discuss the past and the present in reference to the common stone? Do you think he has a particular reason for his choice of examples?

When you as a student writer make a habit of careful reading, you will begin to notice how writers like Olenewa (whose essay is in Unit Three) and Jeff Haas pattern information. Haas combines examples with comparison and other techniques to present his belief that the common stone is both humble and powerful, simple yet sophisticated.

Other writers you read in this text may employ many patterns to structure their ideas and facts, patterns such as classification or process analysis—two of the organizational structures to be discussed in this unit. Reading both student and professional writers can show you the value of learning basic techniques and applying them to your own compositions.

Writing Strategy

The first step in writing an essay is to make sure you have a focus and enough content to write about. In an essay of example, the content is the development of a series of illustrations.

Writing paragraphs using examples can be difficult for several reasons:

A. You write the same example over and over. This is a common error in paragraph development. You write a number of sentences believing that each contains a separate and unique example, but when you read over your work you discover all the examples are really just one, but each is written in different words. In such a case, once students have composed their topic sentence, they say the same thing repeatedly.

> *I find that writing exams is a terrifying experience. I get very nervous. My hands start to shake and I feel sweat breaking out on my forehead. I can't write because my hand is not steady. I feel uncomfortable because I'm feeling clammy and my face is damp. In fact, I'm jumpy and my hands just won't stay still as I try to write and I can't control the pen I'm holding.*

This paragraph *seems* to illustrate its topic sentence but it really doesn't develop the idea very far. Essentially, the student has used only two examples—shaky hands and a wet forehead—and reworded the two a number of times. Thus, the paragraph remains undeveloped. One way to overcome this problem is to isolate each sentence (as you reread your draft) and ask yourself if each contains a complete illustration. Then ask yourself if subsequent sentences introduce related but different illustrations that clearly pertain to the topic sentence. Does each sentence show the reader a new image each time? If not, go back, make a list, and revise.

B. You write examples that illustrate something other than the main idea of the topic sentence. When you write quickly, you may often go "off topic." That means you present examples that may or may not relate appropriately to the topic sentence. This problem may occur because you feel you need more information to fill out the paragraph and thus add material that doesn't belong.

My brother loves to argue. Any time our family sits down to dinner, Kevin is there ready to take on anyone who wants to discuss politics, money, you name it. Kevin loves a cause, either for or against, depending on what others decide to defend. He is an expert on graft and corruption in business and can set up an attack on corporation practices rivalling any lawyer. Kevin got his degree in law at university. He wanted to practise after he graduated, but wasn't able to find a position articling because the job market was full. Kevin can argue about the "lawyer" market, too. He loves to point out how big law firms send out calls for interviews even though they have no real positions to offer. Kevin can attack or defend almost any topic concerning the government or the way we spend our dollars.

Do readers need to know about Kevin's university days? Perhaps in another paragraph, with a different topic sentence, those facts would be pertinent. But in the paragraph above, his school history is "off topic." One way to deal with this excess information is to read your examples out of sequence. While you do this, ask yourself if each separate example relates to or develops the topic sentence. If an illustration doesn't quite fit, remove it and save it for another part of the essay. In the paragraph above, cutting out the text on Kevin's school days would make the paragraph more focused and coherent. Remember, rejecting and revising information are essential parts of the writing process.

C. The order of the examples is misleading. Often you'll find as you write that you forget about arranging your examples so that a reader can follow your train of thought without getting confused. You discover that all your illustrations are pertinent and that you have remained "on topic," but, when you reread, there is something wrong with the unity or the flow of the paragraph. This impression may stem simply from erratic organization. Above all, readers want writers to be logical.

One of the most physically challenging activities I know is the sport of windsurfing. You need a board and a sail, of course, and you need a lot of confidence. You have to know how to stand on the board and lean into the wind. I find the worst part is the cold plunge. Before you start you need to get into shape by lifting weights and getting the biceps in form. Holding onto the mast in the wind is one of the hardest parts of windsurfing. Falling into cold water can take your breath away and may cause mild hypothermia, which can lead to exhaustion if you are out far from shore. Once you've gotten into shape, mainly with bicep curls and leg-strengthening bench-presses, the handling of the board is less of a hassle.

Where is this paragraph going? There are two sets of examples, but they are confusing and jumbled and mislead the reader as to what priorities need to be set. The writer needs to rearrange the examples into two separate sections, one following logically from the other. Both sets of illustrations develop the topic sentence, but, because of the order in which they are written, they don't seem related to it. Always try to structure examples in a logical framework: from least important to most or from smallest to largest. Logical order shows a progression or a flow of development so that readers can understand what you wish to express.

The Thesis Statement

Writing a thesis statement for an essay of example is often done after you've focused your subject, compiled a list of examples, and written out your body paragraphs. Selecting examples and finding details can be time consuming. You may know what you need to say, but you may have to write a draft of the essay first before you can decide on the final form of your thesis statement.

One sure method for determining the validity of your thesis statement in an essay using examples is to make sure you select clear key examples that

a. are comprehensive, so that other supporting examples can be used in the development of body paragraphs; and

b. belong together and relate to each other, as they illustrate the subject you've chosen to write about.

How can you tell if a key example is comprehensive, that it is broad enough in scope to be broken down into smaller examples? In the following demonstration, note how a simple series of ideas is tested with a number of questions.

THESIS STATEMENT:	"A part-time job gives you money, self-confidence, and freedom."
SUBJECT:	part-time job
LINK:	gives
KEY EXAMPLES:	money, self-confidence, freedom

How can you determine that *money* is comprehensive enough to be used as a key example? Ask yourself:

a. What does money buy?

b. Why is money earned in a part-time job a good thing?

c. How much money does a student earn in such a job?

Answers to these questions, written in detailed form, would provide supporting examples to develop your paragraph. If you have written an essay in draft form, apply the same questions, reading through your first paragraph to determine if the supporting examples can be related to a single key example.

Look at the word *freedom*. In the context of an essay about a part-time job, what supporting examples would expand upon the idea of freedom?

Supporting examples:

"A part-time job gives me the freedom to choose and buy the clothes I like, such as a leather vest or a long trench coat."

"With the money I earn from my job, I'm free to go on a holiday without my parents, if I choose!"

"Because I can now afford to pay rent, I have moved to my own place (a small apartment with its own kitchen) and can come and go when I want. I'm free to invite my friends over when I wish, at two in the morning or at six at night."

All three supporting examples relate to the key example, *freedom,* and thus would validate the use of the word in the thesis statement.

The Anecdote

Another writing technique you can use in an essay of example is the **anecdote**. This can be used as a supporting example in a paragraph, and could, in the right essay, make up an entire paragraph in itself. An anecdote is a short story or incident that illustrates a particular point about a person or an object. Banesh Hoffman, a British scientist and teacher, wrote an anecdote about his friend Albert Einstein, the mathematician and brilliant philosopher who stated the theory of relativity.

> *He was one of the greatest scientists the world has ever known, yet if I had to convey the essence of Albert Einstein in a single word, I would choose* simplicity. *Perhaps an anecdote will help. Once, caught in a downpour, he took off his hat and held it under his coat. Asked why, he explained, with admirable logic, that the rain would damage the hat, but his hair would be none the worse for its wetting. This knack for going instinctively to the heart of a matter was the secret of his major scientific discoveries.*

In "The Great Communicator," Margaret Atwood pays tribute to Northrop Frye on the occasion of his death. She uses a series of examples, often in the form of anecdotes, to demonstrate her thesis: Northrop Frye was "the great communicator."

The Great Communicator

Margaret Atwood

1   I first encountered Northrop Frye where so many did: in a lecture room, at Victoria College in the University of Toronto, where he taught for five decades. It was his famous "Bible" course, considered de rigueur for any serious literature student at the time. I don't know what I was expecting: thunder, perhaps, or a larger-than-life talking statue. What actually appeared was an unassuming, slightly plump and rumpled figure, with distracted hair and extremely sharp eyes behind Dickensian spectacles. This person placed one hand on the desk in front of him, took a step forward, took another step forward, took a step back, took another step back. While repeating this small dance pattern, he proceeded to speak, without benefit of notes or text, in pure, lucid, eloquent, funny and engaging prose, for the space of an hour. This was not a fluke. He did it every week.

2   Teaching was not something Northrop Frye engaged in as an unimportant and tedious academic duty. Despite his reputation as the foremost literary critic of his own and many another generation, both nationally and internationally, he always spoke of himself as an educator. He did not lock literature into an ivory tower; instead he emphasized its centrality to the development of a civilized and humane society. As a critic, he did not write for other critics, in an esoteric jargon only a few could comprehend; he wrote instead for the intelligent general reader. His early experiences as a divinity student and preacher stood him in good stead: pick up any of his books and what you will hear (not *see*, for he was enormously conscious of the oral and even the musical values of the word) is a personal voice,

speaking to you directly. Because of its style, flexibility and formal elegance, its broad range and systematic structure, his literary criticism takes its place easily within the body of literature itself.

3   That sounds fairly intimidating, and a lot of people were intimidated by Frye. I suppose it's difficult not to be intimidated by someone so brilliant. But intimidation was not something Frye did on purpose. He didn't suffer fools gladly, it's true, and he could be devastatingly ironic when confronted with malicious or willed stupidity; but he was surprisingly gentle with youthful naivete and simple ignorance. In contrast to the image of austerity and superhuman power others projected on him, he could be quite impish. His students were often startled to find references to current pop songs, comic books or off-colour jokes injected dead-pan into an otherwise serious-minded lecture on *King Lear* or *Paradise Lost,* which probably intimidated them more: Was there anything this man hadn't read? Apparently not; but since one of his major themes was the way in which plots resemble other plots—whether they are found in fairy tales, epic poems or soap operas—there was nothing he refused to consider. He knew also that the way in which we understand ourselves is less through theory than through story. In the life of any individual, as in the lives of communities and nations, stories are primary.

4   So now I will tell a couple: because, when anyone dies one of the first things we do is tell stories about them. What to choose from? The apocryphal one about how he first came to Toronto by winning a speed-typing contest? (Actually, he didn't win; but he *was* a very swift typist.) The one about the adulating woman who said to him, "Oh, Dr. Frye, is there *anything* you don't know?" Norrie, gazing characteristically at his shoes, mumbled that he didn't really know very much about Japanese flower arranging and proceeded to deliver an informed page or two on the subject. Or, from M.T. Kelly, a writer friend with whom he discussed northern-exploration journals: "He came to my book-launch at the Rivoli! Can you picture it? Queen Street West, with the black leather? The man was spiritually generous!"

5   Or the time we had him to dinner and something burnt in the kitchen and the fire alarm went off, waking our young daughter. She wandered downstairs and got into a conversation with Norrie. Despite his well-known social shyness, he had no difficulty talking with a six-year-old, and she herself was enchanted by him. That interlude, not the high-powered adult conversation that surrounded it, was the high point of the evening to him.

6   I think one of the sadnesses of his life was that he never had children. But there are many people, including some who never knew him personally, who will feel orphaned by his death.

RESPONDING TO THE READING

Comprehension

1. Notice how Atwood organizes her examples. She uses a chronological sequence:

    a. What is the first anecdote she tells? When did it happen and what clues assist you in determining this?

    b. What is the final anecdote she tells? When did it happen and what clues assist you in determining this?

2. In both the first and last anecdote in the essay, how does Atwood show that Frye was "the great communicator"? Based on these anecdotes, what qualities are essential to a great communicator, according to Atwood?

3. In both of these anecdotes, Atwood also presents Frye as an endearing human being. What examples achieve this effect?

4. In her second paragraph, Atwood stresses that Frye "always spoke of himself as an educator."

    a. How many examples of his role as educator does she present?

    b. What does Atwood identify as Frye's most powerful qualities as an educator?

5. In the third paragraph, Atwood concentrates on Frye's personality.

    a. How does she support her contention that Frye was brilliant as a communicator?

    b. What does she mean when she says "stories are primary"?

6. In the fourth paragraph, notice how well Atwood has established the transition from her third paragraph.

    a. What is the connection?

    b. What is the purpose of each of the anecdotes told in paragraph four?

Analysis

Read Frye's essay "Don't You Think It's Time to Start Thinking?" in the Additional Essays section in Appendix B. Would you agree with Atwood that Frye was a great communicator?

In the following essay, "Deliberate Strangers," Charlie Angus dissects our society and discusses how we have become estranged from one another. He gives numerous examples of our fascination with horror and violence before presenting an extended example of the life and crimes of serial killer, Ted Bundy. The thesis of this essay is not stated directly until the conclusion. However, readers are made powerfully aware, through reasons and examples, of the impact of turning victims into objects of entertainment.

Deliberate Strangers

Charlie Angus

1   It's Saturday night and the kids want a movie. At the local video store, row after row of neatly packaged carnage assails the eyes. *The Toolbox Murders, Sorority House Massacre,* and *Three on a Meathook* compete with such old-time classics as *Texas Chainsaw Massacre.* There are video covers featuring victims being hunted with knives, chainsaws, hooks, and drills.

2   As you search in vain for an old Disney classic, the kids are crying out to see Jason. Jason? Who is Jason? They hand you a video called *Friday the 13th*, a film that has spawned four sequels and countless imitations. The basic story is rarely changed, movie to movie: a psychopath named Jason dons a mask and mutilates local teenagers.

3   "He's sort of a cult hero," the guy behind the counter explains.

4   Okay, so vampires, werewolves, and things that go bump in the night have always been part of our folklore. People love a good ghost story and always have. Bram Stoker's Dracula, the most famous figure in horror history, has been frightening people for generations.

5   It can be said that horror provides a way of synthesizing unexplainable evil. Tales like *Dracula* provide a safe way of confronting the darker side of human relationships. The reader is able to step over the line of the great unknown, comforted by the fact that the beast is always defeated in the end. The reign of darkness is broken by dawn, and Nosferatu is foiled in his evil plans.

6   Hollywood accepted this basic premise of horror for years. The heroine was always rescued from the fate of the undead, and Bela Lugosi always died before the credits rolled. But then, in 1960, Alfred Hitchcock released the film *Psycho*, and nothing has been the same since. For the first time, the monster in a horror film was another human being—a psychopath. Hitchcock tapped a growing fear that strangers could be monsters. Howling at the full moon was replaced with the brutal depiction of Janet Leigh being slashed in the shower. A generation of filmgoers would never feel the same again about closing the shower curtain. In this one scene, Hitchcock changed forever the way viewers perceive fear.

7   A trip to the video store is enough to realize how far-reaching the effects of *Psycho* have been. Supernatural monsters have been replaced by Jason and the genre of psycho killers. The techniques of presenting horror have also continued to change. In the 1970's, Brian DePalma released *Dressed to Kill*, which used the camera as if it were the eyes of the killer. The audience was allowed to share in the excitement of the hunt, the gore of the kill. Our focus has been shifted from the thrill of stopping the villain to the thrill of hunting down the victim. The modern horror movie has taught us to be wary of seemingly tranquil country roads. Who knows where someone might be waiting with a chainsaw or an axe?

8   Horror has made a clear shift from identifying with victims as subjects to regarding them merely as objects. Is this shift a harmless flight into fantasy, or have the borders of our culture, the substance of our collective soul, been altered? Welcome to the age of Jason, an age when the serial killer has become a culture hero.

9   Meet Ted Bundy, all-American boy. He was popular and good-looking, and it was said that he had an almost Kennedy-like charisma. A former employer described Ted Bundy as a man who believed in the system. In particular, Ted believed in success. At one time he studied law. In 1972, he completed his degree in psychology and worked at a crisis clinic in Seattle.

10   Over the next four years, he raped and killed as many as 50 women. When finally apprehended after murdering two women and assaulting a third in a Florida sorority house, Ted Bundy became an instant celebrity. His trial was a classic event of the 1980s. Two hundred and fifty reporters, representing readers on five continents, applied for press credentials to the first televised murder trial in history.

ABC News set up a special satellite hookup to bring the trial to 40 million American living rooms—a television horror drama.

11   The man of the hour did not let his public down. Bundy presented a persona that was charming and witty. When interest seemed to wane, he resorted to outrageous stunts for the cameras. The case moved further into the realm of absurdity when Bundy announced to the court that he had married a woman who fell in love with him during the trial. Those who missed such highlights the first time round could relive the experience when *The Deliberate Stranger*, a made-for-TV dramatization, was shown on prime time. Even radio claimed a piece of the pie with the songs *The Battle of Ted Bundy* and *Just Say It Ted.* Ted Bundy found the success he had craved.

12   The hype of the trial and Bundy's celebrity status served to underline America's fascination with serial killers. Bundy was a star in the quickly growing field of *lustmord:* killing for the thrill of it. Historically, there have been occasional instances of serial killers, but such cases were rare. According to Elliot Leyton in *Hunting Humans*, in the period between 1920 and 1950, the United States did not average more than two serial killers a decade. In the 1960s, this number rose to five (for an average of one new serial killer every twenty months). In the 1970s, the number of known serial killers rose to seventeen (for an average of one every seven months). Between 1980 and 1984, the figure jumped to 25 known serial killers, signifying a new serial killer every 1.8 months.

13   The rise of serial killers is disproportionate to population growth and to the increase in the murder rate in general. Newspapers are full of information on the latest killers, their particular "styles," their kill ratios in relation to existing "records." The Son of Sam, the Hillside Strangler, John Wayne Gacy, Henry Lee Lucas, Charles Ng, the Green River Killer, Clifford Olson—countless books, movies, and articles chronicle the exploits of these killers with a fascination that borders on adulation.

14   Ted Bundy became something of a spokesperson for this new breed of killer. He showed the world that psychopaths are not deranged. Most serial killers have passed previous psychological testing. They are well liked and never socially suspect. Psychopaths, however, relate to other human beings as objects. They lack the ability to empathize. Psychopathy is the extreme form of self-centredness.

15   The testimony at the trial underlined how easily such a disordered personality could fit in with social convention. At the time of Bundy's arrest, his friends were unable to reconcile the man they thought they knew with the brutal murderer described in the press. "He was one of us," one friend explained. Although it was overshadowed by the revelations of murder and mayhem, this detail is a key to unlocking the world of Ted Bundy. As a young Republican, as a yuppie, and as a brutal killer, he was one of us. His killings, like everything in his life, were a mirror image of the world around him.

16   After his conviction, Ted Bundy spent many hours being interviewed by his biographers, Hugh Aynsworth and Stephen Michaud. Calmly and dispassionately, he articulated the roots of his murderous inclinations: "If we took this individual from birth and raised him, say, in the Soviet Union or Afghanistan, or in eighteenth-

century America, in all likelihood he would lead a normal life. We're talking about the peculiar circumstances of society and of the twentieth century in America." Ted Bundy knew he was a psychopath. Perhaps we all have some of the psychopath in us.

17   This is an age of impersonal violence. Television has brought saturation bombing in Vietnam, genocide in Cambodia, sniping in Beirut, and street wars in Los Angeles into our homes. Every night around suppertime, the living room is filled with footage of strangers killing strangers. Our response to tragedy has become shallow. Horrified for a minute, interested for an hour, we soon turn our attention from the dead and dying on our screen. The victims have become merely objects eliciting prurient interest instead of subjects eliciting heartfelt empathy. We no longer relate to them as human beings. Neither did Ted Bundy. "What's one less person on the face of the earth anyway?" he asked his interrogators.

18   Ironically, while becoming numb in the face of death, we are still aroused by violence. We have witnessed the deaths of thousands, both real and imagined. We have been spectators in an endless parade of shootings, stabbings, bombings, burnings, and stranglings. In the realm of fiction. Jason is just the latest in a long line of cultural figures who testify to the power of violence in solving problems, settling scores, and putting zest into one's day. What makes fictionalized killing palatable is that the audience doesn't have to relate to those killed. Bad guys are dispatched with style and the audience is spared the messy details about grieving families and friends.

19   Ted Bundy did not kill to solve problems or expiate childhood trauma. He killed to possess status goods. His victims were all socially desirable women. "What really fascinated him," Bundy said, "was the thrill of the hunt, the adventure of searching out his victims. And to a degree, possessing them as one would a potted plant, a painting, or a Porsche. Owning, as it were, this individual."

20   In his world view, sex and violence were simply two faces of the same coin. "This condition," he told his interrogators, "... manifests itself in an interest concerning sexual behaviour, sexual images.... But this interest, for some unknown reason, becomes geared toward matters of a sexual nature that include violence." The stimulation we receive from media violence and sex rests on our ability to see others as objects. They become commodities to be consumed. "Once the individual had her [the victim]," Bundy explained, "where he had, you know, security over her, there would be minimum of conversation ... to avoid developing some kind of relationship."

21   This is indeed an era of peculiar circumstances. The days when one's neighbours were like family are long gone. We do not know our neighbours; perhaps we are not even interested in knowing them. This rift has been the price paid in the pursuit of commodity culture. In advanced capitalist societies, everything has a price, and every obligation is judged by its ability to advance individual interests. The ties of community, family, and even marriage have been weighed in the balance and found wanting. The modern ethic chooses pleasure over obligation, career over community, the self over the other. We have become a culture of deliberate strangers.

22   Serial killers are nurtured in this breakdown of community. In the absence of strong social interrelationships, the alienated mind begins to perceive others as objects for personal gratification, whether financial, sexual, or violent. On a spiritual level, *lustmord* is the logical extreme of our cultural sickness. Murder has become the ultimate act of self-worship. Gone are the crimes of passion, the relationships gone wrong, the fated love affairs. The killings reflect a cold brutality, the sterile control of subject over object.

23   Ted Bundy went to his death on January 24, 1989. His execution served as a gruesome conduit of hate and media sorcery. Two hundred reporters, camped out near the grounds of the prison, detailed every aspect of Bundy's date with the electric chair as if it were a major sports event. Cheering crowds gathered outside the prison gates. Street vendors reported a brisk trade in "I like my Ted Bundy well-done" T-shirts.

24   In the eyes of the public, it was not a fellow human being who was dying, but an object, a thing fit for ridicule and murder. His public revelled in the gruesome details, spurred on by reports of his fear and remorse. In the end, it was as mechanical and empty as his own crimes, again the sterile control of subject over helpless object. Ted Bundy died reaffirming America's belief in murder. No wounds were healed, no victims' families made whole once again. The beast is not dead but remains lurking in the gulf between neighbours. The electric chair and the cheering crowds serve only as reminders that Ted Bundy was one of us.

25   Ted Bundy was not a monster. He was a human being, and his path toward the ultimate in evil is a path that is well trodden in our culture. He made the choices that commodity consciousness dictates: pleasure, self-worship, and alienation from true relationships. His obsessions with violence and death were extreme, but the path that led there is a path we have all walked in our viewing and in our minds. If Ted Bundy's life and death are to have any meaning, we have to realize that the pursuit of self-interest is not a harmless choice. It fundamentally affects the fabric of human relationships. It is time to repair the bonds of community and stop being deliberate strangers.

RESPONDING TO THE READING

Comprehension

1. Paraphrase the second sentence in paragraph 1.
2. Explain what is meant by a cult hero.
3. What is the "basic premise of horror" that has been accepted by Hollywood for years?
4. What relationship is drawn between Hitchcock's *Psycho* and DePalma's *Dressed to Kill*?
5. The essay apparently changes its focus in paragraph 9. In what ways has the writer already prepared readers for Ted Bundy? What techniques of unity and coherence organize this essay?

6. Explain where Charlie Angus finds his title. Why is it appropriate?
7. How many examples of other serial killers are presented?
8. Scan for examples of impersonal violence that have numbed us. Define *psychopath* in your own words.
9. What reasons are given for why Ted Bundy killed?
10. What examples does Angus provide to show how serial killers "are nurtured in this breakdown of community"?

Analysis

1. Charlie Angus uses very informal language in the first four paragraphs of "Deliberate Strangers." Why do you think he begins his essay in this manner?
2. Do you believe we need "a safe way of confronting the darker side of human relationships"? Why or why not?
3. How many of the videos referred to in the essay have you ever seen or heard of? How important do you think it is to present examples that can be easily related to?
4. Paraphrase "In the eyes of the public, it was not a fellow human being who was dying, but an object, a thing fit for ridicule and murder." What was your reaction when you read this sentence and then realized later in the same paragraph (24) that Angus was comparing the average person to Ted Bundy?
5. Do you believe that Angus's conclusion follows logically from the examples given throughout the essay?
6. Do you think there is a link between the images we see in Hollywood movies and on TV and how we regard violence?

In his essay, "A Stranger in a Strange Land," Austin Clarke presents numerous examples of the estrangement that resulted from his immigration to Canada from Barbados.

A Stranger in a Strange Land

Austin Clarke

1   One thing you do not know about me, and which I have been thinking of for the past few days: I have no real, true friends in this country, even after all these years; for those persons I hold dear are all in Barbados, or are scattered throughout the other West Indian countries.

2   Those are the persons who grew up with me; went to the same schools, were in the same choir; in the same cadet corps; the same scout troop, the 23rd Barbados; who attended St. Matthias Anglican church, for matins, Sunday school and evensong and service, from the age of 6 until I left Barbados in 1955; who were with me on picnics, outings, excursions; who attended cadet and scout camps up in the country; who were prefects and head boys at Combermere School for Boys, and at Harrison College (also for boys, until recently when it became co-educational);

persons with whom I could, and did, discuss the most personal things—joys and sorrows, and the insoluble and very important crises of growing up.

3   I cannot pick one person in this country, my new "home," with whom I am free to share these confidences. And I am not speaking about the trust a man should put in a woman. I am talking about male children, who grow with you into boys, and eventually into men. A significant part of my history and development ended when I set foot in Toronto. This certainly must be the meaning of alienation, if not of rootlessness. It can manifest itself in what the host society rushes to label as delinquent behaviour. No doubt much of the criminal behaviour of immigrant youths, and not only West Indian youths, may be ascribed to this absence of roots and ruins.

4   The roots I call the mores, and the ruins, the statues and the buildings of glass, steel and concrete, and the sensibility of our new friends of our transplanted "home," which is not always uniformly consistent with the way we see ourselves. This is the only meaning of the statement that, "immigrants behave differently from Canadians."

5   Individually, it is the difference between acquaintanceship and friendship. Metaphorically, it explains the immigrant's reliance upon materialistic accomplishments: large house, loud behaviour, conspicuous tastes. All this to the detriment, perhaps the inability, of transposing the roots and the ruins of the country of birth and of breeding.

6   In Barbados, I breathe in the smell of soil, I taste the scandals of the landscape. The mud through which I trample and the sand that pours through my fingers are the roots and ruins I spoke about. It does tend to make my tentative accomplishment in this country empty, and at the same time, over-important and inflated.

7   "We are the hollow men. / We are the stuffed men. / Leaning together / Headpiece filled with straw. Alas! / Our dried voices, when / We whisper together / Are quiet and meaningless / As wind in dry grass / or rats' feet over broken glass / In our dry cellar."

8   It took T.S. Eliot, himself an outsider in England, to grasp this essence of alienation, even though he may have had other personal crises in mind when he wrote this poem. We do know, however, that he was never accorded his wish to be an Englishman, even though he tried to be one, even though he is known as an English author; and this denial came in spite of the posture of snobbish Britishness he himself affected.

9   By nuance and by innuendo, and in crude sections of English society, he was not permitted to forget that "The Dry Salvages" (a poem that described his background in the United States) was not London. "I do not know much about gods." I would paraphrase his words to read, "I do not know much about Toronto's gods." In Toronto, I forget that back in Barbados are those ruins, roots and mud essential to my mental health, as "that river is a strong brown god"; and in forgetting of this part of Barbados now that I am here in this developed country, "the brown god is almost forgotten by the dwellers in cities." I forget them to the detriment of my psychical well-being.

10   So you see my dear, the reason for my silence, my reticence, sometimes my petulant reticence about things that normally summon passion. You see also, why

we are the hollow men, and why our "voices when we whisper together are quiet and meaningless."

11   I stay awake at night, afraid to accept the reward of my toils during the day, because the night is a conspirator for "death's other kingdom" so I remain awake, alone at an hour when I am trembling with the tenderness of nostalgia, for those broken ruins and roots of Barbados. Awake, trying to delay and to postpone the inevitable behaviour of "dwellers in cities": that for the softest desire, I must face an institution, for relief from stress, I must face an institution, for the solution of a problem of passion, I must face an institution, because there are no persons, no friends of childhood.

12   Good night—this is not my cynicism, nor my vengeance upon you because you were born here, it is simply a benediction, and my recognizing your blessed advantage that you are able to sleep with your ruins and your "river," which are as comforting as they tell me a water bed is.

RESPONDING TO THE READING

Comprehension

1. How do you know Austin Clarke is an immigrant to Canada based on what he says in the opening paragraph?
2. Clarke presents a number of examples in paragraph 2. What purpose does he achieve through these examples?
3. In paragraph 3 Clarke says: "A significant part of my history and development ended when I set foot in Toronto." How is the essay based on this statement?
4. What examples does Clarke use to define "roots" and "ruins"?
5. What relation does Clarke draw between the immigrant's success and the "roots and ruins"? (See paragraphs 5 and 6.)
6. Summarize the impact T.S. Eliot's poem, "The Hollow Men," made on Clarke.
7. Clarke refers to a river in paragraph 9. What is the river and what does it mean to him?
8. To whom do you think this essay is addressed? What evidence can you find to support your view?
9. What are the institutions Clarke must face? Provide an example of each.
10. What is the effect of Clarke's concluding paragraph on you?

Analysis

1. Why do you think Clarke chose to title his essay as he did?
2. Do you think that "real, true friends" are the friends that you make in childhood?
3. How important are "roots and ruins" to you? Provide examples.
4. What do you make of the irony that Clarke, an immigrant from Barbados, finds comfort in the poetry of Eliot, an American immigrant to England?

5. "By nuance and by innuendo" an immigrant is often made to feel unwelcome. Can you explain what Clarke means? Do you think this holds true in your experience?
6. Do you agree with Clarke that it is difficult to bring "roots and ruins" to a new country? Discuss.

Writing Suggestions

1. Northrop Frye had a profound influence on Margaret Atwood. Is there anyone in your life—a former teacher, a relative, a friend—who has affected you in a strong way? Write an essay celebrating that person's qualities. Use examples and anecdotes.
2. Write an essay of example about a simple object that has great significance. You might consider, as Jeff Haas did with the common stone, how greatly that simple object has affected your life.
3. What qualities do you think a great communicator should have? Actors, rock stars, and writers are all communicators. Choose one you know about and show what qualities have made this person effective as a communicator.
4. What lessons in good communication have you learned, or what experiences have you had in good communication? Discuss, using examples from your own life.
5. Both Angus and Clarke discuss estrangement and alienation. Have you ever experienced either one? Write an essay using examples to discuss your experience.
6. Angus outlines how images of violence have affected our society. Using examples from your own experience, write about how violence or its images affected you.
7. Although Clarke's piece is an article written for a newspaper, it reads like a personal letter to a friend, with his use, for example, of the phrase "my dear." Using a similar format, write an essay expressing your strong feelings about an issue in your life.

II. Essay of Process Analysis

Process analysis explains how something can be done, step-by-step, or how something happens. In the first case, readers can follow a process and achieve the same result (e.g., repeating a lab experiment). In the second, readers can understand a process but not repeat the actions (e.g., how World War II began).

All "how to" process analyses have the same purpose: to enable readers to follow a procedure, or a series of steps, to achieve a desired result. You are familiar with a variety of "how to" process analyses: recipes, manuals, and lab experiments. You will also have read articles in magazines, or seen programs on television on such subjects as how to find a mate, how to practise safe sex, or how to get into shape.

Read the following essay, "How to Use Less Communication."

How to Use Less Communication

Stuart Johns

1   First-year composition courses serve no useful purpose. Being able to think and express oneself clearly on paper will never be an asset. Despite the *cri de coeur* from employers who list good communication skills as their #1 job requirement, learning to write clearly and correctly is redundant. Keep all of these ideas in mind as we tackle an essay of process analysis. Follow the steps given you and you will never master this means of communication: disregard the logical order of your content; refuse to think about the mechanics of your composition; and above all, show no consideration for your reader.

2   When you start to write a process analysis remember that this rhetorical mode is really a procedure with a beginning, middle and end. Don't you hate the obvious! Keep your reader in suspense; whatever you do, don't organize steps into a coherent sequence. After all, if a step is missed it really doesn't matter that much. For example, why bother with an introduction? Just leap straight in. If the reader is unsure about the subject or isn't interested enough to read on, that's not your problem. The order of any process isn't carved in stone anyway, so why bother being organized? When you present the steps, assume the results are obvious and don't need to be described or explained in any way. Elaboration is boring. You can achieve confusion in your reader by jumping from one unconnected point to another. In addition, don't warn your reader of any upcoming step or resulting problem; clear signals are not the writer's concern. The reader will know better the next time! "Learn from your mistakes" is a great motto to live by.

3   While the reader will learn from mistakes, you have no responsibility for the mechanics of your composition. By that I mean you shouldn't worry about grammar at all. Just go with the flow! Checking spelling is a waste of time; who cares about using a dictionary anyway? If these errors add to your reader's frustration, don't worry! It doesn't reflect on you at all. In keeping with the disregard for organization of steps, supply no transition words. Smooth style is for teachers of English, not real people. In fact, even the use of paragraphs is entirely optional and you could write the whole process in one long surging paragraph. However you decide to present the process, make sure it has no names, no margins, no double spacing, no pagination. Let the reader figure all that out.

4   Letting the reader figure it out has been the key to this essay so far. Although I've discussed organization and mechanics, our discussion has always related to the reader. With this in mind, the final step in producing a totally useless piece of communication demands a lack of concern for your reader. Don't tell your reader any essential background details and omit any stages that are preliminary to the successful completion of the process you are discussing. Assume your reader knows the meaning of any special terms you might use. Explaining something you know to someone who doesn't already possess that knowledge is time-consuming and requires effort. Finally, an air of superiority will convince the reader you really know what you're talking about.

5   Following these suggestions will ensure that your reader has no necessary background information and makes no allowances for possible variations in the process. Being unaware of your reader's needs will alienate the reader completely if the confusion of the process and the sloppiness of the mechanics haven't already succeeded in this accomplishment. Above all, don't relate your process to any other similar process. This might add relevance to your analysis and that is a waste of your time. Follow the steps given you and you will achieve a complete failure in communication. You will prove that being able to think and express yourself clearly is not an asset you possess. You will have demonstrated that, for you, a first-year composition course serves no useful purpose.

RESPONSING TO THE READING

Comprehension

1. What is the thesis statement in this essay? Identify the focused subject and its key ideas.
2. How does the thesis inform the reader that this is a "how to" process analysis?
3. How is this thesis linked to the opening ideas in the essay?
4. What attention-getting devices are used in the introduction?
5. Because this is a process analysis, each key idea in the thesis is actually a stage or sequence in the process. Each stage is composed of a series of related steps. List the separate steps in each stage.
6. The opening sentence of each body paragraph states a key idea/key stage. It also gives readers a link with the previous paragraph. What is each link and how does this transition work effectively?
7. What is the link or transition between the conclusion and the rest of the essay?
8. How does the conclusion relate to the thesis and to the steps in the essay?
9. How does the title relate to the content of the essay?
10. What is the effect of repeating in the concluding line the idea from the opening line of the essay?

Analysis

If you were misled by the tone of this essay and read it at face value, you would be puzzled by its purpose. After all, who would really want to write badly, insult readers, and be illogical? As you quickly realized, the essay is **ironic**; that is, it says one thing while meaning another.

This essay is complex because of its irony, but most "how to" process analyses are straightforward. What makes "How to Use Less Communication" challenging isn't the process it describes but the ironic tone in which it is written.

1. Based on your reading of this essay, what would you say are the correct steps to communicating effectively?
2. A **pun** is a play on words: words that say two things at once. Explain the pun in the title.
3. Why must writers be aware of readers? The essay talks about frustration, confusion, an and "air of superiority." Why are these negative things? Why should they be avoided by good writers?
4. An essay can be written in a humorous, serious, sarcastic, or ironic tone. How does the ironic tone of this essay create humour?
5. What does the term *cri de coeur* mean? Is the author using this term with an air of superiority?

Writing Strategy

Here is a list of steps on how to compose a "how to" process. These numbered steps can be applied to writing analyses ranging from a lab experiment to directions for finding something to a detailed manual of instructions. Once you've read this list, apply it to the essay "How to Use Less Communication" to determine how closely the writer followed the ten steps.

1. Start with a list. Outline, in steps, what materials you may need and/or what you are going to do.
2. Define your purpose. Why are you doing this? Define your result. What do you want in the end?
3. Are your lists complete? Do some steps or materials need to be dropped? Have you made clear all the things you must do to achieve your result? Do your lists relate clearly to the process you are to describe?
4. Order your steps chronologically, first things first. Do some steps happen at the same time as others?
5. Ask yourself: What must my readers know to repeat these steps? Are any background details or definitions of terms needed?
6. Write up the process. Are three main stages best? Are paragraphs more suitable for readers than a numbered list? How should readers be addressed? By simple commands? Through anecdotes and examples? Through long descriptive passages?
7. Write a thesis statement. Name the process you will analyze. State your purpose and desired result.
8. Write an introduction, mentioning your process and any information that would clarify why or how the process is written.
9. Revise your process analysis. Check for unity and coherence. Be aware of dates, times, measurements, transitions (e.g., *while, at the same time, before, after, first, then, at the end*).
10. Write a conclusion in which you restate your purpose and summarize your stages; remind the reader of what can be achieved by the process you have described, and review the desired result.

Reading Strategy

The second type of process analysis explains how something happens or happened.

Because it first appeared in a newspaper and was intended to tell the general reader how something happened, the following article by Leslie C. Smith uses informal language. In spite of its slang expressions and lighthearted tone, the article, a brief history of blue jeans, is very formal in its structure.

The first paragraph presents a clear thesis statement preceded by an attention-getting question: "What do an 1850s California gold miner, Marlon Brando and you have in common?" Once readers have moved on to the second paragraph, Smith's purpose and the pattern in which her information is organized become apparent: she is presenting a **process analysis** that traces the development of blue jeans, step by step. Since Smith is interested in a historical subject, readers are aware that this process is descriptive in nature and that its purpose is to help readers understand a series of significant events that began in the past and still has influence today. In reading a process analysis, it is essential to note how a writer arranges ideas in separate units or steps and that these units are usually arranged in a time sequence, a chronology. Notice how Smith uses dates to define the stages of blue jeans' development from the canvas tent to the designer pant.

Readers of process analysis should also be aware of how transitions are used—such words as *then, only recently, until*—to clarify the chronology. Examples and reasons are also essential to process analysis as they show readers *how* and *why* steps occurred. To recognize the pattern of organization in a process analysis, readers should find the thesis, note transitions, and identify separate steps.

Blue Jeans Born to Last

Leslie C. Smith

1   Question: What do an 1850s California gold miner, Marlon Brando and you have in common? The answer is jeans—those ubiquitous blue pants that have become, within the short span of a baby boomer's lifetime, the very keystone of our casual wear wardrobes.

2   Jeans weren't intended to reshape the way we wear clothes. In fact, they didn't start out as pants at all. In 1853, they were a mere wagon load of brown canvas cloth, carted over the Sierras by a young, enterprising Bavarian immigrant by the name of Levi Strauss.

3   Strauss had it in mind to turn the canvas into miners' tents, and so make his fortune. But when he reached the California gold fields, an old prospector shook his head and said, "You should have brought pants." It seems regular trousers couldn't quite cut the mustard in the rough-and-tumble world of gold mining.

4   Being a clever businessman, Strauss immediately revised his plans and had a tailor cut the canvas up into tough workpants. From then on, it was a race to keep his supply in line with the enormous demand. The button-flied, brown canvas trousers were alternately dubbed "Levi's" because of their designer's name, or simply "501s," which was the material's lot number for reordering.

5   At the close of the 1850s, a sturdy French cotton, *serge de Nîmes* (hence "denim"), replaced the canvas cloth. By this time, however, many people had started calling Levi Strauss's pants "jeans," a corruption of *Genes,* the French name for Genoa—a rather oblique reference to the cotton-twill trousers worn by Italian sailors.

6   Jeans did not become blue until the year 1873. After much experimentation, Strauss decided that indigo was the best dye for his workpants, as that colour remained entirely consistent throughout the dyeing process. Around this time, too, he added brass rivets to the pants' pockets for better reinforcement.

7   Less precisely documented is the moment when Strauss first chose to add the decorative wing-shaped stitching to the back pockets of his 501s. This was a tribute to his new land of opportunity—America, whose intrepid spirit is symbolized by the bald eagle.

8   Jeans, in their own right, began to symbolize the rugged endurance of the American West. The favoured garb of cowboys, by the 1930s they were an established icon—one that Easterners, fresh from their vacations on popular dude ranches, were happy to appropriate.

9   Yet it took until the 1950s before jeans really took off. In that decade, their rough individuality made them the uniform of nonconformists, as typified by film stars James Dean in *Rebel Without a Cause* and Marlon Brando in *The Wild One.*

10   Anti-establishment chic carried jeans through the turbulent 1960s; and by the 1970s, they had become so much a part of our lives that they moved, along with flower children, into the mainstream. Like their wearers, they, too, were caught up in the excesses of the Me Decade: wherein designers, catering to Yuppie desires, raised jeans (and their own bank accounts) to ever more outrageous heights.

11   Only recently have we seen the wisdom in returning to the original, no-frills, five-pocket jeans. They speak to us of true value—not just of price, but of the tradition they represent.

12   Jeans are functional and down-to-earth, apolitical and unisexual. They are also fundamental: They provide a plain blue backdrop for a wealth of wardrobe options. Such versatility makes them acceptable whether worn well-pressed and dressed-up with a blazer and tie, or faded and torn with a T-shirt and sneakers. And because they tend to conform to our bodies over time, we know that they are ultimately as individual as ourselves.

13   Perhaps the main reason for jeans' enduring popularity is the difficulty of pigeon-holing them. There are no set dress regulations governing the wearing of jeans, no denim dos and don'ts to bone up on. Jeans can go wherever and howsoever one wishes. Jeans are, through every fibre of their being, true wardrobe rebels.

RESPONDING TO THE READING

Comprehension

1.   Locate the thesis statement in the essay and paraphrase it. Could the essay begin without a thesis statement? If not, how could it begin effectively to lead readers through the process?

2. How many separate steps are mentioned in the development of blue jeans? Number them.
3. Using skimming and scanning, answer the following True or False questions.
   a. Everybody owns a pair of blue jeans. _____
   b. Levi Strauss was the inventor of blue jeans. _____
   c. The first jeans were made from tent canvas. _____
   d. The name "jeans" was introduced in 1850. _____
   e. The word "denim" came from Genoa. _____
   f. Indigo was used to reinforce jeans in 1873. _____
   g. Blue jeans became more popular in the 1950s because they represented rebellion. _____
   h. Today, blue jeans are regarded as a basic item of clothing. _____

Analysis

1. How does the title of this article relate to its content? to its structure?
2. How would you explain the popularity of blue jeans? What do you think of the reasons Leslie C. Smith presents for their popularity? Are they valid reasons?
3. Do you think blue jeans really are ubiquitous?
4. Why do you think a national newspaper would print an article like this one?
5. Could the story of blue jeans have been as effective if Smith had reversed the order of her steps, starting with the popularity of blue jeans today and going back into history, to the California gold rush? Why or why not?
6. How effective is Smith in holding the reader's attention throughout the article? What devices does she use to keep interest in the subject? Does she use anecdote? Does she ask questions? Does she use supporting examples effectively?

Writing Strategy

As with the "how to do something" writing process, in preparing to write the process of how something happened, the first thing you must do is make a list of the steps involved. You must determine where the process starts and where it ends.

In Leslie C. Smith's essay, the start of the process was 1853, when blue jeans were born from canvas tents.

You must also ask yourself if anything needs to be explained—background information—before you start writing down the steps of the process. What do readers need to know *before* the process is explained? For instance, if you were to explain how a car engine works, would you have to define the main components of the engine before you began? Would readers need to know a brief history of combustion as a preface to the process? What did Leslie C. Smith do? She provided a brief description of the use of canvas in the California gold rush. This background led the reader to the first step, which described how Levi Strauss "had a tailor cut the canvas up into tough workpants."

The *thesis statement* must state clearly the focused subject and identify where the process begins. Smith stated her thesis in the opening paragraph by answering the question she wrote in her brief introduction. She then stated in her second paragraph the idea that jeans weren't intended to reshape the way people dress. This led to her first step in the historical process.

The *body paragraphs* of the process essay are made up of the chronological steps that you determined in your list. Examples, anecdotes, and definitions may be included to sustain reader interest and to clarify how and why a step occurred.

Steps must develop logically. When writing the body, do not write each step separately. Group steps into *stages,* each stage making up a separate paragraph. Smith arranged her steps into three major stages. She began with details illustrating the birth of jeans in the Gold Rush. Her second stage traced the evolution of jeans as popular clothing due to the influence of Hollywood movie stars. Her final stage discussed jeans in their maturity, as essential clothing for people from all walks of life.

To create unity and coherence, each stage should be defined. Smith used dates in her essay to define her stages, but transition words and phrases also clarify stages for readers. To clarify her chronology, Smith used words like *yet, after,* and *recently* with her dates.

What sort of process analysis is used in the following essay by Nicola Bleasby? *Hint:* Look at the title.

How Can You Mend a Broken Heart?

Nicola Bleasby

Love hurts, but time heals all wounds. So take the high road: Get in touch with your inner philologist. It's as easy as ABC.

1   Who says that a few bad clichés and an expanded vocabulary can't mend a broken heart? After the cookie has crumbled and the fat lady has sung, the last things a bruised ego needs is to be at a loss for words when they're needed most. There may be plenty more fish in the sea, but words aren't as disposable. A good word is hard to find—the perfect word is worth its weight in gold.

2   When the flame in a relationship has been extinguished by someone other than yourself (when you have been dumped), the immediate future looks bleak. The most productive course of action to alleviate the agony is not to drown your sorrows in either liquor or nostalgia but to buy a new dictionary. Yes, a dictionary. A big one. The bigger the heartbreak, the bigger the dictionary required.

3   Within the confines of the alphabet it is possible in one month to conquer the most crushing heartbreak while simultaneously expanding your vocabulary. Greeting each day with a new letter inscribes into your consciousness (1) measured progress through emotional trauma; and (2) a vocabulary that puts you in touch with your emotions.

4   Have you got your dictionary handy? Are you sitting comfortably? Who says this can't be as easy as ABC?

5   The initial period post-*affair de l'amour* is the time for emotional primordiality, not composure. The first week begins with anger, bellicosity, perhaps contrition,

perhaps contempt—another day, another diatribe. Suppress nothing. Draw strength from your dictionary. Delve into the depths of your psyche and come to terms with feelings of abandonment, betrayal, and disaffection. Many scathing expressions can be created using this week's material that can't be used in civil, everyday life. Execrate the—well, take your pick of any number of profane epithets befitting the individual responsible for your diminution.

6   This is also a time of contradictions. Your emotional behaviour will run the gamut between abnegation and the urge to gormandize; between ataraxy and garrulity.

7   On the eighth day, it is necessary to contend with reality. You can't hide from the truth no matter how painful it is. Love hurts. The halcyon days *de l'amour* with your *inamorato* are not coming back. He never loved you anyway. You deserve better.

8   If dealing with the H's seem simple, watch out—this could be the harbinger of an early rebound. Jumping from the frying pan into the fire will solve nothing. Be diligent in your reading for the next few days. If you have any "urges," it is probably best to stay inside and read each letter's section—twice. If libidinal impulses persist, all you really have to do is suppress them until R: On rebound day, at least there is an excuse.

9   Even for the most dedicated philologist, L will be the most difficult day to deal with. Too many L words can bring back memories that might subvert all that has been accomplished in the preceding 11 days. Easy solution: Skip the section of the dictionary that falls between louse and low—there's no need to rub salt into a wound. Instead of sentimental thoughts, you'll be left with reasonably negative words that do not pertain to you.

10   It's clear sailing from M to Z. The valediction on Day 22 will be a piece of cake —with this I offer no hand-holding. I have only reached "I"—dealing with the iniquity of isolation, but I have outlined the intended course of my lexical progression. Tomorrow, I will jettison my filiopietistic tendencies (which I discovered a couple of days ago, but which then seemed unimportant). Then, I'm going to discard all the kitschy memories and synthesize the mantra of my autonomy.

11   When I reach Z, I will be ready to join the Zeitgeist with a potentiated vocabulary. It will be a personal triumph, an act of serendipity. After all, when life gives you lemons you've got to make lemonade.

RESPONDING TO THE READING

Comprehension

1. The first sentence written as a question is the thesis statement of this essay. Paraphrase it by rewriting it as a declarative sentence.
2. How many distinct steps does Bleasby give to readers to mend their broken hearts?
3. The steps are presented as two parallel processes. One is chronological. What is the organizing principle of the other?

4. Using your dictionary, define the word *cliché*. Then skim the article to find ten clichés and paraphrase them using more formal language.
5. After an opening paragraph full of clichés, the level of language in the article changes dramatically in paragraph 2. From then on Bleasby combines clichés with a very sophisticated and precise vocabulary. Scan to find ten words that are not part of your everyday vocabulary. Define each by writing a sentence containing the word.
6. Why is the *L* section of a dictionary the most difficult to deal with according to Bleasby? What words between *louse* and *low* could cause heartache and agony to the rejected lover?
7. Does this essay conclude on a positive or negative note? How does the content of the concluding sentence relate to that of the rest of the essay?

Analysis

1. Terry Johnson says that slang "can reveal as well as conceal secrets." Do you think clichés work in the same way? Do you know people who use clichés constantly? Why do you think they do this?
2. Certain public figures use many clichés in their speech—sportscasters and politicians in particular. Why do you think they speak in this manner?
3. What is meant by the phrase "Get in touch with your inner philologist"? Don't just define the meaning of philologist.
4. Is Bleasby's advice serious? Is it really helpful or even realistic?
5. List the steps you would use to mend a broken heart.

Writing Suggestions

1. Write a humorous and ironic article that tells somebody how *not* to do something, making sure you give explicit instructions but using the appropriate tone.
2. Have you ever asked yourself where an object comes from? How was it manufactured, and where and by whom? (Think about your VCR, for instance. Who designed it? Where and how was it made?) Write a process analysis explaining how something you own was made.
3. If you want to write a historical process similar to Smith's article on blue jeans, you will need to do research in a library. Ever wondered why or how a war occurred? What was the birth and development of the car?
4. Give a friend personal advice on how to deal with a particular problem. Make sure your advice contains steps that can be followed.

III. Essay of Comparison and Contrast

Any act of comparison means making a value judgment. How do you decide which shirt to wear? If you have a lot of clothes, you make a series of judgments about colours, pattern, sleeve length, and coordination. For some, the choice may lie between clean and dirty; nevertheless, a decision has been made based on comparison.

Making the reader draw a conclusion or arrive at a value judgment is the purpose of writing an essay of **comparison and contrast.** The conclusion simply may be to see things in a new way because they have been set side by side.

Writing Strategy

The essay of comparison or contrast presents two subjects side by side. **Comparison** shows how the two subjects are alike or similar; **contrast** demonstrates the differences between the two subjects. Some essays of comparison and contrast (Sandra Stewart's, for example) deal with both similarities and differences.

When composing this sort of essay you must consider why you are comparing or contrasting two subjects. What is your purpose in showing the reader how the two subjects are alike or different? Do you want to demonstrate, for example, that a Big Mac is better than a cheeseburger from Burger King? Do you want to persuade your reader to adopt marketing strategy A rather than marketing strategy B? Do you want to shed new light on Johnny Depp by comparing him to, or contrasting him with, Brad Pitt?

In the introduction to any essay of comparison/contrast you must clearly identify your two subjects and your purpose for considering them together. Then you must establish your approach. There are two methods of organizing your materials for an essay of comparison/contrast: the block method and the point method.

Block Method
With this method you concentrate on your first subject; you present all of your key ideas and supporting details as they relate to this subject. When you finish subject 1, you turn to subject 2 and follow the same procedure.

```
       subject 1 – apples            subject 2 – oranges
       Introduction to apples & oranges + thesis statement
       Block 1 – Apples              – taste
                                     – cost
                                     – storage
       Block 2 – Oranges             – taste
                                     – cost
                                     – storage
       Conclusion to apples & oranges
```

Point Method
With this method you discuss the two subjects together in relation to point 1, the first of your key ideas. Then you discuss the same two subjects in relation to point 2, your second key idea. In this way you go back and forth between your two subjects until you have finished discussing your key ideas.

```
       subject 1 – apples            subject 2 – oranges
       Introduction to apples & oranges + thesis statement
       Point 1 – taste               – apples & oranges
       Point 2 – cost                – apples & oranges
       Point 3 – storage             – apples & oranges
       Conclusion to apples & oranges
```

The following essay by student Sandra Stewart uses the point method. As you answer the questions that follow, you will be teaching yourself how to organize an essay of comparison and contrast.

Aladdin and *Beauty and the Beast*

Sandra Stewart

1   There seems to be a trend in movies recently: more interest in the human element, less in hi-tech spectacle. Ironically, two of the best movies I've seen in the last couple of years that explore the area of human relationships are cartoons. Both are Disney productions exemplifying the highest standards of artwork, complex musical scores, and a strong storyline. *Beauty and the Beast* and *Aladdin* are alike in these ways, but *Beauty and the Beast,* unlike *Aladdin,* is a movie with a message.

2   Both movies open with a narrative voice-over, setting the scene. In each the artwork is wonderful. The story *Aladdin* begins with the terrifying Tiger-God set against a deep, dark sky sparkling with stars. Even though it's all drawings, you feel the emptiness of the open spaces, and you know that the villain, Jafar, is really evil. *Beauty and the Beast* opens by moving the viewer through a forest. You really feel as if you are part of the scenery. Even though it's all a cartoon, the camera leads the eyes of the audience deeper through the tangled growth of forest bushes. What amazes me is how the cartoonists managed to give depth and perspective to that forest. In *Aladdin* the artwork is at its most brilliant in the wild carpet-rides, first through the cave of treasures and then in the romantic flight over the countryside that Aladdin and Jasmine take. In the case of *Aladdin,* the star is undoubtedly the Genie. The changes in his shape and size are so fast. This is amazing, especially when fluid movement is not sacrificed to that rapid pace. *Beauty and the Beast* excels in the flowing movements of all its characters, but especially Belle. She moves like a real ballerina with none of the jerkiness you'd expect from watching Saturday morning cartoons. In addition, Belle's face is so expressive. Her acting is better than some Hollywood movie stars. Moods are shown and she has this unruly lock of hair that is always falling across her face and which she brushes aside gracefully. It is this attention to "real" detail that makes this movie so brilliant technically.

3   The quality of the music in each movie is another example of attention to detail. Part of the energy in *Aladdin* comes from its musical score. The songs, with the exception of the beautiful and romantic "New World," are really lively and entertaining. My particular favourites are the ones my little brother likes best, "Prince Ali" and "A Friend Like Me." The talents of Robin Williams, who plays the Genie, are really outstanding. Just as *Aladdin* allows real actors a chance to shine, so does *Beauty and the Beast.* The spectacular "Be Our Guest" would be a showstopper on stage. Jerry Orbach sings his heart out as Lumière in this particular song. The romantic ballad "Beauty and the Beast" is so melodic that my little brother, who was only three and a half at the time, came out of the movie theatre singing it.

4   Both of the movies are based on really well-loved fairy stories. They have strong plots which everyone knows and the Disney writers have adapted to suit

today's society. In *Aladdin,* Princess Jasmine isn't only a "girl" expecting to be married off. She has her own strong personality and demands the right to choose whom she'll marry. She also helps Aladdin overcome the evil Jafar, so that they can "live happily ever after." However, it is in *Beauty and the Beast* that the most powerful changes to the fairy tale have been made. Belle is definitely the star of this movie, and again she's not a weak little girl. In the movie, Belle is a more fully developed character than in the fairy story. She's an active, intelligent modern woman who respects education more than good looks. She really despises the "macho" Gaston. Gaston is an addition to the original fairy story and this character really modernizes the plot. Through Gaston, the movie is able to make us think about "jock" behaviour, mob violence, and propaganda. It's critical of all of these things. *Beauty and the Beast* has a moral that *Aladdin* doesn't. It's more than a story. This is the real difference between the two movies. *Beauty and the Beast* shows how powerful and fragile love is. Even my little brother knew that this movie showed us that real love is for what a person is and not what a person looks like. He could see that the Beast became a handsome Prince only because he and Belle loved each other.

5   Well, I hope I've convinced you to see these movies. They're both on video now. Believe me you'll enjoy both of them not only because they are spectacular and entertaining but also because they teach you something about human relationships in a very realistic way. If you're embarrassed renting them, borrow a kid to accompany you to the video store. You'll be glad you did.

RESPONDING TO THE READING

Introduction

1. In her introductory paragraph, Stewart identifies her two subjects. What are they?
2. What is her thesis?
3. What are the key ideas she will use to compare/contrast her two subjects?
4. What does Stewart say is her purpose in making this comparison/contrast?

Body Paragraphs

In this section of her essay, Stewart takes each key idea and develops it point by point in a paragraph of its own. She discusses both movies in each paragraph, comparing them on the basis of a key idea.

1. Based on your identification of the key ideas in the essay's introduction, find the topic sentence in each paragraph.
2. If she had chosen the block method of development, Stewart would have concentrated first on *Aladdin* and then on *Beauty and the Beast.* Using Stewart's key ideas and her supporting details write an outline for this essay using the block method.

Columbus and the Moon

Tom Wolfe

1   The National Aeronautics and Space Administration's moon landing 10 years ago today was a Government project, but then so was Columbus's voyage to America in 1492. The Government, in Columbus's case, was the Spanish Court of Ferdinand and Isabella. Spain was engaged in a sea race with Portugal in much the same way that the United States would be caught up in a space race with the Soviet Union four and a half centuries later.

2   The race in 1492 was to create the first shipping lane to Asia. The Portuguese expeditions had always sailed east, around the southern tip of Africa. Columbus decided to head due west, across open ocean, a scheme that was feasible only thanks to a recent invention—the magnetic ship's compass. Until then ships had stayed close to the great land masses even for the longest voyages. Likewise, it was only thanks to an invention of the 1940's and early 1950's, the high-speed electronic computer, that NASA would even consider propelling astronauts out of the Earth's orbit and toward the moon.

3   Both NASA and Columbus made not one but a series of voyages. NASA landed men on six different parts of the moon. Columbus made four voyages to different parts of what he remained convinced was the east coast of Asia. As a result both NASA and Columbus had to keep coming back to the Government with their hands out, pleading for refinancing. In each case the reply of the Government became, after a few years: "This is all very impressive, but what earthly good is it to anyone back home?"

4   Columbus was reduced to making the most desperate claims. When he first reached land in 1492 at San Salvador, off Cuba, he expected to find gold, or at least spices. The Arawak Indians were awed by the strangers and their ships, which they believed had descended from the sky, and they presented them with their most prized possessions, live parrots and balls of cotton. Columbus soon set them digging for gold, which didn't exist. So he brought back reports of fabulous riches in the form of manpower; which is to say, slaves. He was not speaking of the Arawaks, however. With the exception of criminals and prisoners of war, he was supposed to civilize all natives and convert them to Christianity. He was talking about the Carib Indians, who were cannibals and therefore qualified as criminals. The Caribs would fight down to the last unbroken bone rather than endure captivity, and few even survived the voyages back to Spain. By the end of Columbus's second voyage, in 1496, the Government was becoming testy. A great deal of wealth was going into voyages to Asia, and very little was coming back. Columbus made his men swear to return to Spain saying that they had not only reached the Asian mainland, they had heard Japanese spoken.

5   Likewise by the early 1970's, it was clear that the moon was in economic terms pretty much what it looked like from Earth, a gray rock. NASA, in the quest for appropriations, was reduced to publicizing the "spinoffs" of the space program. These included Teflon-coated frying pans, a ballpoint pen that would write in a weightless environment, and a computerized biosensor system that would enable

doctors to treat heart patients without making house calls. On the whole, not a giant step for mankind.

6   In 1493, after his first voyage, Columbus had ridden through Barcelona at the side of King Ferdinand in the position once occupied by Ferdinand's late son, Juan. By 1500, the bad-mouthing of Columbus had reached the point where he was put in chains at the conclusion of his third voyage and returned to Spain in disgrace. NASA suffered no such ignominy, of course, but by July 20, 1974, the fifth anniversary of the landing of Apollo 11, things were grim enough. The public had become gloriously bored by space exploration. The fifth anniversary celebration consisted mainly of about 200 souls, mostly NASA people, sitting on folding chairs underneath a camp-meeting canopy on the marble prairie outside the old Smithsonian Air Museum in Washington listening to speeches by Neil Armstrong, Michael Collins, and Buzz Aldrin and watching the caloric waves ripple.

7   Extraordinary rumors had begun to circulate about the astronauts. The most lurid said that trips to the moon, and even into earth orbit, had so traumatized the men, they had fallen victim to religious and spiritualist manias or plain madness. (Of the total 73 astronauts chosen, one, Aldrin, is known to have suffered from depression, rooted, as his own memoir makes clear, in matters that had nothing to do with space flight. Two teamed up in an evangelical organization, and one set up a foundation for the scientific study of psychic phenomena—interests the three of them had developed long before they flew in space.) The NASA budget, meanwhile, had been reduced to the light-bill level.

8   Columbus died in 1509, nearly broke and stripped of most of his honours as Spain's Admiral of the Ocean, a title he preferred. It was only later that history began to look upon him not as an adventurer who had tried and failed to bring home gold—but as a man with a supernatural sense of destiny, whose true glory was his willingness to plunge into the unknown, including the remotest parts of the universe he could hope to reach.

9   NASA still lives, albeit in reduced circumstances, and whether or not history will treat NASA like the admiral is hard to say.

10   The idea that the exploration of the rest of the universe is its own reward is not very popular, and NASA is forced to keep talking about things such as bigger communications satellites that will enable live television transmission of European soccer games at a fraction of the current cost. Such notions as "building a bridge to the stars for mankind" do not light up the sky today—but may yet.

RESPONDING TO THE READING

Comprehension

1. Which two things are being compared in this essay?
2. Identify the thesis of this essay.
3. Is this essay developed by using the point or the block method?

4. What points of comparison does Wolfe make between Columbus's voyages and NASA's forays into space?
5. Why and how were the governments involved in each of these explorations?
6. What is the purpose of the various anecdotes Wolfe uses?
7. How did rumour affect the reputations of Columbus and the astronauts?
8. How optimistic is Wolfe about NASA's future? What clues led to your answer?

Analysis

1. What revelation does the reader experience from the comparison of Columbus's voyages with NASA's space travels?
2. What is the purpose in comparing these two subjects?
3. Explain the allusion in paragraph 5, "On the whole, not a giant step for mankind."
4. Were the voyages of Columbus glorious achievements or merely self-serving exploits? What is Tom Wolfe's position on this? How do you know?
5. What is the implication of placing the "exploration of the rest of the universe" alongside the idea of transmitting "European soccer games at a fraction of the current cost"?

Rachel Carson draws comparisons and contrasts in her essay, "A Fable For Tomorrow," using the block method.

A Fable for Tomorrow

Rachel Carson

1   There was once a town in the heart of America where all life seemed to live in harmony with its surroundings. The town lay in the midst of a checkerboard of prosperous farms, with fields of grain and hillsides of orchards where, in spring, white clouds of bloom drifted above the green fields. In autumn, oak and maple and birch set up a blaze of color that flamed and flickered across a backdrop of pines. The foxes barked in the hills and deer silently crossed the fields, half hidden in the mists of the fall mornings.

2   Along the roads, laurel, viburnum and alder, great ferns and wildflowers delighted the traveler's eye through much of the year. Even in winter the roadsides were places of beauty, where countless birds came to feed on the berries and on the seed heads of the dried weeds rising above the snow. The countryside was, in fact, famous for the abundance and variety of its bird life, and when the flood of migrants was pouring through in spring and fall people traveled from great distances to observe them. Others came to fish the streams, which flowed clear and cold out of the hills and contained shady pools where trout lay. So it had been from the days many years ago when the first settlers raised their houses, sank their wells, and built their barns.

3   Then a strange blight crept over the area and everything began to change. Some evil spell had settled on the community: mysterious maladies swept the flocks of chickens; the cattle and sheep sickened and died. Everywhere was a shadow of death. The farmers spoke of much illness among their families. In the town the doctors had become more and more puzzled by new kinds of sickness appearing among their patients. There had been several sudden and unexplained deaths not only among adults but even among children, who would be stricken suddenly while at play and die within a few hours.

4   There was a strange stillness. The birds, for example—where had they gone? Many people spoke of them, puzzled and disturbed. The feeding stations in the backyards were deserted. The few birds seen anywhere were moribund; they trembled violently and could not fly. It was a spring without voices. On the mornings that had once throbbed with the dawn chorus of robins, catbirds, doves, jays, wrens, and scores of other bird voices there was no sound; only silence lay over the fields and woods and marsh.

5   On the farms the hens brooded, but no chicks hatched. The farmers complained that they were unable to raise any pigs—the litters were small and the young survived only a few days. The apple trees were coming into bloom but no bees droned among the blossoms, so there was no pollination and there would be no fruit.

6   The roadsides, once so attractive, were now lined with browned and withered vegetation as though swept by fire. These, too, were silent, deserted by all living things. Even the streams were now lifeless. Anglers no longer visited them, for all the fish had died.

7   In the gutters under the eaves and between the shingles of the roofs, a white granular powder still showed a few patches; some weeks before it had fallen like snow upon the roofs and the lawns, the fields and streams. No witchcraft, no enemy action had silenced the rebirth of new life in this stricken world. The people had done it themselves.

8   This town does not actually exist, but it might easily have a thousand counterparts in America or elsewhere in the world. I know of no community that has experienced all the misfortunes I describe. Yet every one of these disasters has actually happened somewhere, and many real communities have already suffered a substantial number of them. A grim specter has crept upon us almost unnoticed, and this imagined tragedy may easily become a stark reality we all shall know.

RESPONDING TO THE READING

Comprehension

1. Carson begins her essay without a formal introduction. What are her two subjects? Because she develops the essay in block method, she concentrates on subject one before turning to subject two. Which paragraphs discuss subject two?

2. Is there a thesis statement? If so, where does Carson place it?
3. Identify Carson's key ideas in each block.
4. Why does Carson devote so much of her supporting detail to bird life?
5. What is her purpose in discussing the "town in the heart of America"?

Analysis

1. The discussion of her second subject is substantially longer than her discussion of the first. What details does she add?
2. Her final two paragraphs provide an explanation, a cause for the changes discussed in the essay. What effect does Carson produce by placing this information at the end of her essay?
3. Do you think this essay could have the same impact if it had been written using the point method?
4. What is fable? What fable does Carson relate and why?
5. Carson's language often suggests the supernatural. How many instances of this type of language can you find? In an essay that deals with the natural world, do you think this supernatural diction is appropriate?

What form of development is evident in George Galt's essay—point or block?

Creative Non-Fiction

George Galt

1   When the 1920s New York journalist Robert Ripley championed the phrase "Truth is stranger than fiction," he obviously had not read William Burroughs or Gabriel Garcia Marquez. Most journalists, in my experience, still find facts more compelling than fiction, but then facts are what they are paid to deliver. Outside of journalism, more and more creative writers are sliding back and forth across the fiction/non-fiction frontier and doing a little cross-border shopping while they're on the other side. Nowadays it's difficult to take Ripley's truth-versus-fiction dichotomy seriously. Truth is more promiscuous than Ripley implied—it's everywhere, of course, in the best of every genre—and invention, which used to be considered the exclusive property of fiction, has migrated quietly into non-fiction and earned, at the very least, squatters' rights.

2   It's worth asking, then, why we cling to the literary distinction between fictional and non-fictional prose. One powerful reason these genres are lodged so firmly in place has nothing to do with perceptive reading or intelligent writing. It's simply that academics, for their own purposes of teaching and conceptualizing, think they need such categories (and literary criticism resides with increasing exclusivity in the universities). Still, I think any garden-variety reader does insist on a few basic ground rules when approaching a work of non-fiction prose. Let me try to enumerate them. The list is short.

3   What you have seen (or read), what you have heard, what you have tasted, touched and smelled, these mark the scope of your material in literary non-fiction.

Within that ambit, the sky's the limit. (If you happen to be Marc Garneau, your outer limit is even higher.) Thoughtful readers know that any writer filters objective reality through unconscious bias, the vagaries of memory, and all the eccentricities of individual intelligence and artistic choice. We know that witnesses remember the same event differently. It's not factual accuracy readers care about so much as writerly integrity. A literary non-fiction writer is not a news reporter, but is nonetheless expected to be an honest witness.

4   Simply put, in non-fiction we trust the writer to tell us about people, places and events that have existed in the world outside the writer's imagination. It's not necessary to engage in an abstruse epistemological debate about this. In fiction you can take a piece of your father, a piece of your uncle, and a piece of your neighbourhood barber and roll them together into a portrait of an invented character. Readers know this is not the same as drawing a picture of your father as you honestly remember him.

5   Such apparently precious distinctions do matter. Part of the reason we so carefully distinguish between drama and documentary, between fiction and fact, between imagined dialogue and verbatim transcript, is sheer cultural conditioning. For centuries Western culture has carefully cordoned off adult fantasy into the restricted areas of religion, madness and make-believe tales, and when it escapes from those cages some people experience deep unease. In our highly rational, legalistic, byte-bound culture, we understand fiction to inhabit another realm. Some of us need to be given a clear signal when we are entering it.

6   But here's another argument for an unambiguous contract between reader and writer. Fiction, whether or not we like to admit it, is essentially an elitist form. I mean elitist in the sense that relatively few people will ever write it—or even have any idea how to write it—themselves. This places even the most potent, gut-wrenching fiction on a pedestal one removed from the reader. However powerful a story, its fictional characters will always remain figures in an imaginary landscape outside the nitty-gritty of our everyday reality.

7   Non-fiction contrasts sharply with this pattern. It is the most democratic of literary forms, because anyone who has completed primary school has written some passage of non-fiction prose, and any high-school graduate knows what an essay is. In Canada far more non-fiction than fiction is published, and read. (If you don't believe me, check any random selection of publishers' catalogues.) In short, every reader can personally lay claim to this genre.

8   Unlike someone deeply involved in a novel, who may identify with a compelling fictional character, a reader of non-fiction can mentally pair up with the *writer,* who inhabits the same palpable world and is travelling on the same mortal roller-coaster. In other words, we have all met the non-fiction writer—and he or she is us. This democratic bond is as good a reason as any, it seems to me, for a non-fiction writer to honour the reader's trust and stay honest.

9   In one way, such a link makes the work of writing non-fiction much easier than that of making up stories. The writer need not create a credible new world nor invent vital new people. But in another way the task requires more agility. You can't change the story line. You can't bring in new characters. You can't change the

past. What's done is done. All you can invent are new ways of seeing and remembering, and new ways of saying what's true.

RESPONDING TO THE READING

Comprehension

1. The thesis statement is the final sentence of paragraph 1. Explain its meaning in your own words.
2. Galt compares fiction to non-fiction. What are the points of comparison he draws?
3. Throughout this essay Galt makes allusions to other writers. Who are Robert Ripley, William Burroughs, and Gabriel Garcia Marquez? What sort of writing are Burroughs and Marquez famous for?
4. How does knowing who Marc Garneau is explain the cliché, "the sky's the limit"?
5. Explain how the allusion to cross-border shopping relates to the discussion of fiction and non-fiction.
6. In your own words, explain why non-fiction is democratic.
7. Galt defines fiction as an elitist form. Scan for and paraphrase his definition.
8. Galt says that writing non-fiction is both easier and more difficult than writing fiction. What reasons does he give for this apparent contradiction?

Analysis

1. What do you understand when Galt claims that truth is promiscuous?
2. Explain what Galt means when he discusses cultural conditioning.
3. Explain how the title, "Creative Non-Fiction," summarizes the comparisons in the essay.
4. What qualities do you think are essential to creating what Galt calls the "unambiguous contract between reader and writer"?

Writing Suggestions

1. Compare and contrast two movies, TV shows, or books that you have enjoyed—or not enjoyed.
2. Using "there are things I will tell my children that my parents never told me" as an essay title, compare and contrast the attitudes and behaviour of your generation with those of your parents' generation.
3. Follow a news story in two different newpapers by collecting articles from each paper. At the end of a week, compare and contrast how the story was written by each by looking at point of view, emphasis, use of photographs, placement of story within the paper, levels of language, and vocabulary. End by discussing which paper you preferred.

IV. Essay of Analogy

"Life is like a bowl of cherries; sometimes it's the pits." When you use an **analogy,** you compare two apparently unlike terms (life and the bowl of cherries). The purpose of the comparison is to explain only the "real" subject (life), not the other item (a bowl of cherries). The comparison, because it is a surprising one, forces the reader to think about the "real" subject in a new way.

In the following brief article by Anthony Lukas, life and pinball are compared. After his first sentence, Lukas doesn't mention life (the "real" subject) directly again until the final sentence. He lets his discussion of pinball represent what he wants to say about life.

As you read the article, list the similarities between the game of pinball and "the game of life" as Lukas sees them.

In what order does Lukas present these comparisons? Do you think Lukas could have strengthened his analogy by pointing out the contrasts between pinball and life throughout the essay?

Pinball

J. Anthony Lukas

1   Pinball is a metaphor for life, pitting man's skill, nerve, persistence, and luck against the perverse machinery of human existence. The playfield is rich with rewards: targets that bring huge scores, bright lights, chiming bells, free balls, and extra games. But it is replete with perils, too: culs-de-sac, traps, gutters, and gobble holes down which the ball may disappear forever.

2   Each pull of the plunger launches the ball into a miniature universe of incalculable possibilities. As the steel sphere hurtles into the eclipse at the top of the playfield, it hangs for a moment in exquisite tension between triumph and disaster. Down one lane lies a hole worth thousands, down another a sickening lurch to oblivion. The ball trembles on the lip, seeming to lean first one way, then the other.

3   A player is not powerless to control the ball's wild flight, any more than man is powerless to control his own life. He may nudge the machine with hands, arms, or hips, jogging it just enough to change the angle of the ball's descent. And he is armed with "flippers" which can propel the ball back up the playfield, aiming at the targets with the richest payoffs. But, just as man's boldest strokes and bravest ventures often boomerang, so an ill-timed flip can ricochet the ball straight down "death alley," and a too vigorous nudge will send the machine into "tilt." Winning pinball, like a rewarding life, requires delicate touch, fine calibrations, careful discrimination between boldness and folly.

Sometimes the comparison in the analogy is implied, that is, it is not stated directly.

The Bonfire and the Ants

Alexander Solzhenitsyn

1   I threw a rotten log onto the fire without noticing that it was alive with ants.

2   The log began to crackle, the ants came tumbling out and scurried around in desperation. They ran along the top and writhed as they were scorched by the flames. I gripped the log and rolled it to one side. Many of the ants then managed to escape onto the sand or the pine needles.

3   But, strangely enough, they did not run away from the fire.

4   They had no sooner overcome their terror than they turned, circled and some kind of force drew them back to their forsaken homeland. There were many who climbed back onto the burning log, ran about on it, and perished there.

RESPONDING TO THE READING

Solzhenitsyn has returned to his native Russia after years of living in exile in the United States. He is a writer noted for his criticisms of the former Communist regime, and in particular for his book *The Gulag Archipelago,* on the imprisonment and death of millions of Russians in Siberia. He himself was sent there as a prisoner and experienced the regime's repression while working in a slave-labour camp. When he first lived in Russia before fleeing to America, he was forced to write his political criticisms in coded form, in some cases using analogy as he did in the selection above.

1. What do you think the ants represent in this story? What about the log or the fire?
2. Why do people want to leave their native country?
3. Is this story about love or hatred of one's homeland?

In much science fiction writing and movies, an implicit criticism of our society is given by comparing it to an imagined alien culture. James C. Rettie sets his essay within that framework. "But a Watch in the Night" is an example of an extended analogy.

"But a Watch in the Night": A Scientific Fable

James C. Rettie

1   Out beyond our solar system there is a planet called Copernicus. It came into existence some four or five billion years before the birth of our Earth. In due course of time it became inhabited by a race of intelligent men.

2   About 750 million years ago the Copernicans had developed the motion picture machine to a point well in advance of the stage that we have reached. Most

of the cameras that we now use in motion picture work are geared to take twenty-four pictures per second on a continuous strip of film. When such film is run through a projector, it throws a series of images on the screen and these change with a rapidity that gives the visual impression of normal movement. If a motion is too swift for the human eye to see it in detail, it can be captured and artificially slowed down by means of the slow-motion camera. This one is geared to take many more shots per second—ninety-six or even more than that. When the slow-motion film is projected at the normal speed of twenty-four pictures per second, we can see just how the jumping horse goes over a hurdle.

3   What about motion that is too slow to be seen by the human eye? That problem has been solved by the use of the time-lapse camera. In this one, the shutter is geared to take only one shot per second, or one per minute, or even one per hour—depending upon the kind of movement that is being photographed. When the time-lapse film is projected at the normal speed of twenty-four pictures per second, it is possible to see a bean sprout growing up out of the ground. Time-lapse films are useful in the study of many types of motion too slow to be observed by the unaided, human eye.

4   The Copernicans, it seems, had time-lapse cameras some 757 million years ago and they also had superpowered telescopes that gave them a clear view of what was happening upon this Earth. They decided to make a film record of the life history of Earth and to make it on the scale of one picture per year. The photography has been in progress during the last 757 million years.

5   In the near future, a Copernican interstellar expedition will arrive upon our Earth and bring with it a copy of the time-lapse film. Arrangements will be made for showing the entire film in one continuous run. This will begin at midnight of New Year's Eve and continue day and night without a single stop until midnight of December 31. The rate of projection will be twenty-four pictures per second. Time on the screen will thus seem to move at the rate of twenty-four years per second; 1440 years per minute, 86,400 years per hour; approximately two million years per day; and sixty-two million years per month. The normal life-span of individual man will occupy about three seconds. The full period of earth history that will be unfolded on the screen (some 757 million years) will extend from what the geologists call Pre-Cambrian times up to the present. This will, by no means, cover the full time-span of the earth's geological history but it will embrace the period since the advent of living organisms.

6   During the months of January, February, and March the picture will be desolate and dreary. The shape of the land masses and the oceans will bear little or no resemblance to those that we know. The violence of geological erosion will be much in evidence. Rains will pour down on the land and promptly go booming down to the seas. There will be no clear streams anywhere except where the rains fall upon hard rock. Everywhere on the steeper ground the stream channels will be filled with boulders hurled down by rushing waters. Raging torrents and dry stream beds will keep alternating in quick succession. High mountains will seem to melt like so much butter in the sun. The shifting of land into the seas, later to be thrust up as new mountains, will be going on at a grand scale.

7 Early in April there will be some indication of the presence of single-celled living organisms in some of the warmer and sheltered coastal waters. By the end of the month it will be noticed that some of these organisms have become multi-cellular. A few of them, including the Trilobites, will be encased in hard shells.

8 Toward the end of May, the first vertebrates will appear, but they will still be aquatic creatures. In June about 60 per cent of the land area that we know as North America will be under water. One broad channel will occupy the space where the Rocky Mountains now stand. Great deposits of limestone will be forming under some of the shallower seas. Oil and gas deposits will be in the process of forma-tion—also under shallow seas. On land there will still be no sign of vegetation. Erosion will be rampant, tearing loose particles and chunks of rock and grinding them into sand and silt to be spewed out by the streams into bays and estuaries.

9 About the middle of July the first land plants will appear and take up the tremendous job of soil building. Slowly, very slowly, the mat of vegetation will spread, always battling for its life against the power of erosion. Almost foot by foot, the plant life will advance, lacing down with its root structures whatever pul-verized rock material it can find. Leaves and stems will be giving added protection against the loss of the soil foothold. The increasing vegetation will pave the way for the land animals that will live upon it.

10 Early in August the seas will be teeming with fish. This will be what geologists call the Devonian period. Some of the races of these fish will be breathing by means of lung tissue instead of through gill tissues. Before the month is over, some of the lung fish will go ashore and take on a crude lizard-like appearance. Here are the first amphibians.

11 In early September the insects will put in their appearance. Some will look like huge dragonflies and will have a wing spread of 24 inches. Large portions of the land masses will now be covered with heavy vegetation that will include the prim-itive spore-propagating trees. Layer upon layer of this plant growth will build up, later to appear as the coal deposits. About the middle of this month, there will be evidence of the first seed-bearing plants and the first reptiles. Heretofore, the land animals will have been amphibians that could reproduce their kind only by depositing a soft egg mass in quiet waters. The reptiles will be shown to be freed from the aquatic bond because they can reproduce by means of a shelled egg in which the embryo and its nurturing liquids are sealed and thus protected from destructive evaporation. Before September is over, the first dinosaurs will be seen—creatures destined to dominate the animal realm for about 140 million years and then to disappear.

12 In October there will be series of mountain uplifts along what is now the eastern coast of the United States. A creature with feathered limbs—half bird and half reptile in appearance—will take itself into the air. Some small and rather unpretentious animals will be seen to bring forth their young in a form that is a miniature replica of the parents and to feed these young on milk secreted by mam-mary glands in the female parent. The emergence of this mammalian form of animal life will be recognized as one of the great events in geologic time. October will also witness the high water mark of the dinosaurs—creatures ranging in size from that of the modern goat to monsters like Brontosaurus that weighed some 40

tons. Most of them will be placid vegetarians, but a few will be hideous-looking carnivores, like Allosaurus and Tyrannosaurus. Some of the herbivorous dinosaurs will be clad in bony armor for protection against their flesh-eating comrades.

13 November will bring pictures of a sea extending from the Gulf of Mexico to the Arctic in space now occupied by the Rocky Mountains. A few of the reptiles will take to the air on bat-like wings. One of these, called Pteranodon, will have a wing-spread of 15 feet. There will be a rapid development of the modern flowering plants, modern trees, and modern insects. The dinosaurs will disappear. Toward the end of the month there will be a tremendous land disturbance in which the Rocky Mountains will rise out of the sea to assume a dominating place in the North American landscape.

14 As the picture runs on into December it will show the mammals in command of the animal life. Seed-bearing trees and grasses will have covered most of the land with a heavy mantle of vegetation. Only the areas newly thrust up from the sea will be barren. Most of the streams will be crystal clear. The turmoil of geologic erosion will be confined to localized areas. About December 25 will begin the cutting of the Grand Canyon of the Colorado River. Grinding down through layer after layer of sedimentary strata, this stream will finally expose deposits laid down in Pre-Cambrian times. Thus in the walls of that canyon will appear geological formations dating from recent times to the period when the Earth had no living organisms upon it.

15 The picture will run on through the latter days of December and even up to its final day with still no sign of mankind. The spectators will become alarmed in the fear that man has somehow been left out. But not so; sometime about noon on December 31 (one million years ago) will appear a stooped, massive creature of man-like proportions. This will be Pithecanthropus, the Java ape man. For tools and weapons he will have nothing but crude stone and wooden clubs. His children will live a precarious existence threatened on the one side by hostile animals and on the other by tremendous climatic changes. Ice sheets—in places 4000 feet deep—will form in the northern parts of North America and Eurasia. Four times this glacial ice will push southward to cover half the continents. With each advance the plant and animal life will be swept under or pushed southward. With each recession of the ice, life will struggle to re-establish itself in the wake of the retreating glaciers. The woolly mammoth, the musk ox, and the caribou all will fight to maintain themselves near the ice line. Sometimes they will be caught and put into cold storage—skin, flesh, blood, bones and all.

16 The picture will run on through supper time with still very little evidence of man's presence on the Earth. It will be about 11 o'clock when Neanderthal man appears. Another half hour will go by before the appearance of Cro-Magnon man living in caves and painting crude animal pictures on the walls of his dwelling. Fifteen minutes more will bring Neolithic man, knowing how to chip stone and thus produce sharp cutting edges for spears and tools. In a few minutes more it will appear that man has domesticated the dog, the sheep and, possibly, other animals. He will then begin the use of milk. He will also learn the arts of basket weaving and the making of pottery and dugout canoes.

17   The dawn of civilization will not come until about five or six minutes before the end of the picture. The story of the Egyptians, the Babylonians, the Greeks, and the Romans will unroll during the fourth, the third, and the second minute before the end. At 58 minutes and 43 seconds past 11:00 PM (just 1 minute and 17 seconds before the end) will come the beginning of the Christian era. Columbus will discover the new world 20 seconds before the end. The Declaration of Independence will be signed just 7 seconds before the final curtain comes down.

18   In those few moments of geologic time will be the story of all that has happened since we became a nation. And what a story it will be! A human swarm will sweep across the face of the continent and take it away from the ... red men. They will change it far more radically than it has ever been changed before in a comparable time. The great virgin forests will be seen going down before ax and fire. The soil, covered for eons by its protective mantle of trees and grasses, will be laid bare to the ravages of water and wind erosion. Streams that had been flowing clear will, once again, take up a load of silt and push it toward the seas. Humus and mineral salts, both vital elements of productive soil, will be seen to vanish at a terrifying rate. The railroads and highways and cities that will spring up may divert attention, but they cannot cover up the blight of man's recent activities. In great sections of Asia, it will be seen that man must utilize cow dung and every scrap of available straw or grass for fuel to cook his food. The forests that once provided wood for this purpose will be gone without a trace. The use of these agricultural wastes for fuel, in place of returning them to the land, will be leading to increasing soil impoverishment. Here and there will be seen a dust storm darkening the landscape over an area a thousand miles across. Man-creatures will be shown counting their wealth in terms of bits of printed paper representing other bits of a scarce but comparatively useless yellow metal that is kept buried in strong vaults. Meanwhile, the soil, the only real wealth that can keep mankind alive on the face of this earth, is savagely being cut loose from its ancient moorings and washed into the seven seas.

19   We have just arrived upon this earth. How long will we stay?

 ## RESPONDING TO THE READING

Comprehension

1. How many paragraphs does Rettie use for his introduction? Why does he need so many?
2. The thesis statement is implied. Write one of your own for Rettie's essay.
3. The body of this essay is a process analysis. What process is analyzed?
4. In paragraph 17, Rettie introduces into his process a profound irony. What is it?
5. What does Rettie say is the only real wealth of the earth? Why does he make this claim?
6. Rettie's conclusion is contained in two short sentences. How do they relate to the implied thesis?

Analysis

1. What analogy does Rettie exploit in this essay?
2. Rettie is an American and is writing for an American audience. How can you tell this from this essay?
3. Why does Rettie spend so much time describing the earth's evolution before turning to his "real" subject (civilization)?
4. What relationship does Rettie establish between geologic time and the final seven seconds?
5. Is his last question rhetorical?
6. A **fable** is a short story that teaches a lesson or a moral. What lesson can readers learn from Rettie's essay?
7. What is the source of the first part of Rettie's title? How then does the title relate to his content? What allusions are conjured up by this title?

Writing Suggestions

1. Use an analogy to discuss your attitude to life.
2. Interpret a current event using an analogy.

Simile and Metaphor

A **simile** makes a comparison using *like* or *as*. For example, the poet Robert Burns used the device in his line: "My love is like a red, red rose."

A **metaphor** states a comparison directly, as in Shakespeare's "Life's but a walking shadow, a poor player that struts and frets his hour upon the stage, and then is heard no more."

Shall I Compare Thee to a Summer's Day?

William Shakespeare

Shall I compare thee to a summer's day?
Thou art more lovely and more temperate.
Rough winds do shake the darling buds of May,
And summer's lease hath all too short a date:
Sometime too hot the eye of heaven shines,
And often is his gold complexion dimm'd;
And every fair from fair some time declines,
By chance, or nature's changing course, untrimm'd;
But thy eternal summer shall not fade
Nor lose possession of that fair thou ow'st;
Nor shall Death brag thou wand'rest in his shade,
When in eternal lines to time thou grow'st.

So long as men can breathe or eyes can see,
So long lives this, and this gives life to thee.

RESPONDING TO THE READING

Comprehension

1. Shakespeare opens with a question to his love. List the ways in which his love is like a summer's day.
2. Does he use similes and metaphors? Where?
3. Line 9 opens with the word "But." How is his love *not* like a summer's day?
4. The last two lines of the poem are the conclusion. Paraphrase them.
5. What is the "eye of heaven" in line 5?
6. How could the gold complexion of the sun be dimmed?
7. In line 11, Shakespeare capitalizes the word "Death," making it a proper noun. This is **personification,** in which inanimate objects or abstract qualities are given human characteristics. What does Shakespeare say Death will not be able to do? Why not?

Analysis

A sonnet has only fourteen lines, yet it is a complex form. Shakespeare compares his love to a summer's day, but she is more beautiful and will survive because he has written about her. This sonnet in fact praises poetry itself, for it can preserve ideas and feelings about love for all time. Thus, poetry becomes the "real" subject of this work through Shakespeare's expression. Ultimately, Shakespeare praises his own creative artistry by proving that his lines and their expression of love will endure. This is a paraphrase of the poem's ideas. Find the lines in the poem that relate to each idea.

V. Essay of Classification

Classification is a process in which information about people, places, things, and ideas is arranged into categories sharing common traits. A strong organizing principle determines the kind and number of traits used.

The Plot against People

Russell Baker

1   Inanimate objects are classified scientifically into three major categories—those that break down, those that get lost, and those that don't work. The goal of all

inanimate objects is to resist us and ultimately to defeat us, and the three major classifications are based on the method each object uses to achieve its purpose. As a general rule, any object capable of breaking down at the moment when it is most needed will do so. The automobile is typical of the category.

2   With the cunning peculiar to its breed, the automobile never breaks down while entering a filling station which has a large staff of idle mechanics. It waits until it reaches a downtown intersection in the middle of the rush hour, or until it is fully loaded with family and luggage on the Ohio Turnpike. Thus it creates maximum inconvenience, frustration, and irritability, thereby reducing its owner's lifespan.

3   Washing machines, garbage disposals, lawn mowers, furnaces, TV sets, tape recorders, slide projectors—all are in league with the automobile to take their turn at breaking down whenever life threatens to flow smoothly for their enemies.

4   Many inanimate objects, of course, find it extremely difficult to break down. Pliers, for example, and gloves and keys are almost totally incapable of breaking down. Therefore, they have had to evolve a different technique for resisting us.

5   They get lost. Science has still not solved the mystery of how they do it, and no one has ever caught one of them in the act. The most plausible theory is that they have developed a secret method of locomotion which they are able to conceal from human eyes.

6   It is not uncommon for a pair of pliers to climb all the way from the cellar to the attic in its single-minded determination to raise its owner's blood pressure. Keys have been known to burrow three feet under mattresses. Women's purses, despite their great weight, frequently travel through six or seven rooms to find hiding space under a couch.

7   Scientists have been struck by the fact that things that break down virtually never get lost, while things that get lost hardly ever break down. A furnace, for example, will invariably break down at the depth of the first winter cold wave, but it will never get lost. A woman's purse hardly ever breaks down; it almost invariably chooses to get lost.

8   Some persons believe this constitutes evidence that inanimate objects are not entirely hostile to us. After all, they point out, a furnace could infuriate you even more thoroughly by getting lost than by breaking down, just as a glove could upset you far more by breaking down than by getting lost.

9   Not everyone agrees, however, that this indicates a conciliatory attitude. Many say it merely proves that furnaces, gloves, and pliers are incredibly stupid.

10   The third class of objects—those that don't work—is the most curious of all. These include such objects as barometers, car clocks, cigarette lighters, flashlights and toy train locomotives. It is inaccurate, of course, to say that they *never* work. They work once, usually for the first few hours after being brought home, and then quit. Thereafter, they never work again.

11   In fact, it is widely assumed that they are built for the purpose of not working. Some people have reached advanced ages without ever seeing some of these objects—barometers, for example—in working order. Science is utterly baffled by the entire category. There are many theories about it. The most interesting holds that the things that don't work have attained the highest state possible for an inan-

imate object, the state to which things that break down and things that get lost can still only aspire.

12   They have truly defeated us by conditioning us never to expect anything of them. When a cigarette lighter won't light or a flashlight fails to illuminate, it does not raise blood pressure. Objects that don't work have given us the only peace we receive from inanimate society.

RESPONDING TO THE READING

Reading Strategy

Russell Baker classifies objects into categories or types and begins his essay with a thesis statement that states his focused subject (inanimate objects) and his three specific categories—objects that break down, get lost, or don't work. You can see that he also defines his organizing principle—the idea on which he has based his categories and their shared traits: the method each object uses to defeat mankind.

In a classification essay, the thesis statement alerts the reader to the *number* of types to be discussed and the *principle* upon which the types have been chosen.

Russell Baker wrote this essay to be humorous. Much of his humour depends on personification, a technique that writers use to give inanimate objects human aspects. In describing objects as having malicious intentions, Baker emphasizes his own frustration with the material world around him. His use of this technique also aids him in outlining the traits or characteristics of the objects that annoy him. Notice how in the first three supporting paragraphs—the ones discussing objects that break down—Baker uses examples to illustrate *how* and *why* the objects behave as they do. Note in the first supporting paragraph how Baker concentrates solely on the car, telling the reader specific instances when it "breaks down" and the aftermath: "Thus it creates maximum inconvenience, frustration, and irritability ..."

Baker uses contrast as a transitional device. He directs readers from objects that break down to ones that get lost, ending his supporting paragraph 3 with a statement of fact that contrasts the style of one type of object with another. Some objects "find it extremely difficult to break down," while others "have had to evolve a different technique."

To add irony to his essay, Baker supplements his humour with allusions to science. He writes parts of his essay as if it were a scientific study and uses the language of a more formal, serious essay that might be found in a scientific journal or a magazine on psychology. Baker imitates such scientific language with phrases such as "struck by the fact" and "constitutes evidence."

The conclusion of Baker's essay is actually a discussion of his third category. Baker considers his last category special because he calls it the "most curious of all," showing that this last type of object is the ultimate one for defeating mankind. Irony once again is used to finish. In spite of the fact that objects of this kind cause frustration, it is ironic to discover an unexpected reversal of effect: "Objects that don't work have given us the only peace we receive from inanimate society." This use of irony strengthens Baker's point of view and reminds readers that he retains a distrust of the objects that surround him.

Comprehension

1. According to Baker's thesis statement, inanimate objects frustrate people because of a shared attitude. What is that attitude?
2. All the objects discussed in this essay are found in a certain environment. Which one?
3. Find three instances in the essay where Baker uses irony to create a comic effect.
4. Personification is a literary device wherein an inanimate object is given human qualities. Find three instances where Baker uses this device. To what effect?
5. Keys, pliers, and purses share a secret method for irritating humans. What is this method?
6. What key trait does the automobile possess that makes it a true enemy of humanity?

Analysis

1. What is the ultimate defeat suffered by humanity in "the plot against people"? Do you share Baker's belief in objects' ability to defeat us?
2. Would Baker's essay be as effective without the use of personification? How does personification create humour?
3. How effective is Baker's use of humour in negating frustration? Do you find humour a useful device for combatting stress and tension?
4. **Satire,** the humorous criticism of events and people to expose their folly, is used by writers like Baker to provoke readers to think and change. What is exposed here? What problems does Baker attack with his satire? Is there a remedy in his humour?

Writing Strategy

You classify all the time. Look around at your fellow students. How would you type them? Put them into categories? By gender, height, clothing style, major program? Consider the world of business and government. Employees are classified according to the work they do and are paid for. What do you think the "pay equity" initiative is based on? That's right—job classification!

In order to classify information, you need to begin your process by asking questions specific to categorization:

1. Can my subject be focused and written about adequately enough in a short essay?
2. Can my subject be broken down into distinct categories, each category having a separate series of related traits?
3. Can my categories relate to one another based on an organizing principle?

To demonstrate how you could classify a subject and create valid categories, traits, and a working organizing principle, let's pick the subject of students. The following questions and answers provide an outline of the information you will later compose as sentences and paragraphs.

Subject: STUDENTS

1. *Can this subject be focused?*
   Which students: preschool, public, private, high school, college?
2. *Can one of these focused subjects be organized into groups?*
   College students can be full-time or part-time. Some college students hold down jobs, live at home, and go to school. Others have temporarily left a job to continue schooling, live on their own, and take classes. What about adult learners? They are a distinct group with their own needs, backgrounds, and goals.
3. *Can you label or sort students based on a principle of organization?*
   For instance, could you organize students according to their behaviour and attitudes? The browner, the workaholic, the party animal, the rebel, the whiner?

All groupings must have an organizing principle upon which to define traits and to limit the scope of the type. When you write out your focused subject and your types or groups, be sure to find an organizing principle that will lend unity and coherence to your essay.

Organizing principle

An **organizing principle** defines a purpose that is common to a group. To determine your organizing principle, ask yourself these questions:

a. What is the purpose behind a group's activities or behaviour?
b. What motivates action or thought?
c. What background is shared by the persons and ideas involved?

Once information has been generated, you can begin by writing the thesis statement. A thesis statement for a classification essay must:

a. state the focused subject
b. outline the groups to be discussed
c. state the organizing principle

If you were to write an essay on types of students in the classroom based on behaviour, you might say:

College students behave in different ways both in and out of the classroom. Three common types are the browner, the workaholic, and the party animal.

In composing the paragraphs for a classification essay, it is essential to discuss each group separately. Your paragraphs would open with topic sentences that state the groups to be discussed. The supporting details would be the *traits* shared by members of the groups. The traits are common characteristics and they must relate to the organizing principle in the thesis. For instance, if you were to discuss the workaholics, talking about how such people stay up late, study for ten hours a day, tend to be quiet and studious, and never hand in work late, you would be certain these traits related to the *behaviour* of each group member. If, however, you talked about what workaholics *feel* about work, or what their religious beliefs were, you would be off topic. These traits do not relate to your organizing principle and would be, for this particular essay, unnecessary information for your reader.

Your conclusion could paraphrase your thesis statement or it could make a comment on the reasons why student behaviour exists in your groups. In the classification essay, the conclusion is written to emphasize one feature of your process. In the essay on student behaviour, you might conclude by pointing out that all behaviour is motivated by needs—for some it is a need for recognition, for others a need to release tension and anxiety.

In the following essay by Lionel Ruby, "What Kind of Language Are You Using?" note that Ruby uses a three-point thesis statement and a series of short paragraphs that outline the traits of each function he assigns to language. Note, as well, that his organizing principle rests on his analysis of levels of spoken language.

What Kind of Language Are You Using?

Lionel Ruby

1   Language has more than one purpose. We might say that language operates on different levels, except that the word "levels" suggests higher and lower planes in a scale of value, and this is not intended here. We shall deal with three functions: the informative, the expressive, and the directive. To say that language has these three functions is to say that there are three different reasons for speaking. One reason, or purpose, is to communicate factual information. This is the informative function. We speak also in order to express our feelings, to "blow off steam," or to stir the feelings and attitudes of the person we are talking to. We shall call this the expressive or "emotive" function. And, finally, we speak in order to get people to act. This is the directive function.

2   Some illustrations are in order. A book on astronomy describes the solar system and the stars. We learn that the diameter of the earth is about 8,000 miles; that of the sun, about 800,000 miles; a ratio of 100 to 1. We learn that the star Betelgeuse has a diameter three hundred times that of the sun. This means that if the earth is represented by a baseball, about three inches in diameter, then Betelgeuse would have a diameter of almost a mile and a half. We may learn that there are as many stars in the heavens as there are grains of sand on all the seashores of the world. I have just been using language to communicate information.

3   Expressive language is a second type. When I talk about the United States Senator I like least, I may let off some steam, and relieve my pent-up feelings. I may even infect you with my feelings, making you feel as I feel. The poet, of course, is a specialist in expressive language, as in the lines:

Comes the blind Fury with th' abhorred shears
And slits the thin-spun life.

4   These lines give expression to John Milton's feelings and perhaps make us feel as he felt. When we tell our friends a funny story, to get a laugh, we express our feelings, too, and affect theirs.

5   The third type, directive or action-provoking speech, is illustrated by examples like: "Do unto others as you would have others do unto you," or "Praise the Lord, and pass the ammunition!" We say these things to get action. Ceremonial language, such as "I am happy to meet you," "What a beautiful baby!" and conversation about the weather, also have a directive purpose: to establish social rapport, and to get a friendly response.

6   There are, then, at least three different purposes of discourse. We may also make a somewhat similar classification for words, that is, for words taken by themselves. A basic distinction here is between what we shall call neutral words and emotive words. Neutral words merely convey ideas to us, as when I say, "The sun rose at six this morning." The words in this sentence do not arouse our emotions. But words like "God," "love," "freedom," and "communism" are so closely connected with our total attitudes to life that they are likely to arouse emotional reactions. This division of words into neutral and emotive, however, is relative to our personal experiences, for there is nothing in the word itself which makes it neutral or emotive. If a word conveys nothing but an idea to you, then it is neutral to you; if it arouses your emotions, then it is emotive to you. The word "bread" is a neutral word to me, but to a "fat boy" or a starving man, it may be fraught with emotion. Nevertheless there are some words which can be counted on to make almost everyone "see red," so to speak, like the word "traitor."

7   This classification of words is independent of our classification of the functions of language, for those who wish to inform may use either type, as may those who want to express their feelings, or to get action. In general, however, neutral words will be used when we wish merely to inform, emotive words when we wish to be expressive.

RESPONDING TO THE READING

Comprehension

1. According to his thesis statement, what types of language does Ruby intend to discuss?
2. What example does Ruby use to illustrate the informative function of language?
3. How many of Ruby's examples illustrate expressive language?
4. Into how many types is directed language subdivided?
5. In paragraph 5, Ruby approaches his subject differently by doing what?

6. How does Ruby relate the functions of language to the classification of words?

7. Consider Ruby's conclusion. Does it summarize, restate, or add new information?

Analysis

1. Before reading this essay, you were probably aware of levels of language: the casual talk of friends, the semi-formal level of the classroom, and so on. What types of vocabulary and sentence structure do you associate with the casual, semiformal, and formal uses of language?

2. What level(s) of language do you associate with each of the following: (a) news anchor, (b) disc jockey, (c) politician, (d) religious leader?

3. Some words are loaded (Ruby calls these emotive words), some are neutral. Look up articles in a newspaper and locate examples of the two kinds of words.

The author of the following essay is a First Nations woman named Pat Deiter-McArthur, whose Native name is Day Woman. She has written about native life and history and she would classify herself as a fifth-generation Cree.

Saskatchewan's Indian People—Five Generations

Pat Deiter-McArthur (Day Woman)

1   It has been about five generations since Saskatchewan Indian people have had significant contact with European settlers. The First Generation strongly influenced by Europeans were treaty-signers. The key characteristic of this generation was their ability to have some input into their future. They retained their tribal cultures but realized that they had to negotiate with the Europeans for the betterment of future generations. They did not give up their language or religion or the political structures of nationhood. They were perceived by government as an "alien" nation to be dealt with by treaty.

2   The Second Generation (1867–1910) of Indian people were objects of legal oppression by the government. This generation lived under the absolute rule of an Indian agent, a government employee. Through the Indian Act, this generation was denied their religion, political rights, and freedom to travel off their reserves. A pass and permit system was strictly adhered to on the prairies; every Indian person required a pass to leave the reserve and a permit to sell any agricultural produce. All children were required to attend residential schools run by the churches. The goals of their schools were, first, to make Christians out of their students and to rid them of their pagan lifestyles and, second, to provide a vocational education.

3   Tuberculosis was a major killer of Indian people during this time and contributed to decimating their population in Saskatchewan to a low of five thousand in 1910. This generation was treated as wards and aliens of Canada.

4   The laws which served to oppress the second generation were in place until the early 1950s. The Third Generation (1910–1945) was greatly affected by these laws and schooling. This generation can be described as the lost generation. These people were psychologically oppressed. They rejected their Indianness but found that because of the laws for treaty Indians they could not enjoy the privileges accorded to whites. This third generation was our grandfather's generation. Many Indians at this time could speak their language but would not because of shame of their Indianness. They were still required by law to send their children to residential schools, to send their sick to Indian hospitals, and to abide by the Indian agent. They rarely had a sense of control over their own lives. This generation was considered wards of the government and denied citizenship.

5   Our father's time, the Fourth Generation since treaty-signing, can best be described as the generation of an Indian rebirth. This generation (1945–1980) is characterized by a movement of growing awareness—awareness that being Indian was okay and that Indian people from all tribes are united through their aboriginality, historical development, and special status.

6   This generation saw the rise of Indian and Native organizations across Canada, the return of traditional ceremonies, and an acknowledgment of the need to retain traditional languages and cultural ways.

7   Indian people of this generation were given the right to vote in 1960. The pass and permit system was abandoned in the late 1930s. In 1956, Indian children could attend either residential schools or the local public schools. However, the effects of this generation being raised within an institution and their parents being raised in the same way had a severe impact on these individuals. The residential school not only taught them to suppress their language but also to suppress their feelings and sense of individualism. The continued attack on Indian languages by residential schools left this generation with an ability to only understand their language, but many were not sufficiently fluent to call their Native language their first language.

8   During the sixties, there was a rise in Indian urbanization, a trend that continues today. This generation also contributed to an Indian baby boom that is estimated to be eight to ten years behind the non-Indian baby boomers. The federal and provincial vote allowed Indian people to legally consume alcohol. Alcoholism, suicides, and violent deaths were on the rise for this generation.

9   This was a period of experimentation by both the Indian communities and the government. Unfortunately, neither side was ready for each other. The intended government goal of assimilation was besieged with problems of racism, poverty, maladjustment, and cultural shock.

10   Today's Indian people are part of the Fifth Generation. The fifth generation is faced with choices: assimilation, integration, or separation. Indian people are now able to intermarry or assimilate with non-Indian without the loss of their Indian status. Indian leaders across Canada are seeking a separate and constitutionally

recognized Indian government. Indian government is to provide its own services within Indian reserves. Integration allows Indian people to retain a sense of their cultural background while working and living within the larger society.

11   The fifth generation people are the first children since treaty-signing to be raised by their parents. Many of this fifth generation are not able to understand a Native language. Their first and only language is English. This generation is generally comfortable about their Indianness without strong prejudicial feelings to others. However, this generation is challenged to retain the meaning of Indian identity for their children.

RESPONDING TO THE READING

Comprehension

1. Identify with dates the five generations of Saskatchewan Native people Day Woman discusses.
2. What distinguishes the first generation from the four that follow?
3. What reasons does Day Woman give to explain why the third generation was the "lost generation"?
4. What changes—both good and bad—took place during the time of the fourth generation?
5. In your own words, explain the three choices open to the fifth generation.

Analysis

1. Write a selective summary that charts the impact of European culture on Native people.
2. What does *pagan* mean? Why would it be offensive to the Christian settlers?
3. Do you believe it is necessary to retain a sense of one's cultural background and linguistic tradition?

In our fourth essay of classification, you will notice how the author, Judith Viorst, introduces a number of elements to clarify her groups. First, she uses numbers and titles to define each group. She also bases her data on personal experience. In reading through Viorst's essay, note that she divides and categorizes the people she knows into types.

Viorst is very clear as to how much her friends mean to her and how certain friends belong to certain groups. Viorst's focused subject is complicated, yet she is able to simplify her groupings and make them accessible to her readers. In particular, she divides her groups very clearly, making sure there is no overlapping. She defines for each group a unifying principle or *central trait* and then adds other traits and examples to fill out her analysis. Notice she does not use generalizations as supporting details. That is, Viorst avoids making vague statements about her types of friends. Each type is portrayed with specific and individual details.

Friends, Good Friends—and Such Good Friends

Judith Viorst

1   Women are friends, I once would have said, when they totally love and support and trust each other, and bare to each other the secrets of their souls, and run—no questions asked—to help each other, and tell harsh truths to each other (no, you can't wear that dress unless you lose ten pounds first) when harsh truths must be told.

2   Women are friends, I once would have said, when they share the same affection for Ingmar Bergman, plus train rides, cats, warm rain, charades, Camus, and hate with equal ardor Newark and Brussels sprouts and Lawrence Welk and camping.

3   In other words, I once would have said that a friend is a friend all the way, but now I believe that's a narrow point of view. For the friendships I have and the friendships I see are conducted at many levels of intensity, serve many different functions, meet different needs and range from those as all-the-way as the friendship of the soul sisters mentioned above to that of the most nonchalant and casual playmates.

4   Consider these varieties of friendship:

1.   Convenience friends. These are the women with whom, if our paths weren't crossing all the time, we'd have no particular reason to be friends: a next-door neighbor, a woman in our car pool, the mother of one of our children's closest friends or maybe some mommy with whom we serve juice and cookies each week at the Glenwood Co-op Nursery.

   Convenience friends are convenient indeed. They'll lend us their cups and silverware for a party. They'll drive our kids to soccer when we're sick. They'll take us to pick up our car when we need a lift to the garage. They'll even take our cats when we go on vacation. As we will for them. But we don't, with convenience friends, ever come too close or tell too much; we maintain our public face and emotional distance. "Which means," says Elaine, "that I'll talk about being overweight but not about being depressed. Which means I'll admit being mad but not blind with rage. Which means I might say that we're pinched this month but never that I'm worried sick over money."

   But which doesn't mean that there isn't sufficient value to be found in these friendships of mutual aid, in convenience friends.

2.   Special-interest friends. These friendships aren't intimate, and they needn't involve kids or silverware or cats. Their value lies in some interest jointly shared. And so we may have an office friend or a yoga friend or a tennis friend or a friend from the Women's Democratic Club.

   "I've got one woman friend," says Joyce, "who likes, as I do, to take psychology courses. Which makes it nice for me—and nice for her. It's fun to go with someone you know and it's fun to discuss what you've learned, driving back from the classes." And for the most part, she says, that's all they discuss.

"I'd say that what we're doing is *doing* together, not being together," Suzanne says of her Tuesday-doubles friends. "It's mainly a tennis relationship, but we play together well. And I guess we all need to have a couple of playmates."

I agree.

My playmate is a shopping friend, a woman of marvelous taste, a woman who knows exactly *where* to buy *what,* and furthermore is a woman who always knows beyond a doubt what one ought to be buying. I don't have the time to keep up with what's new in eyeshadow, hemlines and shoes and whether the smock look is in or finished already. But since (oh, shame!) I care a lot about eyeshadow, hemlines and shoes, and since I don't *want* to wear smocks if the smock look is finished, I'm very glad to have a shopping friend.

3. Historical friends. We all have a friend who knew us when ... maybe way back in Miss Meltzer's second grade, when our family lived in that three-room flat in Brooklyn, when our dad was out of work for seven months, when our brother Allie got in that fight where they had to call the police, when our sister married the endodontist from Yonkers and when, the morning after we lost our virginity, she was the first, the only, friend we told.

The years have gone by and we've gone separate ways and we've little in common now, but we're still an intimate part of each other's past. And so whenever we go to Detroit we always go to visit this friend of our girlhood. Who knows how we looked before our teeth were straightened. Who knows how we talked before our voice got unBrooklyned. Who knows what we ate before we learned about artichokes. And who, by her presence, puts us in touch with an earlier part of ourself, a part of ourself it's important never to lose.

"What this friend means to me and what I mean to her," says Grace, "is having a sister without sibling rivalry. We know the texture of each other's lives. She remembers my grandmother's cabbage soup. I remember the way her uncle played the piano. There's simply no other friend who remembers those things."

4. Crossroads friends. Like historical friends, our crossroads friends are important for *what was*—for the friendship we shared at a crucial, now past, time of life. A time, perhaps, when we roomed in college together; or worked as eager young singles in the Big City together; or went together, as my friend Elizabeth and I did through pregnancy, birth and that scary first year of new motherhood.

Crossroad friends forge powerful links, links strong enough to endure with not much more contact than once-a-year letters at Christmas. And out of respect for those crossroads years, for those dramas and dreams we once shared, we will always be friends.

5. Cross-generational friends. Historical friends and crossroads friends seem to maintain a special kind of intimacy—dormant but always ready to be revived—and though we may rarely meet, whenever we do connect, it's personal and intense. Another kind of intimacy exists in the friendships that form

across generations in what one woman calls her daughter–mother and her mother–daughter relationships.

Evelyn's friend is her mother's age—"but I share so much more than I ever could with my mother"—a woman she talks to of music, of books and of life. "What I get from her is the benefit of her experience. What she gets—and enjoys—from me is a youthful perspective. It's a pleasure for both of us."

I have in my own life a precious friend, a woman of 65 who has lived very hard, who is wise, who listens well; who has been where I am and can help me understand it; and who represents not only an ultimate ideal mother to me but also the person I'd like to be when I grow up.

In our daughter role we tend to do more than our share of self-revelation; in our mother role we tend to receive what's revealed. It's another kind of pleasure—playing wise mother to a questing younger person. It's another very lovely kind of relationship.

6. Part-of-a-couple friends. Some of the women we call our friends we never see alone—we see them as part of a couple at couples' parties. And though we share interests in many things and respect each other's views, we aren't moved to deepen the relationship. Whatever the reason, a lack of time or—and this is more likely—a lack of chemistry, our friendship remains in the context of a group. But the fact that our feeling on seeing each other is always, "I'm *so* glad she's here" and the fact that we spend half the evening talking together says that this too, in its own way, counts as a friendship.

(Other part-of-a-couple friends are the friends that came with the marriage, and some of these are friends we could live without. But sometimes, alas, she married our husband's best friend; and sometimes, alas, she *is* our husband's best friend. And so we find ourself dealing with her, somewhat against our will, in a spirit of what I'll call *reluctant* friendship.)

7. Men who are friends. I wanted to write just of women friends, but the women I've talked to won't let me—they say I must mention man–woman friendships too. For these friendships can be just as close and as dear as those that we form with women. Listen to Lucy's description of one such friendship:

"We've found we have things to talk about that are different from what he talks about with my husband and different from what I talk about with his wife. So sometimes we call on the phone or meet for lunch. There are similar intellectual interests—we always pass on to each other the books that we love—but there's also something tender and caring too." In a couple of crises, Lucy says, "He offered himself, for talking and for helping. And when someone died in his family he wanted me there. The sexual, flirty part of our friendship is very small, but *some*—just enough to make it fun and different." She thinks—and I agree—that the sexual part, though small, is always there when a man and a woman are friends. It's only in the past few years that I've made friends with men, in the sense of a friendship that's *mine*, not just part of two couples. And achieving with them the ease and the trust I've found with women friends has value indeed. Under the dryer at home last week, putting on mascara and rouge, I comfortably sat and talked with a fellow named Peter. Peter, I finally decided, could handle the shock of me minus mascara under the dryer. Because we care for each other. Because we're friends.

8. There are medium friends, and pretty good friends, and very good friends indeed, and these friendships are defined by their level of intimacy. And what we'll reveal at each of these levels of intimacy is calibrated with care. We might tell a medium friend, for example, that yesterday we had a fight with our husband. And we might tell a pretty good friend that this fight with our husband made us so mad that we slept on the couch. And we might tell a very good friend that the reason we got so mad in that fight that we slept on the couch had something to do with that girl who works in his office. But it's only to our very best friends that we're willing to tell all, to tell what's going on with that girl in his office.

The best of friends, I still believe, totally love and support and trust each other, and bare to each other the secrets of their souls, and run—no questions asked—to help each other, and tell harsh truths to each other when they must be told.

But we needn't agree about everything (only 12-year-old girl friends agree about *everything*) to tolerate each other's point of view. To accept without judgment. To give and to take without ever keeping score. And to *be* there, as I am for them and as they are for me, to comfort our sorrows, to celebrate our joys.

RESPONDING TO THE READING

Comprehension

1. Paraphrase Viorst's definition of friendship as stated in her introduction.
2. Is Viorst's thesis statement stated directly or is it implied? If implied, write out a thesis for her article.
3. Could one compare "convenience friends" with "special-interest friends"? On what grounds? Take your details from Viorst's examples.
4. What points of similarity exist between "historical friends" and "crossroads friends"?
5. What problem in friendships between men and women is identified by the author?
6. The author uses a conversational style. Based on your reading of the Ruby essay, why do you think Viorst chose to write in this fashion? Does she ever use loaded (emotive) words?

Analysis

1. Which of Viorst's categories are most meaningful to you? Why?
2. Classification can lead to stereotyping. Do you think the author avoids this danger? What do you think of her treatment of men?

3. On what principles would you classify your friends? Is this an appropriate way of thinking about your friends? Define friendship and tell what it means to you.

Writing Suggestions

1. How would you classify your own personal goals? Short-term, long-term, immediate? Discuss.
2. Read Viorst's essay and then make up your own categories of friends. Find an organizing principle that is based on personal experience. Or, if you wish, take Viorst's principle and apply it to your friends. Do not, however, use her titles. Make up your own.
3. Classify emotions. Here, you could use the research methods discussed in Unit Six of this text and discuss types of emotions based on what you find out, or make references to your own life and to characters you've read about in fiction to add detail to your classification.

Archetype

An **archetype** is a form of classification in which the model for the class of object or person becomes so familiar or famous that it is "in a class of its own." In this way an archetype is not only an ideal model but the original pattern from which copies are made. You may have heard the expression "It's the real McCoy," which means that something is the genuine article, the best you can get. The origin of "the real McCoy" is a 19th-century invention by a Canadian, Elijah McCoy. Here is his story and the story of the source of the expression, as told by Ralph Nader.

The Real McCoy

Ralph Nader

1   On May 2, 1844, Elijah McCoy was born in Colchester, Upper Canada (now the province of Ontario, Canada). The son of fugitive slaves George and Mildred McCoy, who escaped from Kentucky through the Underground Railroad, Elijah would go on to revolutionize the operation of machinery with his inventions. After raising Elijah on a farm in Colchester, the McCoy family left Canada and moved back to the United States after the Civil War, settling in a place about one mile from the Ypsilanti, Michigan. George McCoy opened a cigar manufacturing firm and used the profits to send Elijah to Edinburgh, Scotland, to complete an apprenticeship in mechanical engineering. Since he was a young boy Elijah had shown an interest in machines and things mechanical.

2   In 1870, Elijah returned to Ypsilanti as a full-fledged mechanical engineer, but met with racial prejudice and was forced to take a job as a fireman for the Michigan Central Railroad. He operated a small machine shop on the side, but his main job

involved shovelling coal for the trains' steam engines, and oiling all the moving parts of the trains. At that time, trains and all other machinery had to be shut down periodically so that the moving parts could be oiled or lubricated.

3   McCoy became interested in the problems of lubricating machinery, as he saw the frequent shutting down of engines and other machines for oiling and lubricating as a waste of both time and money. In his machine shop he began working on various devices that would lubricate machines as they worked. The idea was to build into the machine canals to carry lubricant to the parts of the machine that needed it. On July 12, 1872, McCoy received the patent for his first invention, an automatic lubricator for steam engines, patent #129,843. The lubricator consisted of a cup that held oil that was built in as part of the steam cylinder; the bottom of the cup was attached to a hollow rod and the opening closed off by a valve; the cup released oil into the cylinder automatically when the engine's steam pressure pushed a piston up through the rod opening the valve. A year later, McCoy improved upon his original design so that the lubricator oiled the cylinder at the most important time, when the steam was exhausted.

4   In 1873, he married Mary Delaney, and they moved to Detroit in 1882. He opened up Elijah McCoy Manufacturing Co. in Detroit with white friends and promoters and acted as Vice-President for the company. Further improvements patented by McCoy in later years numbered fifty-seven in all for lubricating systems for heavy machinery used in locomotives, steamboats and ocean liners. He also invented an ironing board, a lawn sprinkler, a wagon tongue support, and a rubber heel for shoes—eighty-seven inventions in total. By 1892, his lubricating cups were used in factories everywhere, on all railroads in the West and on steamers on the Great Lakes. Eventually, no piece of heavy machinery was considered complete unless it had the "McCoy system." Buyers of machinery would always inspect to make sure McCoy's lubricators were part of the deal. From this concern for quality in automatic lubricators comes the now widely known saying, "the real McCoy."

5   Unfortunately for Elijah McCoy, this fame did not prevent him from losing control of his investment and inventions. While others made millions from his lubricating systems, McCoy lost his business and his home after his wife's death in 1923 and was committed to Wayne County (Eloise) Hospital in 1928, where he died penniless on October 10, 1929.

RESPONDING TO THE READING

Comprehension

1. In a selective one-paragraph summary, write Elijah McCoy's biography.
2. Explain why Elijah McCoy invented his lubricating cup.
3. What was the Underground Railroad and explain its significance to McCoy's life.

4. Besides industrial tools, what domestic items did he invent or perfect?
5. In your own words explain how the expression "the Real McCoy" came into being.

Analysis

1. Given that McCoy's parents were once slaves, what impresses you about their achievements?
2. Using information from the biography, how do you account for Elijah McCoy's success in spite of racial prejudice?

Stereotype

A **stereotype** is a particular kind of classification. When we classify people (e.g., students as browners, whiners, and workaholics), we have to keep in mind that each category is composed of individuals who will vary from the norm we have established. In the case of a stereotype, the category has become fixed as an accepted image and it represents all the people, ideas, or things that belong to that category. In its oversimplification and falsification, a stereotype is an invalid form of classification.

Stereotypes are most often based on gender, race, or religion. Examples of such are "the dumb blonde" or "the uptight WASP." When a person is denied individuality because of stereotyping, bigotry and prejudice result. Jokes based on stereotypes, while they seem harmless, are nonetheless pernicious because they dehumanize the persons involved.

The following essay by Neil Bissoondath, "I'm Not Racist But …," discusses the dehumanizing effect of stereotypes.

"I'm Not Racist But …"

Neil Bissoondath

1   Someone recently said that racism is as Canadian as maple syrup. I have no argument with that. History provides us with ample proof. But, for proper perspective, let us remember that it is also as American as apple pie, as French as croissants, as Jamaican as ackee, as Indian as aloo, as Chinese as chow mein, as … Well, there's an entire menu to be written. This is not by way of excusing it. Murder and rape, too, are international, multicultural, as innate to the darker side of the human experience. But we must be careful that the inevitable rage evoked does not blind us to the larger context.

2   The word "racism" is a discomforting one: It is so vulnerable to manipulation. We can, if we so wish, apply it to any incident involving people of different colour. And therein lies the danger. During the heat of altercation, we seize, as terms of

abuse, on whatever is most obvious about the other person. It is, often, a question of unfortunate convenience. A woman, because of her sex, easily becomes a female dog or an intimate part of her anatomy. A large person might be dubbed "a stupid ox," a small person "a little" whatever. And so a black might become "a nigger," a white "a honky," an Asian "a paki," a Chinese "a chink," an Italian "a wop," a French-Canadian "a frog."

3   There is nothing pleasant about these terms; they assault every decent sensibility. Even so, I once met someone who, in a stunning surge of naiveté, used them as simple descriptives and not as terms of racial abuse. She was horrified to learn the truth. While this may have been an extreme case, the point is that the use of such patently abusive words may not always indicate racial or cultural distaste. They may indicate ignorance or stupidity or insensitivity, but pure racial hatred—such as the Nazis held for Jews, or the Ku Klux Klan for blacks—is a thankfully rare commodity.

4   Ignorance, not the willful kind but that which comes from lack of experience, is often indicated by that wonderful phrase, "I'm not racist but …" I think of the mover, a friendly man, who said, "I'm not racist, but the Chinese are the worst drivers on the road." He was convinced this was so because the shape of their eyes, as far as he could surmise, denied them peripheral vision.

5   Or the oil company executive, an equally warm and friendly man, who, looking for an apartment in Toronto, rejected buildings with East Indian tenants not because of their race—he was telling me this, after all—but because he was given to understand that cockroaches were symbols of good luck in their culture and that, when they moved into a new home, friends came by with gift-wrapped roaches.

6   Neither of these men thought of himself as racist, and I believe they were not, deep down. (The oil company executive made it clear he would not hesitate to have me as a neighbour; my East Indian descent was of no consequence to him, my horror of cockroaches was.) Yet their comments, so innocently delivered, would open them to the accusation, justifiably so if this were all one knew about them. But it is a charge which would undoubtedly be wounding to them. It is difficult to recognize one's own misconceptions.

7   True racism is based, more often than not, on willful ignorance, and an acceptance of—and comfort with—stereotype. We like to think, in this country, that our multicultural mosaic will help nudge us into a greater openness. But multiculturalism as we know it indulges in stereotype, depends on it for a dash of colour and the flash of dance. It fails to address the most basic questions people have about each other: Do those men doing the Dragon Dance really all belong to secret criminal societies? Do those women dressed in saris really coddle cockroaches for luck? Do those people in dreadlocks all smoke marijuana and live on welfare? Such questions do not seem to be the concern of the government's multicultural programs, superficial and exhibitionistic as they have become.

8   So the struggle against stereotype, the basis of all racism, becomes a purely personal one. We must beware of the impressions we create. A friend of mine once commented that, from talking to West Indians, she has the impression that their one great cultural contribution to the world is in the oft-repeated boast that "We (unlike everyone else) know how to party."

9   There are dangers, too, in community response. We must be wary of the self-appointed activists who seem to pop up in the media at every given opportunity spouting the rhetoric of retribution, mining distress for personal, political and professional gain. We must be skeptical about those who depend on conflict for their sense of self, the non-whites who need to feel themselves victims of racism, the whites who need to feel themselves purveyors of it. And we must be sure that, in addressing the problem, we do not end up creating it. Does the *Miss Black Canada Beauty Contest* still exist? I hope not. Not only do I find beauty contests offensive, but a racially segregated one even more so. What would the public reaction be, I wonder, if every year CTV broadcast the *Miss White Canada Beauty Pageant?* We give community-service awards only to blacks: Would we be comfortable with such awards only for whites? In Quebec, there are The Association of Black Nurses, The Association of Black Artists, The Congress of Black Jurists. Play tit for tat: The Association for White Nurses, White Artists, White Jurists: visions of apartheid. Let us be frank, racism for one is racism for others.

10   Finally, and perhaps most important, let us beware of abusing the word itself.

RESPONDING TO THE READING

Comprehension

1. In his introduction Bissoondath begins with a series of stereotypes. On what basis are they alike?
2. Where does Bissoondath actually define racism?
3. What TV events does Bissoondath refer to in order to discuss the theme of his essay?
4. How many specific examples does the author use of loaded (emotive) language?
5. The author talks about the use of emotive and neutral words, terms you read about in Ruby's essay. Where does Bissoondath show an example of these two functions of word use?

Analysis

1. Why does the author use so many rhetorical questions in paragraph 7?
2. What is the purpose of the anecdote about the cockroach?
3. Read the opening sentence in paragraph 8. Do you think Bissoondath is right?
4. Is it really possible to abuse the word *racism?* How has the author convinced you of this fact?
5. When you read the title, what was your initial expectation as a reader? Did the essay fulfil your expectation? Who is the author's intended audience?
6. Why do so many people make use of stereotypes?
7. The author implies that multiculturalism is a form of stereotyping, if not racism. Is he right?

In the following essay, Michael Dorris describes his and his wife's attempts to raise their daughters in a gender-neutral environment. While Dorris's struggle with stereotyping is as serious as Bissoondath's, it is written in a humorous and self-deprecating style.

The Minnie Mouse Kitchen

Michael Dorris

1   My wife, Louise, and I, well-intentioned parents of two young daughters, are ever vigilant lest our girls limit their horizons because of sexist stereotyping. Each, we believe, should aim for whatever her talents and inclinations dictate—be it president or Nobel Prize physicist, Supreme Court justice or space-shuttle pilot.

2   So, what did we do last year when, for their special Christmas present, five-year-old Persia and four-year-old Palla's collective wish was for the complete Minnie Mouse kitchen?

3   Despair. Despite all of our gender-neutral picture books, they had clearly already been molded by the subtle messages of media and popular culture. White aprons, not lab coats, loomed in their future.

4   How about a chess set? we suggested. A magic kit? An ant farm?

5   No. Persia was firm, Pallas obdurate: It was Minnie Mouse or nothing. Tucked under the pillow of their imaginations was the page torn from a wish book in which two future mommies happily baked miniature angel foods, washed tiny plastic dishes, and planned the week's menu by perusing their stock of brand-name products.

6   Early December became the time for an unstated battle of wills, a contest of aspiration over who knew best what two of us wanted. Louise and I made the issue a symbol that spanned from suffrage to the Equal Rights Amendment. Our daughters, however, remained steadfast in their inclination toward home ec, though ultimately they seemed to resign themselves to the inequities of power. Their complaints would be saved, no doubt, for some future psychoanalyst.

7   Then on Christmas Eve, as I was preparing my grandmother's special sweet-potato balls (whipped, flavored with brandy, formed around a marshmallow, and dredged in cornflake crumbs) and Louise was making a family favorite, wild rice stuffing for the turkey, a string of startling insights simultaneously occurred to us: We loved to cook. We spent lots of time doing it. We were Minnie Mouse.

8   Yikes! It was almost 4:00 p.m., and the stores would soon close.

9   A gentle snow had begun to fall, and here and there as I drove along the road toward town, colored Christmas lights twinkled through the windows of houses with smoking chimneys. New England in winter can, at such moments, seem like one giant Hollywood set, a Currier and Ives scene ready for a heart-warming story to happen. In this version, my part would have been played by Jimmy Stewart: awkward, stalwart, the honest gallumpf who carried the American dream like a red, white, and blue banner. He was out to do a deed, to accomplish one of those minor miracles that make life wonderful and annually bring a smile to Donna Reed's eyes.

10   The problem was, every store within a hundred miles was sold out of the Minnie Mouse kitchen.

11   "The last one went ten minutes ago," the salesman noted, driving a stake through my heart as I finally stood at the head of a long line of shoppers.

12   I was a poor excuse for a father. I looked from right to left in search of any idea, and there it was, suspended by wires from the ceiling: every one of Minnie's treasures—stove, sink, and "frigerator," its doors invitingly ajar.

13   "How about that one?" I pleaded.

14   "Oh, no," the man said. "That's the display model."

15   "It's not for me," I argued, perhaps unnecessarily. "It's for my little girls. They're only four and five." I paused dramatically, then fired my best shot: "It's Christmas Eve."

16   The man hesitated as Minnie teetered between us: rules, or little girls' dreams come true?

17   "Sell it to him," the grandmother behind me snarled menacingly. "What are you, Mr. Scrooge?"

18   "Call the manager," protested a man waiting to buy a snow shovel.

19   "Climb up there and take it down," demanded a very pregnant women with an ominously quiet voice. "Or I will."

20   There were holes in the plywood facades of Minnie's major appliances where hooks had been, but no matter. They fit into the backseat, jauntily red and white. Jimmy Stewart drove home singing carols with the radio.

21   After our daughters were in bed, Louise and I arranged the kitchen beneath the tree, amid the puzzles and books and telescopes. Then we rose early to witness the girls' reaction. Right on cue they ran into the room, stopped still, and stared. What would each do first? Cook? Scour a pot? Clean out the freezer? Anything was possible.

22   Persia and Pallas held hands for what seemed a long time. Then, as one, they turned to where we sat and ran to squeeze between us.

23   "We knew you would," Persia said.

24   And Pallas nodded in agreement. "We knew it all the time."

 # RESPONDING TO THE READING

Comprehension

1. In the opening sentence of the essay, Dorris talks about "sexist stereo-typing." What is it he is afraid of?
2. Explain the meaning of the sentence, "White aprons, not lab coats, loomed in their future."
3. How does Dorris stereotype "mommies"?
4. Paraphrase "a contest of aspiration," "a symbol that spanned from suffrage to the Equal Rights Amendment," and "the inequities of power."

5. Why does Dorris use italics (for the word "we") three times at the end of paragraph 7?
6. What happens to Dorris to make him exclaim "Yikes!" at the beginning of paragraph 8? What do you assume will happen next given the details of paragraph 8?
7. Paragraph 9 exploits a number of stereotypical Christmas scenes. How many can you identify?
8. The three customers in line behind Dorris work *against* stereotype. Explain how.
9. Why does Dorris in paragraph 20 refer to himself as Jimmy Stewart?
10. What final image of Dorris's family does he leave readers with?

Analysis

1. What evidence can you find that Dorris is presenting himself as the stereotypically well-intentioned parent? How does he overcome the stereotype?
2. The ambitions he has for his daughters are expressed ironically. How? Why?
3. The sentence with which paragraph 21 ends, "Anything was possible," appears to have greater implications than the list of tasks (cook, scour, clean) that precedes it. What does this suggest to you? (Hint: reread paragraph 1.)

In the following essay by Judy Syfers, the subject once again is serious, although the author chooses to treat her subject with irony and humour.

I Want a Wife

Judy Syfers

1   I belong to that classification of people known as wives. I am A Wife. And, not altogether incidentally, I am a mother.

2   Not too long ago a male friend of mine appeared on the scene fresh from a recent divorce. He had one child, who is, of course, with his ex-wife. He is obviously looking for another wife. As I thought about him while I was ironing one evening, it suddenly occurred to me that I, too, would like to have a wife. Why do I want a wife?

3   I would like to go back to school so that I can become economically independent, support myself, and, if need be, support those dependent upon me. I want a wife who will work and send me to school. And while I am going to school I want a wife to keep track of the children's doctor and dentist appointments. And to keep track of mine, too. I want a wife to make sure my children eat properly and are kept clean. I want a wife who will wash the children's clothes and keep them mended. I want a wife who is a good nurturant attendant to my children, who arranges for their schooling, makes sure that they have an adequate social life with their peers,

takes them to the park, the zoo, etc. I want a wife who takes care of the children when they are sick, a wife who arranges to be around when the children need special care, because, of course, I cannot miss classes at school. My wife must arrange to lose time at work and not lose the job. It may mean a small cut in my wife's income from time to time, but I guess I can tolerate that. Needless to say, my wife will arrange and pay for the care of the children while my wife is working.

4 I want a wife who will take care of *my* physical needs. I want a wife who will keep my house clean. A wife who will pick up after me. I want a wife who will keep my clothes cleaned, ironed, mended, replaced when need be, and who will see to it that my personal things are kept in their proper place so that I can find what I need the minute I need it. I want a wife who cooks the meals, a wife who is a *good* cook. I want a wife who will plan the menus, do the necessary grocery shopping, prepare the meals, serve them pleasantly, and then do the cleaning up while I do my studying. I want a wife who will care for me when I am sick and sympathize with my pain and loss of time from school. I want a wife to go along when our family takes a vacation so that someone can continue to care for me and my children when I need a rest and a change of scene.

5 I want a wife who will not bother me with rambling complaints about a wife's duties. But I want a wife who will listen to me when I feel the need to explain a rather difficult point I have come across in my course of studies. And I want a wife who will type my papers for me when I have written them.

6 I want a wife who will take care of the details of my social life. When my wife and I are invited out by my friends, I want a wife who will take care of the babysitting arrangements. When I meet people at school that I like and want to entertain, I want a wife who will have the house clean, will prepare a special meal, serve it to me and my friends, and not interrupt when I talk about the things that interest me and my friends. I want a wife who will have arranged that the children are fed and ready for bed before my guests arrive so that the children do not bother us. I want a wife who takes care of the needs of my guests so that they feel comfortable, who makes sure that they have an ashtray, that they are passed the hors d'oeuvres, that they are offered a second helping of the food, that their wine glasses are replenished when necessary, that their coffee is served to them as they like it.

7 And I want a wife who knows that sometimes I need a night out by myself.

8 I want a wife who is sensitive to my sexual needs, a wife who makes love passionately and eagerly when I feel like it, a wife who makes sure that I am satisfied. And, of course, I want a wife who will not demand sexual attention when I am not in the mood for it. I want a wife who assumes the complete responsibility for birth control, because I do not want more children. I want a wife who will remain sexually faithful to me so that I do not have to clutter up my intellectual life with jealousies. And I want a wife who understands that *my* sexual needs may entail more than strict adherence to monogamy. I must, after all, be able to relate to people as fully as possible.

he can play around but she can't.

9 If, by chance, I find another person more suitable as a wife than the wife I already have, I want the liberty to replace my present wife with another one. Naturally, I will expect a fresh, new life; my wife will take the children and be solely responsible for them so that I am left free.

10   When I am through with school and have a job, I want my wife to quit working and remain at home so that my wife can more fully and completely take care of a wife's duties.

11   My God, who wouldn't want a wife?

RESPONDING TO THE READING

Comprehension

1. Syfers begins with a statement of classification. What qualities does she provide to categorize a wife?
2. What motivated Syfers to want a wife?
3. "I want" is repeated throughout this essay. What effect does this repetition have on you?
4. What five major areas of personal life does Syfers suggest a wife should manage?
5. Syfers's definition of a wife depends on the job classification, not on gender. How do you know this?
6. What is the point of the rhetorical question at the end of this essay?

Analysis

1. Is Syfers fair in her assessment of a wife's duties?
2. This essay was written in 1970. Is it still relevant to modern marriage?
3. Do you think Syfers has stereotyped the role of a wife? Why of why not?
4. Do you believe this essay alienates its male readers?
5. In what ways do you think Syfers succeeds in being ironic?

Finally, here is a student essay that tackles stereotyping. Julie-Ann Yoshikuni, a Centennial College student, won first prize for this essay in the CALL (College Association for Language and Literacy) writing competition in 1992.

The Canadian Dream

Julie-Ann Yoshikuni

1   "So, do you speak Oriental?" Not long ago, I was actually asked this disturbing question. I refer to this as "Continental Genericism," a term used to conveniently group all members of like Continents into a single, homogeneous unit. The essence of my Canadian Dream is simple; the mechanics of it, complex. My wish is to be recognized foremost as a Canadian, a difficult task given my unmistakable Asian features. Being classified as an "Oriental" is not always easy: for example,

everyone expects me to be an academic genius, most people simply assume I am of Chinese descent and the general public fears I am a hazard on the road.

2   Many people believe that Orientals are inherently superior in intelligence. I find this somewhat bothersome, but I will not complain. I have worked very hard to perpetuate this popular myth and, consequently, it has driven me to crank out some of my best work. How would I feel knowing that I was not prepared for a test, when three habitual cheaters were counting on me? The pressure to excel in mathematics and computer science is often overwhelming. English is my only haven because everyone "knows" we are incapable of spelling. Despite the fact that academic performance is usually a function of the amount of time spent studying, many people will continue to believe Orientals have a "special" capacity for numbers.

3   Most people assume that all Orientals are Chinese. This is not surprising since the Chinese population in Toronto is very large. However, as a third generation Canadian of Japanese descent, I have certainly had my share of frustrating experiences. For example, I get tired of explaining to people that I really don't know whether 1991 is the year of the pig, snake or rabbit. I have reached the conclusion that people are simply attempting to make polite small talk when saying things such as, "we knew a Chinese guy once, maybe you know him?" or "we really do like chicken balls and egg rolls."

4   In my own little way, I have learned to deal with these situations, but I have yet to conquer the reckless driver presumption. "They can cook, they can count, but watch out, because they sure can't drive." If you are a Canadian, and you have the slightest difficulty figuring out which ethnic group this statement pertains to, then you must be living in a vacuum. I am the first to admit that there are poor drivers who are, indeed, Oriental. However, not all Orientals are incapable of operating a motorized vehicle. Contrary to popular belief, our ability to drive is not hampered by a lack of peripheral vision. This vehicular hostility directed at Orientals has led me to deduce that perhaps this animosity stems from the fact that we make better cars. Unfortunately, as long as there are Oriental drivers, there will always be a good joke.

5   My Canadian Dream come true is simply to be recognized and treated as a Canadian.

6   However, due to circumstances beyond my control, I am left to deal with the stigma attached to being Oriental: that is, being smart, Chinese and careless on the road. All I can say is, it looks like I'm 0 for 3!

RESPONDING TO THE READING

Comprehension

1. Julie-Ann Yoshikuni coins the phrase "continental genericism." What does she mean by it? Can you think of examples of it?
2. Define in your words Yoshikuni's "Canadian dream."

3. Paraphrase Yoshikuni's thesis statement.
4. What aspects of stereotyping does Yoshikuni face because of her appearance?
5. The author suggests advantages and disadvantages in being identified as "an academic genius." What examples can you find of each?
6. How do the examples you found for question 5 reflect stereotyping?
7. What examples of frustrating experiences does Yoshikuni provide?
8. Yoshikuni attacks two "popular beliefs" about Chinese people. How does she attack them and how effective are the attacks?
9. What examples of the author's use of irony and sense of humour can you find?

Analysis

1. Do you agree with Yoshikuni who says the mechanics of achieving her dream are complex?
2. How well do you think the author handles being stereotyped?
3. Will this essay by a fellow student affect your attitude when you hear a racist joke?

Writing Suggestions

1. Have you ever experienced stereotyping? How did you react to it? How did you deal with it?
2. Does stereotyping limit individual achievement? Provide examples and reasons to support your point of view.
3. Do you agree with Bissoondath's position on racial stereotyping. Explain why or why not.
4. In what ways do you believe parents should act as role models for their children?
5. Argue against Syfers's position by claiming that you want a husband.

VI. Essay of Cause and Effect

Cause and effect writing explains why things happen and what results follow. Cause and effect essays link conditions and consequences by showing how and why they are connected.

On Reading Trash

Bob Swift

1   If you want kids to become omnivorous readers, let them read trash. That's my philosophy, and I speak from experience.

2   I don't disagree with The National Endowment for the Humanities, which says every high school graduate should have read 30 great works of literature,

including the Bible, Plato, Shakespeare, Hawthorne, the Declaration of Independence, *Catcher in the Rye, Crime and Punishment* and *Moby Dick.*

3   It's a fine list. Kids should read them all, and more. But they'll be better readers if they start off on trash. Trash? What I mean is what some might call "popular" fiction. My theory is, if you get kids interested in reading books—no matter what sort—they will eventually go on to the grander literature all by themselves.

4   In the third grade I read my first novel, a mystic adventure set in India. I still recall the sheer excitement at discovering how much fun reading could be.

5   When we moved within walking distance of the public library a whole new world opened. In the library I found that wonder of wonders, the series. What a thrill, to find a favorite author had written a dozen or more other titles.

6   I read a series about frontiersmen, learning about Indian tribes, beef jerky and tepees. A Civil War series alternated young heroes from the Blue and the Gray, and I learned about Grant and Lee and the Rock of Chickamauga.

7   One summer, in Grandpa Barrow's attic, I discovered the Mother Lode, scores of dusty books detailing the adventures of Tom Swift, The Rover Boys, The Submarine Boys, The Motorcycle Boys and Bomba the Jungle Boy. It didn't matter that some were written in 1919; any book you haven't read is brand new.

8   Another summer I discovered Edgar Rice Burroughs. I swung through the jungles with Tarzan, fought green Martians with John Carter, explored Pellucidar at the Earth's core, flew through the steamy air of Venus with Carson Napier. Then I came across Sax Rohmer and, for book after book, prowled opium dens with Nayland Smith, in pursuit of the insidious Fu Manchu.

9   In the seventh grade, I ran across Booth Tarkington's hilarious Penrod books and read them over and over.

10   My cousin went off to war in 1942 and gave me his pulp magazines. I became hooked on Doc Savage, The Shadow, G8 and His Battle Aces, The Spider, Amazing Stories. My folks wisely did not object to them as trash. I began to look in second-hand book shops for past issues, and found a Blue Book Magazine, with an adventure story by Talbot Mundy. It led me back to the library, for more of Mundy's Far East thrillers. From Mundy, my path led to A. Conan Doyle's *The Lost World,* Rudyard Kipling's *Kim,* Jules Verne, H.G. Wells and Jack London.

11   Before long I was whaling with Herman Melville, affixing scarlet letters with Hawthorne and descending into the maelstrom with Poe. In due course came Hemingway, Dos Passos, *Hamlet, The Odyssey, The Iliad, Crime and Punishment.* I had discovered "real" literature by following the trail of popular fiction.

12   When our kids were small, we read aloud to them from *Doctor Dolittle* and *Winnie-the-Pooh.* Soon they learned to read, and favored the "Frog and Toad" and "Freddie the Pig" series.

13   When the old Doc Savage and Conan the Barbarian pulps were reissued as paperbacks, I brought them home. The kids devoured them, sometimes hiding them behind textbooks at school, just as I had. They read my old Tarzan and Penrod books along with Nancy Drew and *The Black Stallion.*

14   Now they're big kids. Each kid's room is lined with bookshelves, on which are stacked, in an eclectic mix, Doc Savage, Plato, Louis L'Amour westerns, Thomas

Mann, Gothic romances, Agatha Christie, Sartre, Edgar Allen Poe, science-fiction, Saul Bellow, Shakespeare, Pogo, Greek tragedies, Hemingway, Kipling, Tarzan, *Zen and the Art of Motorcycle Maintenance,* F. Scott Fitzgerald, *Bomba the Jungle Boy,* Nietzsche, *The Iliad, Dr. Dolittle,* Joseph Conrad, Fu Manchu, Hawthorne, Penrod, Dostoevsky, Ray Bradbury, Herman Melville, Fitzgerald, Conan the Barbarian … more. Some great literature, some trash, but all good reading.

RESPONDING TO THE READING

Reading Strategy

Bob Swift's essay claims that children who are encouraged to read popular fiction will become, as a result, avid lifetime readers. His thesis statement is the opening line of his essay. Using personal anecdotes from his own childhood, Swift illustrates how and why he became a reader. Note how he uses specific examples of the books he discovered and what effect they had on his way of seeing the world: "Another summer I discovered Edgar Rice Burroughs. I swung through the jungles with Tarzan, fought green Martians with John Carter …"

Swift relates a chronology of discoveries, charting the times and the books he read as his curiosity for reading grew. His method is simple: he states a single cause and then shows the multiple effects that followed. In support of paragraph 9, Swift points out that his cousin introduced him to pulp magazines. As a result, Swift became "hooked on Doc Savage," and he began searching for more books of the same kind in second-hand bookstores. His interest led him back to the public library, where he became acquainted with more sophisticated writing: the stories of Jules Verne, H.G. Wells, and Jack London.

Swift selects examples that prove the connection between his reading trash (e.g., pulp magazines) and his subsequent desire to explore new books. The final consequence of his devouring of popular fiction was the discovery of "real" literature—the works of Hemingway and Shakespeare.

Comprehension

1. In paragraphs 1 to 4, what does Swift claim is the immediate effect of reading trash?
2. If kids fall in love with reading trash, what happens next?
3. How many of the works listed have you read? How many have you never heard of? Why are so many of them unfamiliar to readers today?
4. What do all the titles of the trash have in common?
5. How many personal anecdotes does Swift use?
6. Give Swift's reasons why kids should read trash.
7. How does Swift's conclusion relate to his thesis?
8. What other ways of teaching kids to read does Swift implicitly reject?

Analysis

1. Do you agree with Swift that all reading—trash and great literature—is good reading?
2. Trash is an emotive word. Why does Swift use it more often than the neutral "popular fiction"?
3. This article was written for a newspaper to be read by the "general public of readers." What assumptions has Swift made about his reading audience?
4. Did you read trash as a kid? Did you go on to read greater things as Swift did? Tell how and why. If you didn't read trash, or were forbidden to do so, how did you learn to read and like reading? Do you like reading, in fact? If you don't, why not?

Writing Strategy

In writing a cause and effect essay it is essential to state from the beginning what your subject is and how it creates a connection between causes and effects.

Writing cause and effect essays requires a number of careful approaches:

1. Make sure the cause and effect relationship between two or more things is logical and valid, and not just based on coincidence.

EXAMPLE: For years it was rumoured that cigarette smoking caused cancer. Without evidence to back up the claim, the statement was regarded as mere coincidence. Now there are ample scientific data to prove there is a real and logical link between the cigarette and lung cancer.

2. In writing a cause and effect essay, be sure to gather adequate data and examples.

EXAMPLE: Bob Swift wrote his essay using book titles and memories from his own life to prove his cause and effect thesis. His data were valid evidence that reading popular fiction can result in an increased desire to read better works. Evidence is essential in cause and effect writing, for without it false assumptions and claims can be presented as truth.

3. Do not create a connection between causes and effects if none readily exists.

EXAMPLE: Sometimes writers say "this is the cause because ... here is the effect." No clear connection has been established. There is crime in a neighbourhood; therefore, there are drugs being sold. Such an assumption may be false. It is tempting to assume proof or to depend on bias, but evidence must be shown before a cause and effect relationship can be considered valid. Consider this situation: If a strict teacher fails you on an essay-answer test, is it because that teacher is unfair and picky? Or is the grade based on errors you missed in proofreading your final copy? The causes might be a combination of both the teacher's methods and your exam fatigue, a combination difficult to measure. Do not assume that because one event follows another, the first *causes* the second. If you inhale and cough, your cigarette may be the cause of your sudden hacking. But there is the possibility that you may have asthma or an allergy and one of those may be the actual reason for your cough.

4. In writing cause and effect essays be aware that there are types of causes:
   a. immediate causes—causes that on first glance are obviously related to effects
   b. ultimate causes—causes that stand out above all others as main motivations

EXAMPLE: If a child is crying, the immediate cause could be a skinned knee. If a child skins a knee frequently and cries, the ultimate cause might be a poor sense of balance or a low pain threshold.

5. Try to balance causes and effects in equal numbers. If that is not possible, realize that a sequence of causes may bring about further causes that then leads to certain consequences.

EXAMPLE: The firing of two employees caused much anxiety in the company, which in turn caused low morale in the office. The results included decreased productivity and an increase in absenteeism on Fridays and Mondays.

In the following essay by Malcolm X, notice how the author describes multiple causes that led to his becoming an educated man.

Prison Studies

Malcolm X

1 Many who today hear me somewhere in person, or on television, or those who read something I've said, will think I went to school far beyond the eighth grade. This impression is due entirely to my prison studies.

2 It had really begun back in the Charlestown Prison, when Bimbi first made me feel envy of his stock of knowledge. Bimbi had always taken charge of any conversation he was in, and I had tried to emulate him. But every book I picked up had few sentences which didn't contain anywhere from one to nearly all of the words that might as well have been in Chinese. When I just skipped those words, of course, I really ended up with little idea of what the book said. So I had come to the Norfolk Prison Colony still going through only bookreading motions. Pretty soon, I would have quit even these motions, unless I had received the motivation that I did.

3 I saw that the best thing I could do was get hold of a dictionary—to study, to learn some words. I was lucky enough to reason also that I should try to improve my penmanship. It was sad. I couldn't even write in a straight line. It was both ideas together that moved me to request a dictionary along with some tablets and pencils from the Norfolk Prison Colony school.

4 I spent two days just riffling uncertainly through the dictionary's pages. I'd never realized so many words existed! I didn't know which words I needed to learn. Finally, to start some kind of action, I began copying.

5   In my slow, painstaking, ragged handwriting, I copied into my tablet everything printed on that first page, down to the punctuation marks.

6   I believe it took me a day. Then, aloud, I read back, to myself, everything I'd written on the tablet. Over and over, aloud, to myself, I read my own handwriting.

7   I woke up the next morning, thinking about those words—immensely proud to realize that not only had I written so much at one time, but I'd written words that I never knew were in the world. Moreover, with a little effort, I also could remember what many of these words meant. I reviewed the words whose meanings I didn't remember. Funny thing, from the dictionary first page right now, that "aardvark" springs to my mind. The dictionary had a picture of it, a long-tailed, long-eared, burrowing African mammal, which lives off termites caught by sticking out its tongue as an anteater does for ants.

8   I was so fascinated that I went on—I copied the dictionary's next page. And the same experience came when I studied that. With every succeeding page, I also learned of people and places and events from history. Actually the dictionary is like a miniature encyclopedia. Finally the dictionary's A section had filled a whole tablet—and I went on into the B's. That was the way I started copying what eventually became the entire dictionary. It went a lot faster after so much practice, helped me to pick up handwriting speed. Between what I wrote in my tablet, and writing letters, during the rest of my time in prison I would guess I wrote a million words.

9   I suppose it was inevitable that as my word-base broadened, I could for the first time pick up a book and read and now begin to understand what the book was saying. Anyone who has read a great deal can imagine the new world that opened. Let me tell you something; from then until I left that prison, in every free moment I had, if I was not reading in the library, I was reading on my bunk. You couldn't have gotten me out of books with a wedge. Between Mr. Muhammad's teachings, my correspondence, my visitors—usually Ella and Reginald—and my reading of books, months passed without my even thinking about being imprisoned. In fact, up to then, I never had been so truly free in my life. ...

10   As you can imagine, especially in a prison where there was heavy emphasis on rehabilitation, an inmate was smiled upon if he demonstrated an unusually intense interest in books. There was a sizable number of well-read inmates, especially the popular debaters. Some were said by many to be practically walking encyclopedias. They were almost celebrities. No university would ask any student to devour literature as I did when this new world opened to me, of being able to read and *understand*.

11   I read more in my room than in the library itself. An inmate who was known to read a lot could check out more than the permitted maximum number of books. I preferred reading in the total isolation of my own room.

12   When I had progressed to really serious reading, every night at about ten p.m. I would be outraged with the "lights out." It always seemed to catch me right in the middle of something engrossing.

13   Fortunately, right outside my door was a corridor light that cast a glow into my room. The glow was enough to read by, once my eyes adjusted to it. So when "lights out" came, I would sit on the floor where I could continue reading in that glow.

14   At one-hour intervals the night guards paced past every room. Each time I heard the approaching footsteps, I jumped into bed and feigned sleep. And as soon as the guard passed, I got back out of bed onto the floor area of that light-glow, where I would read for another fifty-eight minutes—until the guard approached again. That went on until three or four every morning. Three or four hours of sleep a night was enough for me. Often in the years in the streets I had slept less than that.

15   I have often reflected upon the new vistas that reading opened to me. I knew right there in prison that reading had changed forever the course of my life. As I see it today, the ability to read awoke inside me some long dormant craving to be mentally alive. I certainly wasn't seeking any degree, the way a college confers a status symbol upon its students. My homemade education gave me, with every additional book that I read, a little bit more sensitivity to the deafness, dumbness, and blindness that was afflicting the black race in America. Not long ago, an English writer telephoned me from London, asking questions. One was, "What's your alma mater?" I told him, "Books." You will never catch me with a free fifteen minutes in which I'm not studying something I feel might be able to help the black man. ...

16   Every time I catch a plane, I have with me a book that I want to read—and that's a lot of books these days. If I weren't out here every day battling the white man, I could spend the rest of my life reading, just satisfying my curiosity—because you can hardly mention anything I'm not curious about. I don't think anybody ever got more out of going to prison than I did. In fact, prison enabled me to study far more intensively than I would have if my life had gone differently and I had attended some college. I imagine that one of the biggest troubles with colleges is there are too many distractions, too much panty-raiding, fraternities, and boola-boola and all of that. Where else but in prison could I have attacked my ignorance by being able to study intensely sometimes as much as fifteen hours a day?

 ## RESPONDING TO THE READING

Comprehension

1. How did Bimbi inspire Malcolm X to become better educated?
2. Malcolm X outlines the process by which he taught himself to read. Summarize it in your own words.
3. What was the effect of Malcolm's copying the dictionary?
4. What caused Malcolm X to feel so "truly free" in prison?
5. To what use did Malcolm X put his new-gained ability to read?
6. On what grounds does Malcolm X compare his prison studies with a college education?
7. What caused those who met Malcolm X believe he was university educated?
8. Throughout this essay, Malcolm X uses a lot of slang. Find five examples and paraphrase them.

Analysis

1. What is the conclusion of this essay? How does Malcolm X finally end his story of his life in prison? How effective is this ending?
2. For whom did Malcolm X write this essay? What assumptions did he make about his audience? How well do you think he addressed this audience?
3. In what ways do you identify with Malcolm X's self-improvement process? Have you ever taught yourself to do something difficult? Outline the process, if you have, and compare it with the attitude Malcolm X expressed in his essay.
4. Malcolm X claims that prison allowed him to be free. In what ways was that true? Have you ever experienced a limitation that actually helped you to grow and change?
5. In what ways did Malcolm X show his belief in the dignity of humankind— white or black? Do you think he was a revolutionary? How does his essay relate to current race relations among Canada's various groups?

The following essay examines the causes of extinction on earth.

The Biggies Died Out in Earth's Mass Extinctions

Graham Young

1   A while ago, a local area computer network at the University of Manitoba in Winnipeg was knocked out by a computer virus that went by a very melodramatic name—something like "Avenging Angel" or "Dark Destroyer." The virus jumped from the network onto the hard drives of personal computers as their users plugged into and off the network. It spread rapidly, like an epidemic; once it was in a computer, it incapacitated any software the user attempted to open.

2   Nevertheless, one machine was not affected. This computer was an old IBM clone running a version of DOS (disk operating system) that was apparently too primitive for the virus to deal with. The computer had an inherent immunity to the infection.

3   The machine's fortunate owner, a paleontologist and friend of mine, suggested that his computer was like the survivor of one of those mass extinctions that have occurred on Earth, in which most forms of life are driven to their deaths over a relative brief period of geologic time. It seemed to be a particularly apt analogy.

4   Scientists have identified up to 15 mass extinctions in the history of life. The disappearance of dinosaurs (and many other life forms) at the end of the Cretaceous period is by far the most widely known. Evidence indicates this event was probably caused by the impact of a large asteroid on Earth 65 million years ago in what is now the Yucatan Peninsula of Mexico. Such a collision of asteroid and planet could have caused earthquakes and tidal waves and produced a cloud of dust that blocked sunlight and caused the death of plants, the basis of food chains.

5   Although this was one of the five largest mass extinctions, it was not, in fact, the greatest one of all. That honour goes to the one that occurred at the end of the

Permian period about 250 million years ago. In this catastrophe up to 96 percent of all species on Earth became extinct.

6   The major mass extinctions apparently had different causes. (The other three majors occurred in the late Ordovician Period 440 million years ago; the late Devonian 360 million years ago; and the end of the Triassic 210 million years ago.) Some of the earlier global deaths may have resulted, not from bombardment by an object from space, but from changes in global climate, in glaciation or in sea-level and ocean-circulation patterns. There was considerable variation in the length of time global extinctions took place. If the asteroid scenario is correct, then much of the end-Cretaceous event could have happened in less than a year, while other extinctions may have been spread out over several million years.

7   Over the past two decades, much research has been directed at mass extinctions, scientists have discovered that in each of the events, certain types of life forms disappeared while others came to predominate among the survivors. Animals that died off were typically large and/or complex, and had specialized needs for food and resources—dinosaurs are typical of these. Those that survived tended to be small and have simple needs.

8   Other survivors had relatively low food needs. They may have produced very long-lived seeds or eggs or gone into a state of suspended animation.

9   Thus, the simple, clam-like invertebrate Lingula that lives in the sediment of tidal flats and would probably be considered a pretty dull sort of animal has survived every mass extinction of the past 500 million years.

10   Perhaps the comedian's suggestion that the survivors of a future holocaust will be cockroaches driving Plymouth Valiants is not far off the mark, since both animals and cars could be described as ecologic generalists. Similarly, my friend's computer is a simple "life form," and was able to survive a deleterious event that knocked out the more complex and specialized members of the computer ecosystem.

11   A stand-alone computer is much less likely to be infected by a virus than is a computer cabled into a network.

12   In the same way, biologic systems that are largely separated from the rest of Earth's food web are unlikely to be severely affected by mass extinctions. For instance, the ecosystems along deep-sea ridges don't depend on the sun for energy but are based on bacteria that metabolize energy from hot, mineral-rich water flowing out of the ridges. These ecosystems are characterized by strange, giant tube worms and unique bivalves and crabs. Such organisms were probably largely unaffected when the dinosaurs vanished.

13   Other stand-alone or nearly stand-alone ecologic systems include some large cave networks, and microbes that have been discovered living in bedrock deep within Earth's crust.

14   If we take the analogy further, and consider the whole Earth as a single local area network, we have to ask the obvious question: Is there a virus lurking out there that could cause a global system failure? If there is, then the systems likely to be extinguished are the big complex ones, which sadly include any organism that can read this.

RESPONDING TO THE READING

Comprehension

1. Like the friend he refers to, Graham Young is a paleontologist. What does a paleontologist do and how would you know this from reading Young's essay?
2. Young discusses two major extinctions. What are they?
3. Explain how the computer is analogous to the dinosaurs, according to Young.
4. List the causes Young gives for the extinction of the dinosaurs.
5. What effect does a change in global climate have on life on earth?
6. According to Young, what causes certain animals to survive mass extinctions?
7. How can being a part of a network cause failure or extinction?
8. What system and what organism is Young referring to in his final paragraph?

Analysis

1. What is the impact on readers of the analogy Young makes between the old IBM clone computer and primitive life forms that survived mass extinctions?
2. In what ways are we, as a complex organism existing in a sophisticated society, more vulnerable to extinction?
3. Explain the allusion to the "cockroaches driving Plymouth Valiants."
4. Do you believe there is anything we can do to make our extinction less probable?

Smoking Is Good for My Business

David Ginsburg

1   "Do you mind if I smoke?" my travelling companion asked me.

2   "Not at all," I replied. "In fact, I should be most pleased if you would. It would be good for my business."

3   "What do you do?"

4   "I am a cancer specialist and I look after patients with lung cancer."

5   He seemed utterly taken aback.

6   This is a most tasteless anecdote. Would it be any less crass were I to have said that I was a heart surgeon repairing vessels damaged by cigarettes? Or an undertaker?

7   Or would it have been more acceptable if the pleasure that I took in his smoking being good for my business had related to my work as a tobacco farmer

in southwestern Ontario, to my work as a tobacconist, a tobacco company executive, the receiver of revenue benefiting from a tobacco tax, or a social agency anticipating a reduced payout on his old-age-security pension because of his early death?

8   Would it have been more acceptable were I an organizer of a sporting event or an arts festival dependent on a tobacco sponsorship?

When 350 people died in a plane crash last summer, there was appropriate concern and consternation. The police were involved, government agencies were involved, CNN provided 24-hour coverage, and the company may yet be in serious trouble as a result.

9   Three hundred and fifty people died yesterday, another 350 people the day before and 350 the day before that. Three hundred and fifty people will die today and tomorrow and the day after tomorrow—all from the same cause and all involving the same industry. Does anybody care?

10   There seems to be a remarkable lack of concern for the deadly implications of tobacco smoking that does not apply to other areas. Were an aircraft company to build airplanes with the sole problem that one plane each day, filled with 350 people, crashed killing all aboard, this would undoubtedly evoke a response. There would be concern even if the company could justify its existence on the basis that jobs are provided building the plane, flying the plane, servicing the plane, taxing ticket sales and gasoline sales and generally supporting the economy.

11   It would not be acceptable if the company were to claim that there was no proof that the planes, or the pilots, or maintenance policies were in any way at fault; or if it were able to show that many other planes fly without any problems at all. It would not be acceptable if the company promised to build a lighter plane with possibly fewer consequences of the crash.

12   The equivalent toll on human life consequent on cigarette sales is ignored—seemingly on the basis that we need the tax money, need the tobacco sponsorship to promote the arts or sporting events, need the jobs the industry provides, need the conviviality of smoking in bars and restaurants.

13   Do these people know that they are riding on the backs of the three or four hundred people who die each day as a result of smoking? Do they care? Are we blind to the connection between the economic benefits on one side and the human suffering on the other side of this equation?

14   I recently consulted on a mother of three young girls. She had begun smoking when she was 12. Now she had a large lump in her neck, her liver was enlarged, her abdomen swollen, her breathing gasping. She had lung cancer. Could I justify this to her 12-year-old daughter on the basis that her mother was dying for the economic good of society, for a tennis tournament, for a concert?

15   Today I saw a man of 39 who had smoked 25 cigarettes a day since his early teens. He is paralyzed from the spread of lung cancer to his spinal cord. Can I reassure him that his cigarette smoking has benefited farmers and tobacco company employees?

16   My mother died a few years ago with evidence of widespread lung cancer. Should I feel comforted that over time she spent a lot of money at the local drug

store where she bought her daily packet of cigarettes; that she had a short-lived illness which cost the health-care system very little and that she no longer needs her old-age-security payments?

17   In my view, nothing justifies the growing of tobacco, the making, advertising and selling of cigarettes and the exploitation of the people who smoke them. When I see one patient after another dying of lung cancer, of heart disease, of chronic lung disease, I am filled with rage and not at all concerned that smoking is good for my business.

RESPONDING TO THE READING

Comprehension

1. David Ginsburg is an oncologist. What does he do?
2. "This is a most tasteless anecdote." What is Ginsburg referring to and do you think the anecdote is tasteless?
3. Ginsburg gives a number of occupations he could be in rather than that of oncologist. What are they?
4. Two significant associations are connected with the number 350. What are they?
5. Ginsburg presents three cancer patient anecdotes. What is the purpose of each?
6. Ginsburg ends his essay saying he is "filled with rage." What reasons does he have for being enraged?
7. This essay focuses mostly on effects rather than causes. What are the effects?

Analysis

1. How would you feel if you had been the travelling companion of Ginsburg referred to in the opening of the essay?
2. What are the benefits Ginsburg cites that derive from cigarette sales? Does he convince you that the suffering outweighs the benefits?
3. Explain the irony of the title and how the title relates to the cause and effect structure of Ginsburg's argument.
4. Ginsburg presents two causes of death in this article: plane crashes and smoking. What is the difference between how each is treated by the media and society in general? Why do you think this difference exists?
5. In your opinion, what does Ginsburg hope to achieve by writing this essay and having it published in a national newspaper? Does he have a just cause?
6. Throughout the essay Ginsburg offers no proof that smoking actually causes cancer. Why?

Writing Suggestions

1. Is there a book that has had a profound effect on your life? Explain, giving examples.
2. What motivates you to learn? Outline the causes of your own education and what you expect the effect of your education will be.
3. Do you think society is better or worse today than it was when your parents were young? Explain the causes of the changes in society since then as you see them.
4. Do you have a just cause for which you would write articles or take part in demonstrations? State your cause and discuss the changes that would occur in society if your cause were to gain the support of the majority.

Writing That Affects the Reader:

Description, Narration, Argumentation/Persuasion

"Observe always that everything is the result of a change." (Marcus Aurelius)

The following rhetorical techniques—description, narration, and argumentation/persuasion—are used not only to explain but also to create an effect upon readers' feelings, ideas, and actions.

Description

Description is a means of conveying information vividly. It appeals to a reader's senses—sight, touch, taste, hearing—as it attempts to reproduce through words the physical qualities of a previous experience. Affecting a reader's senses heightens emotion.

Descriptive writing depends upon conveying feeling using adjectives, adverbs, similes, metaphors, and other rhetorical devices.

Curtain Up

Catherine George

1   Sit back, relax and enjoy. It's showtime in Ontario. And you're in for an eye-popping treat. In the next few weeks, right here on our country stage, the curtain will rise on a color spectacle to rival the flashiest of show-biz extravaganzas.

2 Watch Mother Nature, the star of the show, in her role as leading lady. Like a classy Vegas showgirl, she'll do a quick change right before your eyes. She'll coyly shed her subdued summer wardrobe and, with a flourish, transform into a brightly-painted vixen, boldly strutting her stuff centre stage.

3 She'll blaze across the hills and down the valleys in a flamboyant cloak of many colors, oranges, crimsons, purples, and a crown of gold, in a season finale that's sure to get rave reviews from even the most jaded of critics. Best of all, everyone gets a free front-row seat.

4 Though the travelling show isn't officially due to open in southern Ontario for a couple of weeks, you can catch a sneak preview in the hardwood forests farther north where the elevations are higher and the climate change occurs a little earlier.

5 And, contrary to what some of us have been told, Jack Frost doesn't have a thing to do with changing the color of the leaves. In fact, he is often the spoiler if he arrives too soon, causing them to shrivel and drop before they get a chance to flaunt their fiery hues. What it takes is sufficient rainfall, cool (not frosty) nights and bright sunny days that cause the sugars in the leaves to produce those red, orange and yellow pigments.

6 With the exception of a few remote areas in Asia, no place on earth puts on an autumn display to rival the one you'll see in Ontario, Quebec, the Maritimes, and over the border in New England and northern New York state. Though no one can predict for certain, late September through Thanksgiving weekend should be the best time for leaf peepers to plan a jaunt into the countryside.

7 If you watch the ads you'll find a number of bus tour operators offering foliage tours in Ontario, Quebec and across the border. Cruise boats operate regularly on the Muskoka, Kawartha and Haliburton lakes, a pleasant day's outing for the family. It's probably too late this year but for next autumn you might think about renting a houseboat and taking the family for a color cruise on the Trent–Severn waterways system.

8 Algoma Central runs a train trip from Sault Ste. Marie into the spectacular Agawa canyon until mid-October. Some of the conservation areas such as the Kortright Centre near Kleinburg sponsor autumn color walks. So there are plenty of ways you can put a touch of color in your life.

9 But the best bet for catching the scenery is in the family car. All you need is a tank of gas, a picnic basket and your camera. When the mood strikes or a particular setting appeals you can stop for lunch under a cathedral of color, buy a pumpkin at a roadside stand or pick up a fresh apple pie at a country bakery.

10 You might try to plan your jaunt to coincide with one of the agricultural fairs or harvest festivals taking place in the small communities all across Ontario from now until Thanksgiving.

RESPONDING TO THE READING

Comprehension

1. George's thesis is "In the next few weeks ... the curtain will rise on a color spectacle to rival ... showbiz extravaganzas." With what sorts of examples does she develop her supporting details?
2. What is the analogy established in the thesis and operating throughout this essay?
3. Paragraphs 2 and 5 contain examples of personification. What are they?
4. What comparison is made between Mother Nature and Jack Frost?
5. Find five examples of George's use of vivid language. What specific words does she use to describe a colour spectacle? How many colours does she present in the first five paragraphs?
6. Does she make use of simile and metaphor? Find examples of each.
7. In the last five paragraphs, George makes a number of suggestions to her readers about how to get a "front-row seat." What are they?

Analysis

1. What sort of language does George use (see Ruby's article) and what is its effect on you? Is it appropriate to her subject? Give examples that show the level of language and vocabulary.
2. This article was written for *The Toronto Star*, and its intended audience was the general reading public. What effects did the writer want to produce in her audience?
3. George places side by side two apparent opposites, comparing the still natural world of the woods to the flamboyant artificial Las Vegas floor show. Is this comparison effective?

Essays that are solely descriptive are rare. Rather, description is a technique employed to enhance the style of a piece of writing—whether it be a process analysis or a comparison and contrast.

The Shack

Margaret Laurence

1   The most loved place, for me, in this country has in fact been many places. It has changed throughout the years, as I and my circumstances have changed. I haven't really lost any of the best places from the past, though. I may no longer inhabit them, but they inhabit me, portions of memory, presences in the mind. One such place was my family's summer cottage at Clear Lake in Riding Mountain National Park, Manitoba. It was known to us simply as The Lake. Before the government piers and the sturdy log staircases down to the shore were put in, we used to

slither with an exhilarating sense of peril down the steep homemade branch and dirt shelf-steps, through the stands of thin tall spruce and birch trees slender and graceful as girls, passing moss-hairy fallen logs and the white promise of wild strawberry blossoms, until we reached the sand and the hard bright pebbles of the beach at the edge of the cold spring-fed lake where at nights the loons still cried eerily, before too much humanshriek made them move away north.

2   My best place at the moment is very different, although I guess it has some of the attributes of that long-ago place. It is a small cedar cabin on the Otonabee River in southern Ontario. I've lived three summers there, writing, birdwatching, river-watching. I sometimes feel sorry for the people in speedboats who spend their weekends zinging up and down the river at about a million miles an hour. For all they're able to see, the riverbanks might just as well be green concrete and the river itself flowing with molten plastic.

3   Before sunup, I'm wakened by birdvoices and, I may say, birdfeet clattering and thumping on the cabin roof. Cursing only slightly, I get up *temporarily*, for the pre-dawn ritual of lighting a small fire in the old black woodstove (mornings are chilly here, even in summer) and looking out at the early river. The waters have a lovely spooky quality at this hour, entirely mist-covered, a secret meeting of river and sky.

4   By the time I get up to stay, the mist has vanished and the river is a clear ale-brown, shining with sun. I drink my coffee and sit looking out to the opposite shore, where the giant maples are splendidly green now and will be trees of flame in the fall of the year. Oak and ash stand among the maples, and the grey skeletons of the dead elms, gauntly beautiful even in death. At the very edge of the river, the willows are everywhere, water-related trees, magic trees, pale green in early summer, silvergreen in late summer, greengold in autumn.

5   I begin work, and every time I lift my eyes from the page and glance outside, it is to see some marvel or other. The joyous dance-like flight of the swallows. The orange-black flash of the orioles who nest across the river. The amazing takeoff of a red-winged blackbird, revealing like a swiftly unfolded fan the hidden scarlet in those dark wings. The flittering of the goldfinches, who always travel in domestic pairs, he gorgeous in black-patterned yellow feathers, she (alas) drabber in greenish grey-yellow.

6   A pair of great blue herons have their huge unwieldy nest about half a mile upriver, and although they are very shy, occasionally through the open door I hear a sudden approaching rush of air (yes, you can *hear* it) and look up quickly to see the magnificent unhurried sweep of those powerful wings. The only other birds which can move me so much are the Canada geese in their autumn migration flight, their far-off wilderness voices the harbinger of winter.

7   Many boats ply these waterways, and all of them are given mental gradings of merit or lack of it, by me. Standing low in the estimation of all of us along this stretch of the river are some of the big yachts, whose ego-tripping skippers don't have the courtesy to slow down in cottage areas and whose violent wakes scour out our shorelines. Ranking highest in my good books are the silent unpolluting canoes and rowboats, and next to them, the small outboard motorboats put-

putting along and carrying patient fishermen, and the homemade houseboats, unspeedy and somehow cosy-looking, decorated lovingly with painted birds or flowers or gaudy abstract splodges.

8   In the quiet of afternoon, if no boats are around, I look out and see the half-moon leap of a fish, carp or muskie, so instantaneous that one has the impression of having seen not a fish but an arc of light.

9   The day moves on, and about four o'clock Linda and Susan from the nearby farm arrive. I call them the Girls of the Pony Express. Accompanied by dogs and laughter, they ride their horses into my yard, kindly bringing my mail from the rural route postbox up the road. For several summers it was Old Jack who used to drive his battered Volkswagen up to fetch the mail. He was one of the best neighbours and most remarkable men I've ever known. As a boy of eighteen, he had homesteaded a hundred miles north of Regina. Later, he'd been a skilled toolmaker with Ford. He'd travelled to South America and done many amazing things. He was a man whose life had taught him a lot of wisdom. After his much-loved wife died, he moved out here to the river, spending as short a winter as possible in Peterborough, and getting back into his cottage the first of anyone in the spring, when the river was still in flood and he could only get in and out, hazardously, by boat. I used to go out in his boat with him, late afternoons, and we would dawdle along the river, looking at the forest stretches and the open rolling farmlands and vast old barns, and at the smaller things close by, the heavy luxuriance of ferns at the water's rim, the dozens of snapping turtles with unblinking eyes, all sizes and generations of the turtle tribe, sunning themselves on the fallen logs in the river. One summer, Old Jack's eighty-fourth, he spent some time planting maple saplings on his property. A year later, when I saw him dying, it seemed to me he'd meant those trees as a kind of legacy, a declaration of faith. Those of us along the river, here, won't forget him, nor what he stood for.

10   After work, I go out walking and weed-inspecting. Weeds and wildflowers impress me as much as any cultivated plant. I've heard that in a year when the milkweed is plentiful, the Monarch butterflies will also be plentiful. This year the light pinkish milkweed flowers stand thick and tall, and sure enough, here are the dozens of Monarch butterflies, fluttering like dusky orange-gold angels all over the place. I can't identify as many plants as I'd like, but I'm learning. Chickweed, the ragged-leafed lambs' quarters, the purple-and-white wild phlox with its expensive-smelling perfume, the pink and mauve wild asters, the two-toned yellow of the tiny butter-and-eggs flowers, the burnt orange of devil's paintbrush, the staunch nobility of the huge purple thistles, and, almost best of all, that long stalk covered with clusters of miniature creamy blossoms which I finally tracked down in my wildflower book—this incomparable plant bears the armorial name of the Great Mullein of the Figwort Family. It may not be the absolute prettiest of our wildflowers, but it certainly has the most stunning pedigree.

11   It is night now, and there are no lights except those of our few cottages. At sunset, an hour or so ago, I watched the sun's last flickers touching the rippling river, making it look as though some underwater world had lighted all its candles down there. Now it is dark. Dinner over, I turn out the electric lights in the cabin so

I can see the stars. The black skydome (or perhaps skydom, like kingdom) is alive and alight.

12   Tomorrow the weekend will begin, and friends will arrive. We'll talk all day and probably half the night, and that will be good. But for now, I'm content to be alone, because loneliness is something that doesn't exist here.

RESPONDING TO THE READING

Comprehension

1. The first two paragraphs act as Laurence's introduction based on her opening line, "The most loved place …" What is this place and how do you know?
2. What was the first place she loved most?
3. What is the controlling pattern of organization Laurence uses from paragraph 3 to the end? How does she organize her supporting details within this pattern?
4. Paraphrase her "pre-dawn ritual."
5. Paragraph 4 focuses on the trees around Laurence's cabin. Find examples of simile and metaphor at work here.
6. The bird is often used as a symbol of our imagination. In paragraph five what is the implied analogy that Laurence uses?
7. In paragraph 7 how many classifications of boats does Laurence present to her readers?
8. In paragraph 9 Laurence pauses in her description of her day to tell an anecdote about Old Jack. What kind of anecdote is it?
9. In paragraph 10 Laurence employs cause and effect. Find other examples of this pattern of organization.
10. Do you think Laurence's final sentence could stand as her thesis statement? Why or why not?

Analysis

1. Do you think there is a distinction between being lonely and being alone? How does Laurence's essay support your point of view?
2. Laurence succeeds in condensing the details of Old Jack's life into a single paragraph. How is it that we feel we know him and "what he stood for"?
3. Compare Laurence's attitude to nature to that of Catherine George. You might wish to consider their word choice and techniques.
4. "The black skydome (or perhaps skydom, like kingdom) is alive and alight." The play on words—skydome/skydom—is a *pun*. What does Laurence achieve by the use of this pun?
5. Laurence presents a typical day at her cabin. The simple events she relates, through their repetition—both in action and words—take on a greater

significance for Laurence; that is, they become a *ritual,* a form of celebration or praise, often having spiritual overtones. To what extent is this true in Laurence's account of her day? What rituals are important to you? What do they celebrate?

Writing Strategy

Margaret Laurence had a keen eye. She saw shadows, colours, and shapes, and she drew comparisons. She knew the names of objects and animals, and she knew how to talk about what they did and why they existed. Her descriptions are full of details that express her strong love of the Canadian outdoors.

To use description effectively, you must first of all observe closely. Descriptive writing rests on details—colours, smells, sounds, and shapes. It is important to select details for effect. Ask yourself, what *main effect* do I want to create for the reader? Do you wish to re-create a scene in its physical dimension or do you want to describe a moment in time and the feelings you experienced? Description must rely on a selection of details that will be most useful for creating the main effect. A writer must also decide on a point of view in using descriptive details. Should you re-create in words the entire scene in front of you or only a part? If you were to describe an object, would you begin your description at the top or the bottom?

Above all, descriptive writing must be concrete. You must use specific words and a variety of details in order to create a vivid impression. For example, compare the two passages below. The first is by Laurence. The second is a paraphrase of her passage written in a vague and general style.

LAURENCE: By the time I get up to stay, the mist has vanished and the river is a clear ale-brown, shining with sun ... Oak and ash stand among the maples, and the grey skeletons of the dead elms, gauntly beautiful even in death.

PARAPHRASE: By the time I'm up, the river is clear and the sun is shining. I look at trees, some of which are dead.

Writing Suggestions

1. Describe in detail a favourite place where you have recently spent time. Use as many words as you can to relate to readers the colours, smells, shapes, and sizes found in this place.
2. Describe your feelings for a person by telling the reader the concrete effects that person has on you. For instance, how do you physically react when you first see someone you really like or despise? Do you blush? Do you feel hot and cold at the same time? What happens to the palms of your hands, the pit of your stomach?
3. Describe a vivid memory of an incident in your childhood and then describe your feelings about it. How would you describe joy or anger, for instance?

Narration

Narration is a story-telling technique. It can be as brief as an anecdote, as casual as a joke, and as exciting as gossip about the weekend.

Reading Strategy

What you will notice with all narrative is that there is a beginning, a middle, and an end. Readers are impelled by the forward movement and development of a story. They become increasingly interested in "what happens next" when a clear chronological ordering of events is presented. A narrative may be interrupted from time to time by a flashback, foreshadowing, or a description of a scene, yet readers have an expectation that the events in the story will eventually reach some kind of end or resolution. Narrative writing arranges events in time to make a point. A joke, for instance, leads a listener through a series of events and moments up to a punchline. The events must be selected and related carefully and accurately for the punchline to make sense. Narrative depends on logical order, clear detail, effective transitions, and a believable outcome.

The following story by the brothers Grimm seems very simple, at first. The plot structure—the order of key events—is linear; one event follows another in a simple line of cause and effect.

The appearance of simplicity is deceptive, however, for this story has profound implications. As you read it, see if you can detect the turning point, that is, the moment when the story changes direction and meaning. Ask yourself whether the end met your initial expectations.

The Old Man and His Grandson

Jacob and Wilhelm Grimm

1   There was once a very old man, whose eyes had become dim, his ears dull of hearing, his knees trembled, and when he sat at table he could hardly hold the spoon, and spilled the broth on the tablecloth or let it run out of his mouth. His son and his son's wife were disgusted at this, so at last they made the old grandfather sit in the corner behind the stove, and they gave him his food in an earthenware bowl, and not even enough of it. And he used to look toward the table with his eyes full of tears. Once, too, his trembling hands could not hold the bowl, and it fell to the ground and broke. The young wife scolded him, but he said nothing and only sighed. Then they bought him a wooden bowl for a few pennies out of which he had to eat.

2   They were once sitting thus when the little grandson of four years old began to gather together some bits of wood on the ground. "What are you doing there?" asked the father. "I am making a little trough," answered the child, "for father and mother to eat out of when I am big."

3   The man and his wife looked at each other for a while and presently began to cry. Then they took the old grandfather to the table and henceforth always let him eat with them and likewise said nothing if he did spill a little of anything.

RESPONDING TO THE READING

Comprehension

1. In paragraph 1, what background details are you given? Summarize the facts.
2. **Setting** tells readers when and where the story happens. It can also inform the reader of the social, economic, and political status of the characters. Setting can also convey an emotional atmosphere. How firmly can you establish where and when the story took place?
3. In paragraph 2, what has the child learned from observing his parents' treatment of the grandfather?
4. Although this is a simple story, readers can discover complex motivations for the characters' actions. Why do the man and wife start crying?
5. List in point form the plot—the outline of the events—of the story.

Analysis

1. A story is not only its plot; it has a central **theme,** an idea that it develops. What is the theme of this story? Look at the title for a clue. Why does the title exclude mention of the parents?
2. An **archetype** is an assumed ideal pattern used as a model. Could this story be read as an archetype of family life?
3. What lesson does this folk tale teach us about human behaviour?
4. Folk tales often transcend time and culture. Does this story succeed in doing so?
5. This narrative is told in the **third-person** point of view (using *he, she, they, it*). The narrator may or may not be directly involved in the events of the story. The **first-person** point of view (using *I, my, we*) tells the story either as a participant or an observer. Retell this story from the first-person point of view of one of the characters. Compare your version with those of your classmates.

Writing Strategy

Most stories of everyday life have already happened before they are told on paper. Thus, the use of the *past tense* is common in writing a narrative. Events in a story are arranged by writers in chronological order—the order in which they occurred in time. Some narrative structures reverse the order of events—going from last to first to make a certain point—but this structure is rare. Often narrative requires some background information. For example, readers need to know details about the people in a story before the actual events are described.

If you use narrative in essay form, you must have a central point. Telling a joke without a punchline would be similar to writing a narrative without a reason. If you wish to tell a story, say, about a friend who won a lottery, the point of your story could be to show what the friend did with the money. You would have to restrict your narrative to the events that are crucial to the friend's winning of the jackpot, pointing out in detail the series of events that took place once the money was in your friend's hands. The point of your story would be to show readers what happened to your friend; perhaps it would tell how sudden wealth brought both happiness and despair.

John Allemang's essay tells a first-person story consisting of a series of anecdotes.

Bedtime Stories

John Allemang

1   In my nine years as official family storyteller, I figure I've taken on about 727 parts. Before a fidgety audience of two, I've played genies, princesses, bickering hippopotami, a Teutonic witch (the movie role went to Anjelica Huston), God, the Hardy Boys, an Alsatian chef, neurotic mice, two nuns and, my personal favourite, Nancy "Boss" Chicken, failed telephone operator.

2   Of all the nice surprises lying in wait for parents—outweighing the nasty ones, you'll be happy to hear, if only because sleepless nights come as no surprise—one of the nicest has been bedtime. Late at night, I've discovered, my children will listen to me. This is the next thing to a miracle, as you'll know if you've ever tried to tell a child not to inspect his baseball cards in the middle of the road.

3   For someone whose stage career never got much beyond the role of Lettuce in the Grade 1 production of Peter Rabbit, there is a wonderful pleasure in giving a nightly performance. And my audience gives me the actor's supreme compliment: they stay awake. Now I realize that what my children enjoy hearing are the squawks and howls and bad French accents, not the moral at the end of the story. But I like to think of it as a softening up. Listen to my rendition of *The Church Mice* 50 times and you'll pay closer attention next time I tell you to take your feet off the table.

4   What both children and adults enjoy about bedtime stories is that they are make-believe. They are a quick escape from a way of life that no longer tolerates many fantasies or escapes. And that's why I was surprised when my six-year-old daughter said to me the other night, after I'd sent my son off to his room, "Daddy, tell me a story about when you were little."

5   Playing a pompous chicken in front of your child is easy. Playing yourself is much harder. I have this odd feeling that my children admire me more the less I'm like myself. Part of the pleasure in reading stories comes from convincing these

hereditary skeptics that their meek father really is part-genie, part-witch, that he is able to turn into whatever he pleases.

6   The past imposes its own limits, and I don't always like to remind myself of them. We didn't have an enchanted wardrobe or a magic looking glass when I was young. We had shopping centres and open ditches and three transit connections to downtown Toronto. It is not a past I want to escape—it seemed like paradise at the time—but as a realm of fantasy, it always seemed to be lacking.

7   But my daughter was asking, and she must have had her reasons. I turned out the lights, thought hard, and came up with a memory of my grandparents' garden in the Niagara peninsula. I told her about climbing cherry trees and playing hide-and-go-seek among the sunflowers, and before long the discarded bits and pieces of this ordinary life started coming back together again. I remembered for my daughter the stale, musty smell of the basement where my grandfather, who was a dentist, had his office. I talked about the crisp, new comic books that my grand-mother kept ready for our surprise visits, and the ancient organ we pretended to play, and the earaches we got after a summer's swimming in Lake Erie.

8   These stories have no end, as my wily daughter must have known. She was trying to match the *1,001 Arabian Nights* for staying power. Every night since my debut I have felt a little dread when the storybook comes to an end and I have to improvise my life. How can I hope to match the last book we read, which was about a giant who collected dreams and blew them into children's ears and saved the world?

9   But the plain, simple stories that leave my mouth enter my daughter's ears almost as a dream. I remember the trivia from my childhood, but she hears myths. "Once upon a time …" I should say, as I begin my tales of breakfast hamburgers at Woolworth's and babysitters who died on the job and the boy who crossed the busy street against the rule so he could buy his Mom a present.

10   Not a princess anywhere. But for my daughter, who hears stories about princesses and giants every night, family stories have their unreal charm. And at the very worst (such were the joys) they put her to sleep.

RESPONDING TO THE READING

Comprehension

1. What is the central point of Allemang's essay?
2. Allemang tells a story about himself telling stories. How many separate stories are told within this framework?
3. What setting is presented in the first paragraph?
4. Explain the allusion to the actress Anjelica Huston. Can you explain any of Allemang's other references to children's stories?
5. Give examples of how Allemang makes this a funny narrative.
6. Find an example of Allemang's use of cause and effect.

7. How does he compare storybook stories to stories about when he was little?
8. "The past imposes its own limits." What does this mean?
9. In paragraph 8, Allemang refers to the "giant who collected dreams." How does Allemang implicitly compare himself to that giant?
10. How many different audiences is Allemang addressing in this essay?

Analysis

1. In spite of its humour, how do you know this is a serious essay?
2. Allemang says people enjoy stories because "they are a quick escape from a way of life that no longer tolerates many fantasies or escapes." Do you think this is true? Do you find it ironic that Allemang offers so many escapes?
3. Even though this was written for a North American reading audience (just look at all those allusions), do you think this essay can appeal to people worldwide? Why?
4. Almost every family has its official storyteller. Who told you your stories and what were they about?
5. "I remember the trivia from my childhood, but she hears myths." What does Allemang mean by this?
6. Many writers, including Shakespeare, claim that literature gives humankind a sense of the eternal. In "Bedtime Stories," simple, mundane events of one's life are transformed into stories that engage the imagination. How important is imagination in your life? Does telling stories make your life more meaningful to you? Do you think telling stories can give people both a history and a future?

The next narrative essay is a travel narrative, an account of Peggy McCann's journey on an icebreaker through the Northwest Passage. The power of her writing comes from the intense descriptions of the ice, "the most important thing." Ice itself seems to be a character in the narrative.

Water Sky

Peggy McCann

Dark patches on low clouds, sometimes almost black in comparison with the clouds, indicates the presence of water below them. This is known as "Water Sky."

Canadian Coast Guard,
Ice Navigation in Canadian Waters

1   Ice's birthday is in October. That is the first thing I learn. As first-year ice survives its first summer's melting it becomes second-year ice, and if it lasts at least two summers it is multi-year. This old ice is hard and thick, three metres or more. The oldest is as unyielding as granite. The salt has leached out of it and its colour,

where bare, is usually blue. The mariners read the ice like a great page, deciphering its textures, variations in blue, pressures of current and wind, the way the sky reflects it, its geography. Multi-year ice looks like continents with ancient, worn-down mountains, and lakes, and plains, and systems of rivers running through them to the ocean.

2   When we reach night in Baffin Bay, the ship's spotlights are turned on, two great blue beams searching for icebergs ahead. The captain says that sea-birds sometimes smash themselves into the lights, and the next morning the crew has to sweep up the bodies. I hear regret in his voice, but that may only be his dignified way of speaking and his careful English.

3   The bridge is homey, with the arms of the captain's chair upholstered in a fading, cream-coloured cloth, rich with flowers. I imagine it came from some living room in Vladivostok, a scrap from a sewing basket. Vladivostok is this ship's home port. She is the Kapitan Khlebnikov, an icebreaker of the Far Eastern Shipping Co. fleet. She is used to escort freighters to and from Siberia, but now she is on her way to Germany to be refitted as a tourist vessel. This is the first time a Russian ship has entered these waters, besides the odd secret submarine; it is the first time a Russian icebreaker will transit the Northwest Passage, and she is taking me with her. North, to a place Mary Shelley only dreamed of.

4   The bridge soon became my favourite place on the ship. It was always warm, with the sun pouring in the wide windows and the radiator running all the way beneath them. It was quiet when the rest of the passengers weren't there; you could not hear the engines, and the sound of the ship breaking ice was muted, that high up, to a shudder, a crunching and a sudden shifting underfoot. Quiet Russian conversations, the telephone or the radio breaking in, commands to the helmsman and his reply.

5   Some days, maybe because the air was dry, you could hear the music of the ice. The song is high and delicate, like glass, but sustained. The sun hitting pieces of ice thrown up by our bow caused rainbows. At other times the ice stayed quiet, until a resisting sound and a crash as it broke. And cracks, starting with the tiniest crack at our bow, spread swiftly, almost suddenly to become a road in front of us, a path to follow through the weakened ice for two miles ahead. I remember that muffled explosive sound, like chains of firecrackers going off, hearing it and skating hard to get away. The pond beside our house, a childhood form of ice.

6   The log and charts are in Russian. The place names gain articles in translation. 14.08.92 Anchor up. Leaving the Cambridge Bay. 17.08.92 Barrow Straight. Resolute. 05.15 Drift near the Resolute. East to Bylot Island and Pond Inlet, then north, to the limit of navigation, the northern tip of Tanquary Fiord, Ellesmere Island. The North Pole is 525 nautical miles north of here; the rest of the world is south. In other places I've been the sea reflects the sky. Here it seems the other way around. It can easily be imagined that the ice, or its absence, governs the sky. Light rises from the ice itself. We sail into solid walls of fog, then into light so blinding, with low mist still on the ice, you can hurt your eyes simply by turning toward a window.

7   The ice is the most important thing. The land seems secondary, hardly born, still raising itself from beneath the glaciers. I see yellow traces of plankton on the

broken slabs of ice that rise ponderously and turn over beside us, hints of the life underneath: krill, fish, seals, whales. Snow buntings nest in the great silence on Axel Heiburg Island. Muskox tracks in the frozen mud, wolf tracks following. Ravens and fulmars, murres, jaegers, muscular gulls as big as small calves. We saw a polar bear with a freshly killed seal, a few metres ahead of the ship. As we came up on him he dragged it beside us, his face and front legs covered in blood, leaving a scarlet living path straight across the ice.

8   The ice is the most important thing. My father told me a story from his merchant navy days, of being caught in fog on the Grand Banks. They couldn't see the icebergs around them but they knew they were there because they could smell them. So they cut the engines and drifted with them. That story was the one that stayed, that was most clear to me when he died. He died in March, 1992, and I saw the ad for the Khlebnikov in June. I cannot describe how strong the wish to go was except to say that it was a calling. It was the ice that drew me. I wanted to know if what he said was true, if the ice really had a smell. If it contained him.

RESPONDING TO THE READING

Comprehension

1. What does Peggy McCann mean by her first sentence, "Ice's birthday is in October"?
2. What are the differences among first, second, and multi-year ice?
3. What nationality is the icebreaker on which McCann is travelling?
4. Why is the bridge McCann's favourite place on the icebreaker?
5. In paragraph 5, to what does McCann compare the different sounds of ice?
6. Explain McCann's reference to "a childhood form of ice."
7. What evidence is presented that shows that "the ice governs the sky"?
8. There is an abundance of life on and beneath the ice. Find examples in McCann's description.
9. Why does Peggy McCann decide to take the trip on the icebreaker?

Analysis

1. In your own words explain what the term "water sky" means.
2. Write a selective summary of the narrative in this passage. Do not include any descriptions.
3. How is personification used in this piece? What is the effect of this device in the narrative?
4. How can ice have a geography?
5. Explain the allusion to Mary Shelley in paragraph 3.
6. Why does McCann repeat the statement "the ice is the most important thing"?

7. Explain the image of "a scarlet living path" in paragraph 7.
8. What is the significance of McCann's father's story?

In this final narrative essay, by Maya Angelou, the author appears to be telling a simple story about a group of people listening to a boxing match on the radio. In fact, Angelou tells a number of stories at the same time—each one relating directly to the boxing match and its effect on the people in the room.

The Fight

Maya Angelou

1   The last inch of space was filled, yet people continued to wedge themselves along the walls of the Store. Uncle Willie had turned the radio up to its last notch so that youngsters on the porch wouldn't miss a word. Women sat on kitchen chairs, dining-room chairs, stools and upturned wooden boxes. Small children and babies perched on every lap available and men leaned on the shelves or on each other.

2   The apprehensive mood was shot through with shafts of gaiety, as a black sky is streaked with lightning.

3   "I ain't worried 'bout this fight. Joe's gonna whip that cracker like it's open season."

4   "He gone whip him till that white boy call him Momma."

5   At last the talking was finished and the string-along songs about razor blades were over and the fight began.

6   "A quick jab to the head." In the Store the crowd grunted. "A left to the head and a right and another left." One of the listeners cackled like a hen and was quieted.

7   "They're in a clench, Louis is trying to fight his way out."

8   Some bitter comedian on the porch said, "That white man don't mind hugging that niggah now, I betcha."

9   "The referee is moving in to break them up, but Louis finally pushed the contender away and it's an uppercut to the chin. The contender is hanging on, now he's backing away. Louis catches him with a short left to the jaw."

10   A tide of murmuring assent poured out the doors and into the yard.

11   "Another left and another left. Louis is saving that mighty right ..." The mutter in the Store had grown into a baby roar and it was pierced by the clang of a bell and the announcer's "That's the bell for round three, ladies and gentlemen."

12   As I pushed my way into the Store I wondered if the announcer gave any thought to the fact that he was addressing as "ladies and gentlemen" all the Negroes around the world who sat sweating and praying, glued to their "master's voice."

13   There were only a few calls for R.C. Colas, Dr. Peppers, and Hire's root beer. The real festivities would begin after the fight. Then even the old Christian ladies who taught their children and tried themselves to practice turning the other cheek

would buy soft drinks, and if the Brown Bomber's victory was a particularly bloody one they would order peanut patties and Baby Ruths also.

14   Bailey and I lay the coins on top of the cash register. Uncle Willie didn't allow us to ring up sales during a fight. It was too noisy and might shake up the atmosphere. When the gong rang for the next round we pushed through the near-sacred quiet to the herd of children outside.

15   "He's got Louis against the ropes and now it's a left to the body and a right to the ribs. Another right to the body, it looks like it was low ... Yes, ladies and gentlemen, the referee is signalling but the contender keeps raining the blows on Louis. It's another to the body, and it looks like Louis is going down."

16   My race groaned. It was our people falling. It was another lynching, yet another Black man hanging on a tree. One more woman ambushed and raped. A Black boy whipped and maimed. It was hounds on the trail of a man running through slimy swamps. It was a white woman slapping her maid for being forgetful.

17   The men in the Store stood away from the walls and at attention. Women greedily clutched the babes on their laps while on the porch the shufflings and smiles, flirtings and pinching of a few minutes before were gone. This might be the end of the world. If Joe lost we were back in slavery and beyond help. It would all be true, the accusations that we were lower types of human beings. Only a little higher than the apes. True that we were stupid and ugly and lazy and dirty and, unlucky and worst of all, that God Himself hated us and ordained us to be hewers of wood and drawers of water, forever and ever, world without end.

18   We didn't breathe. We didn't hope. We waited.

19   "He's off the ropes, ladies and gentlemen. He's moving towards the center of the ring." There was no time to be relieved. The worst might still happen.

20   "And now it looks like Joe is mad. He's caught Carnera with a left hook to the head and a right to the head. It's a left jab to the body and another left to the head. There's a left cross and a right to the head. The contender's right eye is bleeding and he can't seem to keep his block up. Louis is penetrating every block. The referee is moving in, but Louis sends a left to the body and it's the uppercut to the chin and the contender is dropping. He's on the canvas, ladies and gentlemen."

21   Babies slid to the floor as women stood up and men leaned toward the radio.

22   "Here's the referee. He's counting. One, two, three, four, five, six, seven ... Is the contender trying to get up again?"

23   All the men in the Store shouted, "NO."

24   "—eight, nine, ten." There were a few sounds from the audience, but they seemed to be holding themselves in against tremendous pressure.

25   "The fight is all over, ladies and gentlemen. Let's get the microphone over to the referee ... Here he is. He's got the Brown Bomber's hand, he's holding it up ... Here he is ..."

26   Then the voice, husky and familiar, came to wash over us—"The winnah, and still heavyweight champeen of the world ... Joe Louis."

27   Champion of the world. A Black boy. Some Black mother's son. He was the strongest man in the world. People drank Coca-Colas like ambrosia and ate candy

bars like Christmas. Some of the men went behind the Store and poured white lightning in their soft-drink bottles, and a few of the bigger boys followed them. Those who were not chased away came back blowing their breath in front of themselves like proud smokers.

28   It would take an hour or more before the people would leave the Store and head for home. Those who lived too far had made arrangements to stay in town. It wouldn't do for a Black man and his family to be caught on a lonely country road on a night when Joe Louis had proved that we were the strongest people in the world.

RESPONDING TO THE READING

Comprehension

1. How does Angelou set the scene to let readers know this is an important event?
2. The events of the story are interspersed with dialogue. What is the effect of the dialogue on the telling of the story?
3. Explain the reference to "their 'master's voice.'"
4. What is the dramatic effect Angelou creates by describing the people's reactions to the radio commentary on the Joe Louis fight?
5. How many stories are actually told here? Identify each one.
6. "The real festivities ... Baby Ruths also." Explain the irony in this passage.
7. In the paragraph beginning "My race groaned," Angelou uses syntactical repetition ("It was ..."). What is the effect of this?
8. What are the implications of the phrase "hewers of wood and drawers of water, forever and ever, world without end"? What does the phrase allude to?
9. A lot of brand names of products are included in the story. What do these tell you about the young narrator?
10. What is the reaction of the crowd in the store to the Brown Bomber's victory?

Analysis

1. Joe Louis became a symbol for his people. What passages or single details demonstrate this in the story?
2. What are the people in the store really like? What is their social standing? What are their fears and dreams? What is their daily life like? Base your answer on the details Angelou provides.
3. What does the store represent to the people in the story?
4. Angelou presents this narrative based on her own childhood memories. Just like Allemang she shapes those memories for a purpose. Define it.
5. Discuss the irony in the final paragraph.

Writing Suggestions

1. Write a narrative about a very happy moment in your life. Tell it first in third person and then in first person.
2. Write a simple narrative about a series of events that had several meanings. For example, write about your high-school graduation but point out how the actions in that story had broader implications in your life.
3. Write a narrative about an incident in which you were misunderstood by someone.

Writing about a Short Story

Before reading the short stories below, review the following information on literacy terms.

Literary Terms

Character:	Participant in a story. Developed through thoughts or behaviour. **Round characters** possess multiple aspects and undergo changes or growth. **Flat characters** possess one aspect and do not change. A main character, or **protagonist**, is central to the action of a story.
Conflict:	Opposition between two sides (individual characters, groups of people, ideas, ways of behaving, moral or psychological choices) in a story.
Image:	Word picture that stimulates the senses.
Irony:	Contradiction in statement or situation. **Dramatic irony** occurs when a character is ignorant of or misjudges a situation that the reader or another character fully understands.
Plot:	Sequence of actions related by cause and/or motive. Plot is result of credible or real human responses to a problem or conflict.
Point of view:	Position from which author tells story.
	First person/ third person: Story told by I. Third-person story told through *he/she*.
	Participant/onlooker: Acts in the story/Observes actions in story.
	Limited/omniscient: Knows selected amount/Knows everything.
Setting:	Place, physically and socially, of story. Physical setting can describe climate, dwellings, jobs, institutions, and landscapes. Social setting includes status, cultural background, relative wealth, education, and state of mind.
Symbol:	Idea or object standing for values, people, ideas, or ways of life.
Theme:	Main idea of story, expressed through plot, character, setting, and imagery.
Voice:	Narrator of the story. Related to point of view. Can be character imagined by author to tell the story.

The Man Who Loved Flowers

Stephen King

1   On an early evening in May of 1963, a young man with his hand in his pocket walked briskly up New York's Third Avenue. The air was soft and beautiful, and the sky was darkening by slow degrees from blue to the calm and lovely violet of dusk. There are people who love the city, and this was one of the nights that made them love it. Everyone standing in the doorways of the delicatessens and dry-cleaning shops and restaurants seemed to be smiling. An old lady pushing two bags of groceries in an old baby pram grinned at the young man and hailed him: "Hey, beautiful!" The young man gave her a half-smile and raised his hand in a wave.

2   *She passed on her way, thinking: He's in love.*

3   He had that look about him. He was dressed in a light gray suit, the narrow tie pulled down a little, his top collar button undone. His hair was dark and cut short. His complexion was fair, his eyes a light blue. Not an extraordinary face, but on this soft spring evening, on this avenue, in May of 1963, he *was* beautiful, and the old woman found herself thinking with a moment's sweet nostalgia that in spring anyone can be beautiful … if they're hurrying to meet the one of their dreams for dinner and maybe dancing after. Spring is the only season when nostalgia never seems to turn bitter, and she went on her way glad that she had spoken to him and glad he had returned the compliment by raising his hand in half-salute.

4   The young man crossed Sixty-third Street, walking with a bounce in his step and that same half-smile on his lips. Partway up the block, an old man stood beside a chipped green handcart filled with flowers—the predominant color was yellow; a yellow fever of jonquils and late crocuses. The old man also had carnations and a few hothouse tea roses mostly yellow and white. He was eating a pretzel and listening to a bulky transistor radio that was sitting kitty-corner on his handcart.

5   The radio poured out bad news that no one listened to: a hammer murderer was still on the loose; JFK had declared that the situation in a little Asian country called Vietnam ("Viet-num" the guy reading the news called it) would bear watching; an unidentified woman had been pulled from the East River; a grand jury had failed to indict a crime overlord in the current city administration's war on heroin; the Russians had exploded a nuclear device. None of it seemed real, none of it seemed to matter. The air was soft and sweet. Two men with beer bellies stood outside a bakery, pitching nickels and ribbing each other. Spring trembled on the edge of summer, and in the city, summer is the season of dreams.

6   The young man passed the flower stand and the sound of the bad news faded. He hesitated, looked over his shoulder, and thought it over. He reached into his coat pocket and touched the something in there again. For a moment his face seemed puzzled, lonely, almost haunted, and then, as his hand left the pocket, it regained its former expression of eager expectation.

7   He turned back to the flower stand, smiling. He would bring her some flowers, that would please her. He loved to see her eyes light up with surprise and joy when he brought her a surprise—little things, because he was far from rich. A box of

candy. A bracelet. Once only a bag of Valencia oranges, because he knew they were Norma's favorite.

8   "My young friend," the flower vendor said, as the man in the gray suit came back, running his eyes over the stock in the handcart. The vendor was maybe sixty-eight, wearing a torn gray knitted sweater and a soft cap in spite of the warmth of the evening. His face was a map of wrinkles, his eyes were deep in pouches, and a cigarette jittered between his fingers. But he also remembered how it was to be young in the spring—young and so much in love that you practically zoomed everywhere. The vendor's face was normally sour, but now he smiled a little, just as the old woman pushing the groceries had, because this guy was such an obvious case. He brushed pretzel crumbs from the front of his baggy sweater and thought: If this kid were sick, they'd have him in intensive care right now.

9   "How much are your flowers?" the young man asked.

10   "I'll make you up a nice bouquet for a dollar. Those tea roses, they're hot-house. Cost a little more, seventy cents apiece. I sell you half a dozen for three dollars and fifty cents."

11   "Expensive," the young man said.

12   "Nothing good comes cheap, my young friend. Didn't your mother ever teach you that?"

13   The young man grinned. "She might have mentioned it at that."

14   "Sure. Sure she did. I give you half a dozen, two red, two yellow, two white. Can't do no better than that, can I? Put in some baby's breath—they love that—and fill it out with some fern. Nice. Or you can have the bouquet for a dollar."

15   "They?" the young man asked, still smiling.

16   "My young friend," the flower vendor said, flicking his cigarette butt into the gutter and returning the smile, "no one buys flowers for themselves in May. It's like a national law, you understand what I mean?"

17   The young man thought of Norma, her happy, surprised eyes and her gentle smile, and he ducked his head a little. "I guess I do at that," he said.

18   "Sure you do. What do you say?"

19   "Well, what do *you* think?"

20   "I'm gonna tell you what I think. Hey! Advice is still free, isn't it?"

21   The young man smiled and said, "I guess it's the only thing left that is."

22   "You're damn tooting it is," the flower vendor said. "Okay, my young friend. If the flowers are for your mother, you get her the bouquet. A few jonquils, a few crocuses, some lily of the valley. She don't spoil it by saying, 'Oh Junior I love them how much did they cost oh that's too much don't you know enough not to throw your money around?'"

23   The young man threw his head back and laughed.

24   The vendor said, "But if it's your girl, that's a different thing, my son, and you know it. You bring her the tea roses and she don't turn into an accountant, you take my meaning? Hey! She's gonna throw her arms around your neck—"

25   "I'll take the tea roses," the young man said, and this time it was the flower vendor's turn to laugh. The two men pitching nickels glanced over, smiling.

26   "Hey, kid!" one of them called. "You wanna buy a weddin' ring cheap? I'll sell you mine ... I don't want it no more."

27   The young man grinned and blushed to the roots of his dark hair.

28   The flower vendor picked out six tea roses, snipped the stems a little, spritzed them with water, and wrapped them in a large conical spill.

29   "Tonight's weather looks just the way you'd want it," the radio said. "Fair and mild, temps in the mid to upper sixties, perfect for a little rooftop star gazing, if you're the romantic type. Enjoy, Greater New York, enjoy!"

30   The flower vendor Scotch-taped the seam of the paper spill and advised the young man to tell his lady that a little sugar added to the water she put them in would preserve them longer.

31   "I'll tell her," the young man said. He held out a five-dollar bill. "Thank you."

32   "Just doing the job, my young friend," the vendor said, giving him a dollar and two quarters. His smile grew a bit sad. "Give her a kiss for me."

33   On the radio, the Four Seasons began singing "Sherry." The young man pocketed his change and went on up the street, eyes wide and alert and eager, looking not so much around him at the life ebbing and flowing up and down Third Avenue as inward and ahead, anticipating. But certain things did impinge: a mother pulling a baby in a wagon, the baby's face comically smeared with ice cream; a little girl jumping rope and singsonging out her rhyme: "Betty and Henry up in a tree, K-I-S-S-I-N-G! First comes love, then comes marriage, here comes Henry with a baby carriage!" Two women stood outside a washateria, smoking and comparing pregnancies. A group of men were looking in a hardwarestore window at a gigantic color TV with a four-figure price tag—a baseball game was on, and all the players' faces looked green. The playing field was a vague strawberry color, and the New York Mets were leading the Phillies by a score of six to one in the top of the ninth.

34   He walked on, carrying the flowers, unaware that the two women outside the washateria had stopped talking for a moment and had watched him wistfully as he walked by with his paper of tea roses; their days of receiving flowers were long over. He was unaware of a young traffic cop who stopped the cars at the intersection of Third and Sixty-ninth with a blast on his whistle to let him cross; the cop was engaged himself and recognized the dreamy expression on the young man's face from his own shaving mirror, where he had often seen it lately. He was unaware of the two teen-aged girls who passed him going the other way and then clutched themselves and giggled.

35   At Seventy-third Street he stopped and turned right. This street was a little darker, lined with brownstones and walk-down restaurants with Italian names. Three blocks down, a stickball game was going on in the fading light. The young man did not go that far; half a block down he turned into a narrow lane.

36   Now the stars were out, gleaming softly, and the lane was dark and shadowy, lined with vague shapes of garbage cans. The young man was alone now—no, not quite. A wavering yowl rose in the purple gloom, and the young man frowned. It was some tomcat's love song, and there was nothing pretty about *that*.

37   He walked more slowly, and glanced at his watch. It was quarter of eight and Norma should be just—

38   Then he saw her, coming toward him from the courtyard, wearing dark blue slacks and a sailor blouse that made his heart ache. It was always a surprise seeing her for the first time, it was always a sweet shock—she looked so *young*.

39   Now his smile shone out—*radiated* out, and he walked faster.

40   "Norma!" he said.

41   She looked up and smiled ... but as they drew together, the smile faded.

42   His own smile trembled a little, and he felt a moment's disquiet. Her face over the sailor blouse suddenly seemed blurred. It was getting dark now ... could he have been mistaken? Surely not. It *was* Norma.

43   "I brought you flowers," he said in a happy relief, and handed the paper spill to her.

44   She looked at them for a moment, smiled—and handed them back.

45   "Thank you, but you're mistaken," she said. "My name is—"

46   "Norma," he whispered, and pulled the short-handled hammer out of his coat pocket where it had been all along. "They're for you, Norma ... it was always for you ... all for you."

47   She backed away, her face a round white blur, her mouth an opening black O of terror, and she wasn't Norma, Norma was dead, she had been dead for ten years, and it didn't matter because she was going to scream and he swung the hammer to stop the scream, to kill the scream, and as he swung the hammer the spill of flowers fell out of his hand, the spill spilled and broke open, spilling red, white, and yellow tea roses beside the dented trash cans where cats made alien love in the dark, screaming in love, screaming, screaming.

48   He swung the hammer and she didn't scream, but she might scream because she wasn't Norma, none of them were Norma, and he swung the hammer, swung the hammer, swung the hammer. She wasn't Norma and so he swung the hammer, as he had done five other times.

49   Some unknown time later he slipped the hammer back into his inner coat pocket and backed away from the dark shadow sprawled on the cobblestones, away from the litter of tea roses by the garbage cans. He turned and left the narrow lane. It was full dark now. The stickball players had gone in. If there were bloodstains on his suit, they wouldn't show, not in the dark, not in the soft late spring dark, and her name had not been Norma but he knew what his name was. It was ... was ...

50   *Love.*

51   His name was love, and he walked these dark streets because Norma was waiting for him. And he would find her. Someday soon.

52   He began to smile. A bounce came into his step as he walked on down Seventy-third Street. A middle-aged married couple sitting on the steps of their building watched him go by, head cocked, eyes far away, a half-smile on his lips. When he had passed by the woman said, "How come *you* never look that way anymore?"

53   "Huh?"

54   "Nothing," she said, but she watched the young man in the gray suit disappear into the gloom of the encroaching night and thought that if there was anything more beautiful than springtime, it was young love.

RESPONDING TO THE READING

Comprehension

1. How many separate examples of love can you find in this story?
2. Using the examples you have found in question 1, what kinds of love are represented: romantic, cynical, innocent, alien?
3. Stephen King gives readers many examples of springtime. Scan to locate them.
4. King uses concrete details to set this story in May 1963. List the details.
5. How many people does the young man encounter and affect before he meets "Norma"? Each of these people believe that the young man is in love. What is the effect of this belief on each of them?
6. What sorts of details does King give his readers after the young man "turned into a narrow lane"?
7. How do the young man and Norma react to one another when they first meet?
8. Many examples of repetition are contained in paragraph 47. What are they?
9. How many examples of "dark" are in paragraph 49? Compare this darkness with the details in the rest of the story.
10. How does the conclusion of this story relate to the opening?

Analysis

1. This short story deals with love. How does the title relate to the story?
2. What do you think the young man's idea of love is? How is he "love"?
3. Throughout the story the young man is assessed by those he meets or who see him as someone in love. We, the readers, and "Norma" find out what he really is in paragraphs 46 and 47. In light of this, how would you interpret the conclusion of the story?
4. After you read the story, certain details about the young man achieve significance. Find examples of these details. Why are they significant? Were they clues—of any sort—to you when you began reading the story?
5. What is the purpose of presenting the young man through so many different characters' points of view?
6. This story seems to focus on love, beauty, and hope—all the things that spring traditionally represents. However, the young man is in fact the hammer murderer. In what ways does the irony of situation add to the effect of the story? (**Irony of situation** is the occurrence of events that are the opposite of those expected.)
7. What were your expectations when you began reading the story?
8. Stephen King's stories frequently place evil in everyday situations. Do you think this story was written only to shock the reader?

Writing Strategy

An essay based on a piece of literature analyzes the work by focusing on specific aspects and using examples from the story as **supporting details.** For instance, the essay could focus on **point of view, character development, theme, plot,** and **setting.** Any of the rhetorical modes could be appropriate for your essay. The subject of your essay could be arrived at through **brainstorming** or **asking questions** about the story. The two strategies below are developed from answers to the questions that follow King's story.

Model One

In answering the first two comprehension questions on Stephen King's story, "The Man Who Loved Flowers," you focused on the theme of love. If you adapt your answers to make them the basis for an essay about King's short story, you would be considering its thematic development and your subject would be kinds of love. Your answers to the two questions would also provide you with supporting details for your body paragraphs.

Your thesis statement could be written in the following way:

In his exploration of evil in everyday life, Stephen King presents three kinds of love in his short story "The Man Who Loved Flowers": innocent, romantic love; mature, cynical love; and violent, psychopathic love.

If you developed your essay based on the above thesis statement, you would be writing an essay of classification (see page 86). Your **focused subject** is love, the **categories** are the three types, and the **organizing principle** is King's fascination with evil.

Model Two

Analysis questions 3 and 5 about King's story guided you to consider the purpose of King's employment of point of view. Based on your answers you could develop an essay of comparison and contrast using point of view as your subject. As you know comparison and contrast means making a value judgment. In his manipulation of point of view King presents a central irony of our lives: we are often deceived by appearances. In composing your essay, you would most likely follow the block method of development.

Your **thesis statement** could then be written in this way:

In his exploration of evil in everyday life, Stephen King demonstrates how easily we can be deceived by appearances; King contrasts a series of similar perceptions of his protagonist with the shocking reality of the young man.

Regardless of how you choose to develop your essay, remember you must still write paragraphs of introduction and conclusion. In your body paragraphs you prove your thesis by making specific references to the short story. Here you will employ such skills as summarizing, paraphrasing, and quoting. Be careful, however, of two common pitfalls:

1. **Retelling:** Supporting details must prove the idea in your thesis statement. Sometimes students simply repeat the plot or parts of it without any analysis or without relating it to the thesis statement.
2. **Unsupported opinion:** Sometimes students will give an opinion of a story but fail to validate the opinion with specific references to the narrative.

When you are asked to read a piece of literature and discuss it. It each case, specific references made to or details taken from the source in question must be properly documented.

Documentation within the body of your essay is recorded by use of *parenthetical references.* It does not matter whether you have paraphrased, summarized, quoted, or merely mentioned an idea, you still must use a parenthetical reference.

A parenthetical reference means that you cite in parentheses (round brackets) the source of your quote, information, or idea. You cite this source as briefly as possibly, saving the full details of the text for the *Works Consulted* at the end of your paper.

The *MLA (Modern Languages Association) Style* is usually used for Humanities, Social Studies, and Business papers.

Short Quote (MLA Style)

A short quote can vary from a few words to four lines of text. What you need to include are the name of the author and the page number of the reference (MLA). The quote is written as part of your paragraph. It is not indented.

Stephen King says of his protagonist, "He had that look about him" (157).

Here, because the author's name is already mentioned, you don't need to add it in the parentheses.

The protagonist "had that look about him" (King, 157).

When you don't introduce the quote with the author's name, then the author's surname is cited followed by a comma and the page number in parentheses. In each case the words taken from the source are in quotation marks and the period is included *after* the parentheses.

Reference (MLA Style)

The young man seems oblivious to the effect he has on others; he is unaware of his impact on the two women outside the Washeteria, the young policeman, and the two teenagers (King, 159).

Here, you are referring to specific instances in the story, using *paraphrasing,* so you must cite the source.

Long Quote (MLA Style)

This is a quote longer than four lines of text. The crucial difference between a long quote and a short quote is that a long quote is *indented* and so does *not* use quotation marks.

Stephen King makes use of repetition as he describes the murder of the young woman in the sailor blouse:

She backed away, her face a round white blur, her mouth an opening black O of terror, and she wasn't Norma, Norma was dead, she had been dead for ten years, and it didn't matter because she was going to scream and he swung the hammer to stop the scream, to kill the scream, and as he swung the hammer the spill of flowers fell out of his hand, the spill spilled and broke open, spilling red, white, and yellow tea roses beside the dented trash cans where cats made alien love in the dark, screaming in love, screaming, screaming (160).

In the above, because King's name is used to introduce the long quote, only the page number is required in the parentheses. If the quote had been set up without King's name introducing it, information in the parentheses would have been (King, 160).

The American Psychological Association (APA) Style is usually used for scientific or technical papers.

The difference between MLA and APA styles is simple. For APA, the parentheses contain the author and the *date*, not the page number.

The protagonist "had that look about him" (King, 1977).

Additional short stories and questions about them are included in Appendix B (pages 231–43). They are "Jack" by Gary Anderson, "Magi" by Steven Heighton, "To Everything There Is a Season" by Alistair MacLeod, and "Jassie" by Shauna Singh Baldwin.

Essay Topics on Short Stories

1. Compare and contrast the father/son relationships presented in "Jack" and "To Everything There Is a Season" or "Jassie."
2. "To Everything There Is a Season" deals with the theme of transition from childhood to early adulthood. Consider how the story explores this theme.
3. "Jassie" presents a richly detailed character study of its protagonist. Discuss.
4. "Magi" and "Jack" both present the imaginative lives of children. How is the imagination important to the child in each story? How does imagination enable the children in the stories to deal with life issues and difficult situations?
5. Focusing on one or more of the short stories, examine how the author uses language and symbols to create an effect.
6. Setting is important in all the stories. Remember that setting can relate to the emotional landscape as well as the physical landscape of the protagonist. Choose one or more of the stories and discuss how setting adds to the reader's understanding of the protagonist.

7. What personal values and social conflicts are explored in one or more of the following: "Jassie," "To Everything There Is a Season," and "Jack."
8. Did any one of the short stories strongly touch you emotionally? Analyze why.
9. Analyze the use of irony in two or more of the short stories, showing how irony adds to the impact of the story.
10. Choose one of the two thesis statements (page 164) suggested for the Stephen King story and develop it into an essay.

Argumentation and Persuasion

Argumentation and **persuasion** are each written with the express purpose of influencing the reader by effecting a change in the reader's opinions, attitude, or actions. The essay of argumentation or persuasion issues a challenge. To be successful, this type of essay may exploit all of the other patterns of organization and prose techniques. Written effectively, such an essay will sway the reader to think, feel, and act differently.

The analogy of trial by jury can teach you much about writing an argumentation or persuasion essay. Similar methods and presentation of data are useful in setting up your essay of persuasion.

Consider Patrick O'Flaherty's essay. Could you imagine this as a lawyer's speech presented in a courtroom? Look ahead in this section and read Michele Landsberg's essay on capital punishment. Notice how she presents her subject and her evidence. What does she appeal to in her audience?

Read the following essay by Patrick O'Flaherty, "Stupidity is Alive and Well (Thanks to TV)." How does it make you feel? Does it challenge your way of thinking?

Stupidity Is Alive and Well (Thanks to TV)

Patrick O'Flaherty

1   I have been a university teacher of English for more than 20 years. Despite entreaties, threats and a variety of subterfuges aimed at getting students to open and turn the pages of books, I have found myself more and more trying to communicate with people who haven't read the text.

2   Spending 50 minutes in a classroom talking about *King Lear* to glassy-eyed pupils who have yet to discover that Cordelia is not another name for the Cliffs of Dover can be quite a challenge. It is even perilous to address one's remarks to the tiny minority who have actually managed to peruse the assigned book, since many of those have read it with so little attention that they can remember only scattered incidents.

3   Now it is dawning on educators that concentration, memory and factual knowledge, the concomitants of reading, are more than just manifestations of intelligence; they are the building blocks of intelligence.

4   The mind is not a bucket that can hold a fixed quantity. It is like a muscle that is strengthened and expanded by the kind of exercise reading supplies.

5   If our students are less and less willing to read books of any description, then they are not getting smarter. Quite the contrary. And if these are the best and brightest of adolescents, one hesitates to hypothesize about what is happening to the level of intelligence in the general population.   *symptoms*

6   What is responsible for this melancholy syndrome? An assortment of causes, no doubt. But one source of juvenile stupefaction is surely television. Experience has shown that many of the non-readers who inflict themselves on English teachers are inveterate TV watchers. As the book is laid down, if indeed it was ever picked up, the button is switched on.

Statement *gloomy*

7   The invigorating effect of TV on the modern world that was predicted by Marshall McLuhan and others in the sixties and seventies has failed to materialize. The complete opposite seems to have happened. We might ask why.

8   What McLuhan failed to take account of in his analysis of TV was the actual content of most programming. "The medium is the message" was a brilliant piece of hyperbole that did not, however, adequately describe the impact of television. The medium is no more the message than the Chivas Regal bottle is the whisky.

9   The medium of TV comprises transmitters, radio waves, receivers and related equipment. Similarly, books are printed leaves of paper, sewn together between covers. I would not argue that either of these media is a neutral instrument. But it is surely what is in or on the medium that matters.

10   And what is on TV? Most of what is there is of such a nature that it not only fails to test the powers of concentration and memory in the way a book does, but it compels—I would even say invites—a kind of instinctive jettisoning.

11   I am convinced that the mind of a habitual TV viewer develops an automatic erasing or blotting mechanism that operates like a trigger once the show is over, or perhaps like an escape valve while it is actually in progress. The mind is only slightly engaged by the show in any case; the act of discarding it from memory is an entirely rational one. Readers who have watched a number of episodes of, say, *Friends* or the *Fresh Prince of Bel Air* might try to recollect them. Bet you can't.

12   I am not calling attention to the banality, repetitiveness and shallowness of most sitcoms and soaps—the absence in them of anything worth remembering or concentrating on—to suggest that their makers have failed in some way and should try to do better. Their makers know exactly what they are doing.

13   Continuity is not insisted on. It is not why a car spins out of control and crashes that matters, or what the effect of the crash will be on the ensuing action; just watching it happen is the whole point.

14   These shows are manufactured by enterprising executives and producers to appeal to a mind just turning over slowly. Many stories can be dropped for five minutes and picked up again, or used as a backdrop for eating or talking. A novel requires us to recall what happened in chapters one and two. The sitcoms virtually relieve us of this responsibility. Even in the soaps, it hardly matters what happened beyond yesterday.

15   A yet more thorough job of casting off is done by the mind as it views TV advertisements—beer ads, for example, an endless preoccupation of the Canadian networks. In a newspaper there is no need to read the ads, but in watching television they must be endured because their end signals the resumption of the program.

16   The already semi-conscious mind of the TV addict switches into an even lower idling speed as the ads appear, with their message about the wonderful lifestyle associated with beer drinking, a message we know is wrong, since we are all acquainted with the effects of alcohol in society.

17   Watching TV ads is sitting in the corner watching all the lies go by. The mind at some level recoils from this torrent of deceit and spits the stuff out, though hour after hour of partial absorption no doubt leaves an imprint that helps to keep breweries in business.

18   These influences have been at work since early childhood on the numbed psyches of those who find their way into university classrooms. The mental powers that students bring to the new setting are those that have proved sufficient for television. But the essence of TV watching, the continual passive receiving and rejecting of images, together with the low level of exertion such a process entails, is so destructive of the alertness and retentive faculties demanded by the study of books that it constitutes a real handicap.

19   Some will argue that what the children of the television age have to offer is something special, a kind of "Third World" education. But it looks distressingly like plain, new-fashioned stupidity.

RESPONDING TO THE READING

Comprehension

1. What is the effect of O'Flaherty's starting his essay with an anecdote on teaching *King Lear?*
2. Paraphrase paragraph 3.
3. What sort of learning would take place if the mind were a "bucket"?
4. O'Flaherty claims reading supplies a kind of exercise. Find examples of this exercise.
5. What does "this melancholy syndrome" refer to?
6. Explain the allusion to Marshall McLuhan.
7. What is hyperbole? Give an example. Explain the use of the word in O'Flaherty's essay.
8. In a selective summary, outline O'Flaherty's argument against TV.
9. List examples from O'Flaherty's essay that show the differences between TV and reading.
10. O'Flaherty builds up to his thesis statement, placing it near the end of his essay. Locate and paraphrase his thesis statement.

11. How does O'Flaherty write this conclusion? How does it relate to his opening paragraphs?

Analysis

1. Why do you think O'Flaherty begins his argument by stating how long he has been teaching English?
2. Do you agree with his statement that "concentration, memory and factual knowledge ... are the building blocks of intelligence"?
3. Brainstorm for examples of what you can learn from watching TV.
4. How biased is O'Flaherty? Does he ever present the other side of the issue, which is that TV can be intelligent and make watchers think?
5. Who is he ultimately attacking? Is it "the children of the television age" or TV itself?

Appealing to Your Audience

An important feature in argumentation or persuasion is respect for your audience. How you wish to influence your readers is based on three means of **appeal**: logical, ethical, and emotional.

What appeal did Patrick O'Flaherty use? Did he use only one of the three above means or combine two or more of them? Argumentation and persuasion can combine all three, depending on the content of the essay and its dominant patterns of organization.

1. **Logical**
   The **logical appeal** is based on reason: facts, figures, and statistics are of key importance. A clear relationship between your stated position (your thesis statement) and reasons for adhering to it must be established. Evidence and proof are of prime importance in this appeal. As in the writing of an expository essay, you must have verifiable data. See the section that follows, on evidence.

2. **Ethical**
   The **ethical appeal** rests on a system of defined values or a code of morality shared by both writer and audience. In the analogy of the lawyer, the jury's beliefs in justice and fair play should complement those of the lawyer. As part of your position you must clearly define your set of values. Readers will find your argument *credible* if your principles are clear. Credibility, in fact, is important in ethical appeals, as your audience must believe that you are not only knowledgeable but honest and fair-minded. Ethical appeals require proof and evidence as much as any other kind of appeal does. Simply stating an opinion without back-up facts can destroy your credibility as a writer of argument.

3. **Emotional**
   The **emotional appeal** is one made first of all on the basis of your feelings for or against some idea or issue. Second, you must appeal to your readers'

feelings. You may want to arouse their feelings of shame or anger concerning an issue, and thus attempt to use facts and examples that would make them react with their hearts. For instance, in reading Michele Landsberg's essay you will see how her language and her examples appeal to our emotions. She also uses logic in her argument, but she combines it with examples that arouse shame and doubt. This is a popular appeal: you will see it in newspaper editorials, and in television lawyer dramas, as most audiences act on how they feel—their gut reactions!

Presenting the Evidence

Often writers separate argumentation into the logical category and persuasion into the emotional, but this division is based on personal choice and is not an established rule. Persuasion, for instance, can combine both logical and emotional appeals. Likewise, the ethical category can be included in both, or used exclusively on its own.

In constructing an essay of argumentation or persuasion, the evidence you present is crucial. Logical appeals, for example, must have verifiable facts. Opinions must be examined for their validity and cross-checked to make sure they are not lies. Facts in an argument must be logically arranged. In arguing for or against an idea or a belief, you may need to find **primary sources**: first-hand evidence from interviews or personal observations. **Secondary sources** are also valuable—records and reports. Evidence must be *reliable* as well; verifying your facts often depends on doing research and cross-checking (that is, looking up the facts about something as reported by one person or in one book against what has been reported about the same thing by another person or in another book). Some of the techniques for locating data for the research paper you will read about in Unit Six would be helpful in argumentation.

Evidence in the form of supporting details is grounded in three general areas:

1. **Authority** is citing, quoting, or summarizing the views of a well-known and respected person or institution.

EXAMPLE: In arguing for a sandbox in a local day-care, one could cite the ideas of Jean Piaget, a noted child psychologist. In persuading citizens of your small town against hunting, you could biblically proclaim: "Thou shalt not kill."

EXAMPLE: Patrick O'Flaherty refers to Marshall McLuhan, even though he argues against McLuhan's ideas.

2. **Experience** can be presented in the form of personal anecdote or historical example. The process of the experience—how something happened—or the cause and effect relationship between historical events could be related.

EXAMPLE: In arguing for an improvement in the college's registration process, you could recount the horrors of your first day, starting with the line-ups you had to endure. To persuade readers that scientific discoveries are often simple, retell the story of Sir Isaac Newton and the apple.

EXAMPLE: Patrick O'Flaherty starts his essay by talking about his students and their reading habits.

3. **Facts** are information that can be validated or verified. All argumentation and persuasion rests on the use of clear facts. To argue that the ancient Egyptians were great engineers, one need only cite the proportions of the pyramids. To persuade the public against smoking, the government has made tobacco manufacturers include health warnings on packages.

Once information, wording, and appeal have been determined, the overall structure of the essay must be designed. Such structure will depend on the issue you wish to discuss, how much you decide to appeal to logic or emotion, and the needs of your audience. Classical logic presents writers with two forms of setting up an argument: deduction and induction.

Deduction

Deduction accepts a *general principle* (the **main premise** or thesis statement of the essay) as true, then applies it to a specific case or cases (the **minor premises** explored in the body paragraphs) and arrives at a rational **conclusion.** This three-part form is called a **syllogism.** It is used in argumentation to clarify the placement of evidence and to test the validity of the appeal to the audience. In a simple format, the syllogism can be expressed as follows:

MAJOR PREMISE:	All humans are mortal.
MINOR PREMISE:	Tom Cruise is human.
CONCLUSION:	Tom Cruise is mortal.

In building an argument on a syllogism you must be careful, when examining your evidence and deciding on your appeal, not to make the mistake of using faulty reasoning. Here is an example where the syllogism can work against itself:

MAJOR PREMISE:	All mothers are women.
MINOR PREMISE:	Mary is a woman.
CONCLUSION:	Mary is a mother.

These examples are simplified, of course, to show you how the structure of deduction can be applied to information and thought. You must be careful in using deduction not to lead your audience to a false conclusion. Your evidence must be logical and not contradictory.

Induction

Induction examines particular cases and then formulates a general principle or conclusion based on those cases. Induction is often called the *scientific method* and is commonly used in such things as lab experiments and mathematical problem solving. Lawyers use induction to prove guilt or innocence. To be sure your inductive reasoning is sound, you have to substantiate your evidence. Induction depends on facts and dependable supporting information.

Lawyers who prosecute a murder suspect must have dependable and verifiable data to prove guilt. As we know from television, false evidence is misleading and unacceptable. Lawyers often try to appeal to our emotions or our sense of morality when they want to persuade us of their client's innocence, but the inductive approach must rest on solid evidence or no amount of emotion can sway us to believe in the lawyer's case.

Try the following exercises to test your knowledge of deduction, induction, premises, and conclusion.

Missing Premises/Conclusions

In the following sentences, determine what the missing statement is and whether it is a premise or conclusion.

1. All of my students are intelligent, so Kevin can't be one of my students.
2. Only roses grow in the east garden, and those flowers on the table were picked from there this morning.
3. The woman who committed the robbery had long blonde hair, but Heather is a curly-haired brunette.
4. Dictatorial people aren't popular, so Delphine can't be dictatorial.
5. Tony dresses very stylishly, and we know what that implies because all successful businessmen dress stylishly.
6. Someone must be burning leaves because the scent of burning leaves is in the air.
7. Dr. Kent can't be a psychiatrist because his name isn't listed in the Medical Directory.
8. You know the saying "None but the brave deserve the fair," and Bruce's bravery is beyond question.
9. Whenever it snows, Mai Li gets excited about skiing, and it's snowing now.
10. This can't be a rosebush because it doesn't have thorns.

Fallacies

To make sure an argument is sound, you must be aware of what are known as **fallacies**. In presenting an argument, writers sometimes get caught up in their own feelings or their overwhelming sense of right and wrong. Unknowingly, they may "bend" their facts to suit their premise, or express a bias in their choice of data. A lawyer might do this, for instance, in order to win a case, leaving out certain details or overstating others. The lawyer may make personal remarks that appeal to a jury's prejudices. To avoid being accused of lying or distortion, be wary of the following.

Hasty generalization: Generalizations are assumptions based on weak or incomplete evidence. They lead readers toward false or irrelevant conclusions:

EXAMPLE: Corporations are evil and do not benefit society because all they want to do is make a profit at the expense of the environment.

Begging the question or **Arguing in a circle**: A writer presents an argument proving nothing because it gives no clear reasons, but simply restates the original premise.

EXAMPLE: No one who cares about children will oppose the building of a new day care because a day care is something that those who love children know is necessary.

Non sequitur or **Unclear reasoning**: Non sequitur is a Latin term meaning "It does not follow." Writers include information that makes the conclusion or the order of the argument unclear or illogical.

EXAMPLE: Playing a lot of sports builds stamina and speed. Thus, sports are the best way to teach young men manners and morality.

Ad hominem or **Attacking the person**: A writer makes personal, even untrue, remarks about a person or an idea rather than presenting facts against the issue.

EXAMPLE: All politicians are criminals and have never done any good for the people of Canada.

Bandwagon emotionalism or **Ad populum**: Writers appeal to popular prejudices or claim that since everyone thinks in a certain way, that way must be true.

EXAMPLE: Everyone knows today that governments are out to tax honest people to death—just look at the increase in consumer and private income taxes over the past few years!

Refutation

Refutation, another structural device in the essay of argumentation or persuasion, means dealing with counterarguments by showing how they are in error. In taking into account opposing views, even presenting the opposition's full case, you can demonstrate that you are willing to acknowledge two sides of an issue and are able to show how your argument is reasonable and why the opposing view is not. This technique helps to establish your fairness and credibility. It also gives you the opportunity to demolish the argument of the opposition.

The following essay by journalist Michele Landsberg is about an emotional issue—capital punishment. Examine how Landsberg appeals to readers' emotions but avoids fallacies that could mar the credibility of her point of view. Note, also, how she uses the inductive method to build her argument and refutation.

*talking
to people who
are in favor of
death penalty*

*persuading
argument*

*overall main
point: eye
eye for an eye*

Let's Just Shamble Back to the Cave for Some Bone Gnawing

Michele Landsberg

1   It's not because I have any special compassion for murderers that I oppose the death penalty—I enjoy, as much as anyone, the national fantasy of putting a bullet through Clifford Olson's brain—but because it's so useless.

2   The death penalty turns a country into a nation of fools. What has the long, wavering struggle of civilization been but an effort to control, shape and raise us above our most primitive impulses? Now we are about to commit our political energies to a protracted debate on capital punishment, and, according to an Angus Reid survey, 75 per cent of Canadians hope to reinstate the killing of murderers. We might as well shamble back to the cave and gnaw on bones if we are going to distort the whole structure of the law to enshrine our thirst for vengeance.

3   And vengeance it is, because there is no logical basis for the death penalty. This does not seem to have occurred to many pro-death penalty Canadians.

4   Some say it's a waste of good tax money to keep murderers alive in jail. Wrong. At a conservative estimate, every death sentence costs the U.S. Government $2-million in court costs, legal fees, endless appeals and delays, more than twice as much as it costs to keep a killer in jail for life. Right now, each Canadian pays $23 a year for all federal correctional services. We would have to kill off the whole population of a penitentiary to cut the cost significantly.

5   Canadians seem to think that an execution is a painless, modern and scientific way to rid ourselves of an inconvenient human who will never be worth saving. Amnesty International, now campaigning against the death penalty (only two Western nations, the United States and Turkey, have it), says that even the most streamlined methods of gassing, strangling, burning and poisoning entail gruesome agony.

6   In Alabama in 1983, it took three charges of 1,900 volts over a period of 14 minutes to kill a prisoner—smoke and flames erupted from his flesh before he died. A Mississippi murderer writhed in convulsions for eight minutes after he was gassed, until finally the legal witnesses were asked to leave. Prison officials have blocked their nostrils with Vaseline so they won't smell the burning flesh of electrocuted men. In Florida last year, a prison doctor and six guards engaged in a long and brutal struggle to subdue a frantic prisoner and force him into the electric chair.

7   It isn't neat and scientific: it's grotesque, filled with stench and horror, and we turn officials and doctors into legal torturers—"Is he dead yet, doctor?" "No, give him more voltage"—to carry out our fantasy of revenge.

8   Canadians who favor the death penalty think it's only fair to kill those who kill others. But fairness in capital punishment is a sick joke. In the United States, it's the poor, unemployed and black who are executed. There's irrefutable bias in sentencing. Kill a white person and you have more than doubled your chances of being executed. A study of 11,000 U.S. executions shows only two cases of whites put to death for killing a black man. In fact, U.S. law officials have pointed out that

the application of the death penalty is freakishly quixotic: accomplices have been electrocuted while the trigger-puller went free; the retarded and mentally ill and even those who committed crimes as juveniles are gassed; and a man's life or death often depends on a legal labyrinth of technicalities and accidents.

9   Do Canadians think we will never execute people out of racial prejudice? Do we assume that our court officials and legal procedures are free of stupid mistakes, malfeasance and public pressure for conviction? Do we think we would never be capable of hanging an innocent man? Donald Marshall, Donald Marshall, Donald Marshall.

10   If you've ever been in court, you'll know there's truth in the cliché about one law for the rich and one for the poor. If Canada had the death penalty, we could well see a parade of the colored to the hanging room—native Indians, Sikhs, Haitians—while the Helmuth Buxbaums pay a million dollars for expensive lawyers and live. Is this what we want?

11   Many people think the death sentence is a deterrent, but all the evidence points the other way. After Florida reinstated the death penalty, the homicide rate went from a record low to a record high; in non-executing states and in Canada, the murder rate, since abolition, has fallen. The causes of murder are far more complex than the simple absence of capital punishment.

12   And there's an ominous sidelight: only a tiny fraction of those who spend time on death row are eventually executed. Many of the others literally go crazy in their tiny isolation cells—and then they are released. Life sentences may be safer for society.

13   We seem to be in the grip of a fevered delusion, fed perhaps by U.S. media violence. Canadians believe the murder rate is seven times higher than it really is. We use "compassion for the victims' families" as our excuse for insisting on death for the murderers, but, if we genuinely cared about victims, we would spend our time and resources on prevention of the economic and family stresses that lead to murder.

14   Why, when it offends reason and reality, do we turn now to such a pointless debate? We are angry people living in a frightening time. Never have so many felt so threatened, with so much reason. What a spectacle: "The gods are rumbling. Let's smear on the woad and have a human sacrifice." The death penalty is our magic dance, the superstition of savages.

RESPONDING TO THE READING

Comprehension

1. Unlike Patrick O'Flaherty, Michele Landsberg introduces her thesis statement (main premise) immediately. What precisely is her thesis?
2. State the first point in her argument against the death penalty.
3. How does she refute the argument that it's expensive to keep murderers alive?

4. With what evidence does Landsberg refute the argument that modern execution is painless and scientific?

5. What appeal does Landsberg make in her fourth point? How does she refute this particular argument?

6. What comparative evidence does Landsberg provide to refute the notion of the death sentence as a deterrent to crime?

7. What impact does the United States have on how Canadians see themselves, according to Landsberg?

8. What powerful emotional images of humanity does the author conjure up in her last two sentences?

9. Explain the allusions to the following: Clifford Olson, Donald Marshall, Helmuth Buxbaum.

10. Only two Western nations—the United States and Turkey—retain the death penalty. Why does Landsberg state this fact?

11. Why does Landsberg use only American examples of executions?

Analysis

1. The structure of Landsberg's essay is logical. Her appeal is also to logic. How then does this essay achieve its highly emotional tone and effect?

2. The author in her title and conclusion writes with a different attitude from the one she uses in the body paragraphs. How and why?

3. "Life sentences may be safer for society." Do you agree?

4. After reading Landsberg's argument, was your mind changed?

In the following essay, Gary Pinder uses humour in his argument, but how serious is he?

Clone Farms: Let's Bring a Capital Idea to "Life"

Gary W. Pinder

1   It is a melancholy object to see each day, on the streets and on the television, the many people wearing prostheses or confined to wheelchairs, the blind or deaf struggling to cope ... victims of drunk drivers, freak accidents, or birth defects due to illicit drug use.

2   Equally joyless is the increasing number of bedridden souls patiently awaiting organ transplants, dying on expensive waiting lists.

3   And how sobering are the thousands of people hampered by polluted lungs and livers, the undernourished and the undernutrified, the underdressed and the overstressed, unable to work, made impotent by high cholesterol and low self-esteem, outcast by their deficiencies.

4   Even more disturbing, in the present deplorable state of the economy, is the additional grievance to society in the form of welfare and health-care costs and workers-compensation payments. Not only do many individuals suffer, but so does society as a whole.

5   Now, we have just learned, we have the technology to clone human embryos. With what sincere and silent determination, with what furitive ingenuity, with what stealthy creativity this knowledge came upon us. And with what binding obviousness has it been suggested that this is a source for organ donations. Every compassionate taxpayer has an interest in the matter.

6   I therefore humbly offer it to public consideration that we establish immediately, and with equitable distribution throughout the country, clone farms.

7   Each member of society should be entitled to his or her own clone. When a person is born, the parents or the government will authorize a clone to be made for that person. This clone would live "its life" on a clone farm. If an individual, for whatever reason, needs a heart, say, or a hand, it would be supplied by the clone. There would be no worry about finding a perfect match. And if that individual should happen to die, total replacement is an option to ease the pain of a grieving family. Or if the family prefers not, the clone could be auctioned or sold, whole or in parts.

8   Of course, some scrupulous people are likely to censure this idea as a little bordering on cruelty; however, once the overwhelming benefits are explained to them, they will surely give full support to the implementation of this scheme.

9   First of all, thousands of people will be able to lead happy, healthy, normal lives they otherwise would not have been able to lead, no longer restricted by a dialysis machine or the clumsy self-consciousness of a prosthesis. Think of all the Baby Jane and Baby Moe stories with happy endings. In time, they will not even be stories; they will be a matter of course.

10   Individuals will enjoy a higher quality of life and be able to fully participate in daily activities once again or for the very first time. They would be able to contribute to a healthy economy. This in itself would cut welfare and health costs. Millions of dollars would be saved in long-term disability payments.

11   As for the clone farms, they would be entirely self-sustaining. They would not just be farms but places of diverse productivity. Clones would be kept busy with agriculture or working in factories. Their work would pay for their own maintenance, which would be minimal. (Clones can do without steaks and CD players.) All surplus would be split between the "farmers" and the "originals" in the form of dividends, and both would be taxable income, the proceeds of which would go to fight the deficit.

12   Furthermore, as a source of cheap labour, clone farms would ensure that industry would locate here instead of abandoning Canada for other countries like, say, Mexico. This would lead to the production and consumption of inexpensive, high-quality merchandise here at home and an increase of exports to other countries. The economy would grow to be as healthy and as strong as its citizens.

13   Some of those same scrupulous people may fear that the pace of change is "too swift." But the apparatus of society, complex as it is, will remain intact. Government commissions formed to develop regulatory policies and industry standards would employ a few people for a few years. New employment opportunities would open for genetic technologists and clone farmers. Clones-rights activists would form lobby groups and demonstrate. Psychologists and self-help groups would help people with identity crises. Lawyers would argue issues of

ownership and copyright. Scholars would argue issues of originality, authenticity, and creativity.

14   Young people could become pen pals with their clones. They would have someone who understands them. They could even take school trips to clone farms.

15   Parents could better control naughty children: "You can be replaced, you know!" "Settle down, or your clone will get your Christmas presents!"

16   We can all anticipate the sitcoms, the dramas, the bestsellers and the eventual fabrication of nostalgia for life on the farm.

17   So, in essence, things would be exactly the same. Only better.

18   These are not just vain, idle, visionary thoughts. This is a practical and compassionate solution to some of society's problems. We could waste time thinking this through. But we see that after a while, we don't even have to think things through—we just have to take the next step.

19   Yes, we've come a long way from wooden teeth and wooden legs. Let's not stop now.

RESPONDING TO THE READING

Comprehension

1. What are the images in Pinder's introduction that lead up to his main premise?
2. What features of Pinder's sentences in the introduction are different from the style of sentences used by Landsberg?
3. Paraphrase Pinder's main premise.
4. What benefits would society enjoy as a result of clone farms?
5. How would an individual find his or her life improved as a result of clone farms?
6. Describe how a clone farm would work.
7. Why would it be necessary to create regulatory policies if clone farms were in fact put into practice?
8. At what point in the argument does Pinder make it clear to readers that his proposal is not serious?
9. What types of evidence does Pinder give to readers to make his argument seem valid?
10. Comment on the puns in the subtitle of the article.

Analysis

1. Pinder has in the above essay written an imitation of Jonathan Swift's *A Modest Proposal* (which is reprinted on pages 254–60 in Appendix C). What is Pinder's purpose for doing so?
2. "So, in essence, things would be exactly the same. Only better," Pinder says near the end. Do you agree?

3. Although Pinder's proposal is a joke, does it have any merit?
4. What assumptions has Pinder made about his reading audience? How do you know this?
5. What would you like best about having a clone? Would Judy Syfers perhaps like to have one?

Michael Cobden has written the following essay of persuasion in addressing the question in his essay's title.

Why Can't a Man Be More Like a Woman?

Michael Cobden

1   I envy women. I envy the intimacy of their friendships. I especially envy the way they talk to each other—so naturally, easily, personally—while we men banter and talk about sports, politics, business, cars, and other safe subjects. We never ask each other how we're feeling or how our children are. We never raise anything that's troubling us. And we don't hear each other the way women do. We compete: "Guess what I saw today ..." "Well, that's nothing. Guess what *I* saw ..." Yes, I envy women.

2   And I wish they would recognize how fortunate they are, at least in some ways. I wish they'd allow that they have a lot of advantages over us men, that they're privileged in as many ways that matter as we are.

3   I wish men could learn to talk to each other the way women do and get to know each other the way they do. The things they talk about over lunch at my wife's workplace! Body things. Health things. Things about their marriages. Things we men would never, never talk about. The difference between the relations my wife and her (mostly women) colleagues enjoy and my relations with my (mostly men) colleagues is as marked as the difference between the culture of dogs and cats.

4   I envy the way women support each other, and the way they share each other's delights. They have more laughs than we do, and they're real laughs, happy laughs at the pleasure of their intimacy. We men laugh at the things we pretend to find funny but that really serve to keep us apart.

5   Why can't a man be more like a woman? Some men try. They join men's groups and meet once a week or once a month and get in touch with their feminine side and, in a very real sense, civilize each other. Trouble is, most men don't want to meet with the kind of men who go to men's groups, or don't think they do. We like the men we mix with. We just wish we could get to know them the way women get to know each other.

6   You can see the pattern forming in elementary school, even in day care. The boys are on the playground throwing a ball at each other; the girls are standing in a tight circle, talking.

7   Late Saturday morning my wife and two friends did something they enjoy doing once every so often. They went up to Quinpool Road, a nearby shopping

area that always looks in need of rejuvenation. They went to mooch around, hang out, browse in Canadian Tire and have lunch at the third-ranking greasy spoon on the street. And be friends.

8   I said I wanted to go along. Not to browse. Whenever I'm in Canadian Tire I only wish I could find what I'm looking for and get out of there. I wanted to listen to what they'd say to each other, watch how they'd show their friendship. Jane said of course I could come along. Straightaway I decided not to. I said I didn't want to cramp their style—as if I could!—but really I was afraid I'd be bored or uncomfortable with all the personal stuff, the day-to-day stuff. So I said I'd do some housecleaning.

9   I swept the bathroom floors. How, I wondered (though I did not think to ask my friends Chris or Dick or Don) could "my floors" get so dirty? Did their floors get that dirty? And then I got out the squeeze mop.

10   The doorbell rang. Jane's friends had arrived. One, Barbara, had bought a present for me. (Another thing women are so much better at doing than men.) It was a book: *Heidegger For Beginners*. I'd talked when I last saw her about going to an introductory lecture meant for people like me who knew nothing about Heidegger and not understanding the lecture, even though it was in English. She'd noticed (another thing women do better than men) how upset I was about this. She remembered (another thing ...) and bought the book for me.

11   The four of us talked about the book. Barbara explained Heidegger, simply enough even for me. She wanted us to understand. A man might have wanted us not to understand. We could have talked more, but I said I had to get on with the bathroom floors.

12   "And I won't forget the toilets," I said as Jane and her friends went off for a couple of hours of friendship.

13   Yes. I envy women.

RESPONDING TO THE READING

Comprehension

1. In his introduction, what does Cobden imply women talk about?
2. How many examples of repetition does he use in the first paragraphs? Why do you think he uses so many?
3. How does Cobden compare the ways in which men and women laugh?
4. What pattern does he say we can see forming in elementary school?
5. Because Cobden's major pattern of development is comparison and contrast, list the things he says women do differently from men.
6. The anecdote that concludes the essay has three parts. What are they?
7. How would you classify the sort of work Cobden stays home to do?
8. Does the essay have a thesis statement?

Analysis

1. Cobden is attempting to persuade both men and women in this essay. What is he attempting to persuade each sex to do?
2. What kinds of evidence does Cobden use to persuade his readers?
3. What is Cobden's major appeal. Locate specific vocabulary that reveals his particular appeal.
4. There is a seeming contradiction in paragraph 8 when Cobden says, "I was afraid I'd be bored or uncomfortable with all the personal stuff." How do you account for this?
5. How does the anecdote of Barbara and the book support Cobden's major premise?
6. Do you agree with the way Cobden describes men's and women's attitudes and behaviour today?

Writing Suggestions

1. Persuade your reader to see a movie. For this assignment, use all of the skills developed in this text. Write a concise thesis statement recommending the movie, with clear reasons for your recommendation. You may choose a movie currently in the theatre or one now on video. Here are some questions you might want to ask yourself as you proceed: What is your major premise? What was it about this movie that sparked your admiration of it? What examples of characters, dialogue, special effects best support your thesis?

   Remember to consider using summary and paraphrase when recounting plot details. Use narrative when necessary. You may also wish to classify the movie by its genre: science fiction, action, drama, western, etc.
2. Argue for or against any one of the essays used in this unit. Be sure to state a strong main premise and to decide on an appeal that is appropriate to your chosen audience.
3. Is there an issue you feel strongly about? First define it, then structure your argument to persuade readers of the rightness of your position.

6

Reading and Writing from Sources:

The Research Paper

"A man will turn over half a library to make one book." (Samuel Johnson)

The research paper is your presentation of what others have said about a subject. Regard this challenging task of reading and writing as a long essay in which you present your point of view with a thesis statement, topic sentences, and supporting details *gathered from sources.*

Remember, you have at your command a variety of methods for acquiring information and organizing the facts (see Unit Three). Often a research paper may be organized as a process analysis or a combination of patterns such as comparison/contrast with cause and effect (see Unit Four). Student Cecile Dean's research paper in this unit uses comparison, classification, and cause and effect. Here is a process you can follow for writing a research paper.

1. Assign (or choose) a topic.
2. Focus the subject.
3. Do background research to test viability of focused subject.
4. Take information from sources by skimming, scanning, underlining, note-taking, paraphrasing, summarizing, and quoting and citing of sources.
5. Write a working thesis statement and select key ideas from collected data.
6. Read collected data closely and make an outline of your research paper.
7. Write a thesis statement and research paper with proper documentation.

Focusing and Testing the Subject

Whether or not your instructor has assigned a specific topic, you will have to define your subject for this long essay. You may need to brainstorm (see Unit Three), then focus the topic, and finally locate supporting details before you can organize your paper and decide how to pattern your selected information. A research paper may be written using one dominant expository pattern of organization; it may also be persuasive. The form of the paper is defined by your topic and how you wish to express it to your readers.

Let's suppose your instructor assigned a topic related to education. This is a broad field of information; you must narrow it down and find a focus. Let's assume you have brainstormed and decided to discuss math, often a subject either intensely loved or deeply hated. Finding that focused subject still too broad and general, you ultimately choose to centre your research paper on the currently "hot" topic of women and math. A major concern in education, industry, and government today is that at some point during their high-school years, the majority of women become "turned off" by math.

SUBJECT: Women and Math—Why are women turned off? What are the causes of, the reasons for, the solutions to the problem?

Is this topic viable? You will need to test the subject to see if it lends itself to a longer paper by heading to the library. Talk to the personnel there. They will help you to locate information in subject catalogues, encyclopedias, indexes, periodicals, books, and CD-ROMs. Using the questions posed above, you can begin to search for answers in various articles. Be sure as you begin your library search to keep in mind the focused subject—*women and math*. Do not waste time looking up theories of math or the history of math unless you feel they pertain to your essay. As you go through various articles, you may find that some are useful and some are not. Research means *searching, selecting,* and *rejecting.*

What you have been doing at this point is background research to test the potential of your focused subject.

A word of advice: as you read through books, look at their lists of works consulted, or bibliographies. There you will find references to additional information that may be useful. Other likely sources are:

- interviews with experts in the field, classmates, or friends;
- information from local organizations (on the subject of women and math, try phoning a school board or your old high school), institutions, or government.

Once you've gathered a number of pieces of information you must read them carefully. This part of doing research can be time consuming. Here, *skimming* and *scanning* are very useful reading techniques for getting through your preliminary data. Always keep in mind your focused subject and use it as a guide for selecting information you will later use to write your paper.

When you search for sources, even before you choose which ones you will ultimately use, be sure to keep a record of what you have read. Write down all the details you will need for your list of sources, the separate page at the end of your paper that tells readers where you found your details. At this stage of your research it is best to do the following:

- For a book, record—exactly as they are printed—the author's name, the full title, place of publication, name of publisher, date of publication, page numbers.
- For an article in a magazine or newspaper, record—exactly as they are printed—the author's name, title of article (including subtitles under the main title), title of publication, date of the publication, page numbers.
- For an article from an electronic source, record the title, the author, and the directory path you followed to locate the information.

At this early point in your research, it is essential to record these details accurately. Put such information on an index card or on a separate record sheet so you can have an easy reference. Later in this unit we will explain how to arrange this information in proper documentation format, using one of two standard methods.

Be sure to be accurate in your recording of data; you won't want to go back to the library to find your source a second time.

If you find a passage that is well expressed and you wish to quote it, copy it out word for word or photocopy a few pages. Don't forget to write down the source reference details in the manner discussed above. *Always* record the source information, so that you will not be accused of plagiarism.

Plagiarism

Plagiarism, a serious form of cheating, is claiming information written by another as your own. Even unintentional plagiarism can have severe penalties ranging from a grade of zero on the research paper, to failing the course or even expulsion from college.

Plagiarism happens when you write down facts or opinions from someone else but *do not* acknowledge your source. Copying without identification of source is plagiarism. Even if you identify your source, but quote someone without using quotation marks, you are still guilty of plagiarism.

Writing your own paper is difficult and you may find you are overwhelmed by other writers from whom you are taking information. Some research papers rely on sources for 80 percent of their data. How do you then avoid plagiarism? First, be aware that you are selecting data and re-arranging it in a new manner—your own, in fact—to make a point or to argue from a different point of view. Think of researched data as raw material from which you will build up your paper. Explain and then use data in quotes or in paraphrase form. Don't be alarmed if many of your paragraphs begin with your own topic sentence but then are supported by data from a number of other writers. (For example, see Cecile Dean's essay on pages 192–95 of this unit, particularly paragraph 5. See also in this unit the section on quoting. It explains how selected material can be used creatively in your paper.)

But be yourself! Being influenced by a writer you admire is fine, but use your source as a springboard for your own thesis and essay. Take a look at the essay "Clone Farms," from Unit Five, and compare how it reflects but does not copy its famous model, Swift's *A Modest Proposal,* which is reprinted in the Additional Essays section in Appendix B of this book.

Taking Material from Sources: Reading and Recording Skills

A word of warning at the start: *do not* write in library books or journals. Photocopy the passages you need and use your underliner on your own photocopy. Too often, you may find that other students have marked up books with coloured underlining. Such markings can be distracting—not to mention "off topic" for *your* essay—let alone a defacement of public property.

A problem common to many students is figuring out just what to underline. As a result, more than half an article ends up highlighted. If you underline too much, you ultimately create more work for yourself because you haven't actually read and digested the information you really need.

What should you do?

Underlining is helpful for finding key ideas. Thus, underline the thesis statement and the key ideas in the article. Look at each paragraph and select what you think are pertinent supporting details—ones that relate to or discuss your focused subject. It is helpful if you are systematic in your underlining. For instance:

- Use two lines for the thesis statement and a single line for the key ideas and topic sentences. If the thesis is not directly stated, write out one in your own words and record it next to the opening paragraph. (Underlining does not simply mean drawing lines or colouring with a highlighter. It also means asking questions, making notations in the margin, numbering ideas for future reference.)
- Number the supporting details in each paragraph. Highlight the ones that pertain to your focused subject.
- Record the organizational patterns used by the author (cause and effect, classification, etc.).
- Highlight the key words or terms in the article. Highlight words or terms you don't know and define them in the article's margins for future reference.
- Check or highlight what you agree or disagree with in the article, based on your focused subject. Comment when you feel provoked either favourably or negatively. These quick comments can be developed later into points of interest or key ideas in your paper.

Try this method on the article "Maths a Plus," by Jennifer Lewington, keeping in mind the focused subject: sometime in their school career, women were "turned off" math. What were the reasons? Are there any solutions?

Maths a Plus, Schoolgirls Assured

Jennifer Lewington

1 Above the din of pounding hammers, as a roomful of teen-aged girls build wooden tool boxes, apprentice carpenter Deb Harvey delivers a not-so-subtle message about the importance of math and science in their lives.

2 "How are you going to read a tape measure?" she says to an inquiring 12-year-old named Susi Porter, who is wielding her hammer with the two-fisted determination of a tennis player.

3 "How will you know how to read a blueprint?" continues Ms. Harvey. "That's why it's really important to know math."

4 Ms. Harvey, serving for the day as a role model for women in non-traditional jobs, makes herself heard above the staccato rhythms reverberating from the workshop at Northern Secondary School.

5 The former telephone operator, courier driver and landscape gardener, now in the second year of her four-year apprenticeship, was one of the hits yesterday at an annual event sponsored by the Toronto Board of Education. The board is trying to break down the barriers that deflect girls from math and science in high school and beyond. Yesterday's workshop came in the wake of a new international study that shows Canadian children have only middling abilities in mathematics and science compared to those in 19 other countries.

6 "Everything can be fixed ...," begins Ms. Harvey, 34, pounding away at her women-can-do theme. But 13-year-old Suzette Marsh, a Grade 8 student at Lord Dufferin Public School and one of 450 Grade 7 and 8 girls from elementary schools across Toronto who spent the day at Northern, finishes the sentence with a grin: "... if you take physics."

7 Judging by student reaction to the event, a mixture of hands-on activities and speeches, the riddle of women, stereotypes and non-traditional ambitions—such as careers in math and science—becomes less mysterious.

8 Susi, for example, says she used to "hate" math but now loves it, and science too. Her Grade 7 math teacher "spends a whole lot of time explaining it" and, says Susi, he is patient. Her science teacher, also a man, is "sciency" and "neat." She confides proudly that her teacher has taught the class about the periodic table of the elements, a topic other students do not get until Grade 12.

9 Self-esteem, says Edite Flaum, a co-chair of the Horizons '92 event, "is at the top of the list" of factors that influence girls to pursue math and science in high school and beyond.

10 But some old habits, and stereotypes, die hard.

11 On their way to the carpentry workshop, Susi and Suzette swap stories about their schools. Susi, a Grade 7 student at Winona Drive Public School, is frustrated that her girl friends cannot join the hockey team—there is one for the boys, but not for the girls. She says the girls are not allowed to play tackle football or soccer either.

12 How does she square that message with the can-do mantra of yesterday's conference? "It's confusing," admits Susi, who has already rejected a career as an actress as too superficial. "We don't need any more pretenders; we need more real people."

13   Myra Novogrodsky, also co-chair of the event, concedes that a one-day work-shop that tries to sell girls on math and science cannot compete with the mixed messages they receive from society in their daily lives.

14   Janet Reid, a senior physics teacher at Lawrence Park Collegiate Institute, recalls one girl who attended several years ago and switched her career plans from business to engineering. She went on to stand first in her engineering class at the University of Toronto for four years in a row and is now in a master's program.

15   Ms. Reid says that girls and boys have different attitudes towards success in school, one of the factors that hold young women back from non-traditional academic and career tracks. "Even girls who are very capable don't think of pursuing math and science," she says. "They want to feel assured they will do well."

16   When asked about her career plans, Suzette rattles off a rich assortment: archeologist, journalist, poet, biologist, part-time ballerina, psychiatrist. Yet she chafes because her father doesn't think women can do heavy lifting and other tasks.

17   "There are still a lot of men who think carpentry is a man's job," says Suzette.

18   Ms. Harvey has an answer. Just before the girls leave her workshop, new tool boxes in hand, she tells them how she dealt with the male carpenters who always challenged her—even when she was right.

19   "They seemed to see a sign on my forehead that said 'Don't believe a thing this woman says,'" she told the girls. "When they argued, I would tell them 'Stop, read my forehead' and it worked." Now, she says, she is proud of her working partnership on the job with the men carpenters.

Note-taking   When you first read the article "Maths a Plus" and decided it could be useful, you may have noticed a number of things:

1. It presents a series of anecdotes from "authorities" and high-school girls. How many?
2. The article reports "an annual event sponsored by the Toronto Board of Education." What is that event dedicated to? Why is the event important? Who organized it this year? Who participated in it?
3. The author focuses on a particular role model. Who is this person? Why does the author choose her to represent solutions?

These questions are typical of ones you could use when reading through an article and questioning its viability for your paper. Asking such critical questions helps you absorb the article's content and choose what details you will put into your research paper. Writing out your answers in note form may provide you with necessary supporting details.

One of the most important steps in research is the taking of notes.

Taking notes means reading, questioning, writing down brief answers, selecting pertinent answers based on your focused subject or working thesis statement.

Another aspect of taking notes is **paraphrasing** and **summarizing**, two skills taught in Unit Two. As you read an article, you may find a whole paragraph that could be useful and you will want to summarize its content. Certain passages from paragraphs may strike you as important and may contain ideas you will want to paraphrase. Be careful, however, not to include information that doesn't relate to your subject. For example, Susi in "Maths a Plus" expresses frustration at being denied the chance to play contact sports. While this is an interesting social observation, it is not directly related to the problem of women and math, which is the focus of your research. Such an example may seem pertinent because it shows how Susi was frustrated, as women are with math, but it may not ultimately be useful information and therefore can be rejected.

Quoting   (See Unit Four.) Students often ask, "How much should I quote?" or "How much can I quote?" Quoting is useful as a research device only if it is backed up by analysis. Too often, students include short and long quotations and assume their readers will draw connections between the thesis of the paper and the quotations. Quotations are only *recorded references* and do not stand alone. You as a writer must explain the meaning of the quotation or use it to illustrate a point of your own in the paper. Simply quoting an author is not a part of research writing. Readers want you as the writer to interpret the material you have selected, and this is especially true with quotations.

> *Quote to provide a detail, support a conclusion, or show readers the tone and wording of an original source.*

A word of warning: when you use quotations, remember that they are included to validate the point you are making. Too often, students string together a series of quotes believing that this proves their point and shows readers they have researched thoroughly. However, this often seems no more than "padding." Readers may believe that the writer has not thought out the thesis of the essay and has thus included quotations to fill out the length of the paper. Readers may also interpret too many quotations as a sign that the writer is intimidated by the sources chosen as references.

Style

It is important to keep a consistent style in your writing of the research paper. Thus, try to use quotations sparingly and judiciously. Where possible, paraphrase or summarize in your own words to create your own voice in your paper. Always be sure, however, to acknowledge sources. If you need to include a long quotation, you may place the quotation in an indented paragraph of its own in the middle of your paper. Or, if you wish, omit irrelevant sections of the quote by using **ellipses,** devices made of up three or four dots, that show readers you have deleted material. An ellipsis using three dots (...) is used in a passage where a part of a sentence has been removed. An ellipsis using four dots (....) is used in a passage where a complete sentence is quoted but material that follows it has been removed. In the following example paragraph, note the two forms. The reference quoted is the essay "Maths a Plus," by Jennifer Lewington. (Note that the number of the page on which the quotation originally appeared is given also.)

> *There are many examples to show that math anxiety can be overcome. "Janet Reid ... recalls one girl who attended several years ago and switched her career plans from business to engineering" (Lewington, "Maths" A6). However, there are problems that remain. "Ms. Reid says that girls and boys have different attitudes towards success in school" (Lewington, "Maths" A6).*

Writing a Working Thesis Statement   Once you have read through your material and decided what you need, it is time to form a thesis statement. You do this in the same manner as taught in Unit Three. Read through the five articles we have chosen as the basis for our model research paper (the Levington article on pages 143–44 and four more on pages 158–71) and then read the outline below with its working thesis statement. A working thesis statement is a guide to keep you on track as you write out drafts of your research paper. It may, in fact, become your actual thesis statement and thus be included in your opening paragraph.

Outlining   An outline is like a skeleton. It is the "bare bones" of your essay. These "bones" are the basic structure of the ideas of your paper. Outlines can be written in point form or short sentence form.

Bare bones outline
1. Write a title and your focused subject.
2. Describe introduction. Write out thesis statement.
3. Draw up a diagram for your paragraphs indicating what key ideas will be discussed. Make sure ideas connect with each other and relate to the thesis statement.
4. Finally, write out your conclusion.

   This outline may seem simple to do. You can modify it according to the amount of information you have. Here are two outlines based on student Cecile Dean's research paper on the subject of women and math. One is a working outline, the other an annotated outline.

Working outline of Cecile Dean's paper, "Math Anxiety: The Real Social Disease."

TITLE: Math Anxiety: The Real Social Disease

FOCUSED SUBJECT: 1. Math anxiety—what is it? Define.
                                        2. Describe solutions

1. a. define math anxiety.
   b. show its impact on
      i. individuals
      ii. society
   c. problem recognized: research by individuals and institutions to discover causes

      i. peer pressure
      ii. stereotyping
      iii. gender bias

2. Solutions: deal with causes
    a. educate girls before peer pressure
    b. educate families about stereotyping
    c. provide positive role models
    d. educate teachers about math stereotypes
    e. change curriculum
    f. educate society

3. Conclusion

Annotated rough draft of Cecile Dean's research paper, "Math Anxiety: The Real Social Disease."

In this draft, the "skeleton" has been fleshed out with specific references to the five articles Dean decided to use for her raw material. Note how she refers to specific authors and that she writes in point-form sentences.

TITLE: Math Anxiety: The Real Social Disease

FOCUSED SUBJECT: Women and Math: The reasons why women are "turned off" math. Solutions to the problem in Canada.

INTRODUCTION: A personal anecdote. "I am a pioneer because I am a woman who loves math and escaped the disease of math anxiety." Consider putting story about Rosalyn Yalow from Jacoby article here.

THESIS STATEMENT: Math anxiety has severe repercussions for women and society as a whole. It is a type of "social disease," and in Canada steps are being taken to remedy it.

- Tell story of Nobel Prize winner Yalow taken from Jacoby article. Idea: not a lot has changed from Yalow's time in 1930s.
- No one tells girls in the 1990s they can't take physics and must instead be secretaries but attitude still exists: girls stay away from science and math. Quote Finlayson study. Key detail: girls still see math as bad, as a "sickness."
- Causes of math anxiety: Math is a male thing; it is not what girls take to be attractive. Quote Jacoby. Key detail: girls drop out of math by Grade 12; want to avoid being seen as "brains" and competing with guys.
- Women and their parents are also to blame for math anxiety. Quote Jacoby on the theory of "conspirators." Social cost of limiting women. Women are cut off from career options because of math anxiety. Key detail: women still see lives in traditional way; women "cut themselves off from careers based on science and math"; an old prejudice exists. Use Finlayson here.
- Mention more effects of women seeing themselves only as wives and mothers. Bring in idea of pay equity.
- Why are girls still turned off math in spite of the research being done? Quote Estrich. Discuss her idea of the "invisible student." Boys are favoured

over girls in classroom. Role of teacher is important. Key detail: quote Griffith—"boys learn competence, girls lose it."

- Gender bias adds to the problem. Sexism is institutionalized. But there are initiatives to deal with the problem. Quote Lewington on workshops in Ontario. See Finlayson on reactions to the workshops.
- Discuss role of parents in breaking down the sexism prejudice against girls and math. See Finlayson on the Grade 7 program. Key detail: program attempts to get rid of stereotypes.
- More examples on workshops. But here, ask question: What is being done to educate teachers about the problem? Quote Estrich and Finlayson. Draw contrast between the ways boys and girls think and learn.
- Discuss Ministry of Education and Training forum on making math "more fun." Show how it recommends that teachers make math relevant and appealing. See data in "Math Myths."
- Pose question: are separate schools better for girls to learn math? Quote Estrich. Emphasize that new programs and forums are taking place to help girls, parents, and teachers overcome age-old prejudices.
- (CONCLUSION): State the idea that girls can do math well has to be made a reality! Summarize ideas about effects of math anxiety—no career, jobs, etc.

Here is the completed essay by Cecile Dean.

Math Anxiety: The Real Social Disease

Cecile Dean

1   I know I'm stubborn, although I never thought of myself as a pioneer. But that's just what I am. I am a woman: I love math and I'm enrolled in the Environmental program, one of two women. Somehow I escaped the ravages of "math anxiety." "Math anxiety" is the term Susan Jacoby uses to describe the attitude most high school girls have toward this subject. This attitude has severe repercussions not only for the women but for society as a whole. The seriousness of this social "disease" has been recognized and here in Canada steps are being taken to attempt to remedy it.

2   Jacoby refers to Rosalyn Yalow, who won a Nobel Prize for Physics in the 1930s (2). Rosalyn Yalow was advised to train as a secretary because no university would accept her as a graduate student in physics. What would be the reason for the refusal? Rosalyn Yalow was a woman. Before we become smug and think "we've come a long way baby," let me tell you, things have not changed a great deal since 1930.

3   No one openly tells girls they can't be physicists and that secretarial courses are more appropriate for them, but somehow this is the message that most girls in high school subliminally pick up. Judith Finlayson quotes research by the Toronto Board of Education.

> ... even at the introductory level, the ratio of students in computer science courses is two-thirds male to one-third female. By Grade 13, approxi-

mately two-thirds of girls in Toronto schools have dropped out of maths and sciences. (8)

4   Here we are nearly half way through the 1990s and most girls still see math as a sickness they should avoid. Why?

5   Jacoby states that the first symptoms of "math anxiety" occur with adolescence. She quotes a 1981 American study on "Female Achievement in Mathematics," which found that girls in Grade 9 typically did well in math. However, by Grade 12, those same girls had lost their ability and desire to succeed in this area. Jacoby identifies two main causes for this: math is considered a "male" subject; also, girls who are "brains" are unattractive to boys, and in order to avoid this classification and direct intellectual competition with males teenage girls drop out of math.

6   Social stereotyping and peer pressure create "math anxiety." Jacoby goes on to say "the current generation of adolescent girls—and their parents, bred in old expectations about women's interests—are active conspirators in limiting their own intellectual development" (2). These young women are not just limiting their own intellectual development. There is a social cost too. Judith Finlayson points out that high school math is required for admission to many university and community college programs, so many women cut themselves off from career options. Finlayson quotes the conclusion of a 1985 Canadian Advisory Council on the Status of Women report: "adolescent girls still see their lives in very traditional and romanticized terms" (7).

7   What this means is that most high school girls see their lives in terms of a husband, family and job in the clerical or "helping" professions like nursing, E.C.E. or social work. None of these jobs pays as well as math occupations and are seen as traditional "women's work." Failure in math then has severe repercussions that pay equity is only beginning to address.

8   If all this research has been done, why then are girls still being turned off by math? Susan Estrich goes further than Susan Jacoby in answering this question. Basing her findings on a study done by the American Association of University Women, Estrich claims, "Girls are the invisible students; boys get the bulk of the teachers' time" (39). This study, which focused on the progress of girls in school, showed that regardless of the sex of the teacher, boys are favoured in the classroom. Estrich quotes historian and headmistress Elisabeth Griffith, who says, "boys learn competence, girls lose it" (Estrich 39).

9   While girls may "conspire" in infecting themselves with math anxiety, as Jacoby points out, the additional problem of gender-bias in education certainly adds to the disease. Sexism is as institutionalized as racism is and only by recognizing that can we begin to deal with it. Fortunately there are a number of initiatives focusing on math in Canada that attempt to deal with the bigger problem of sexism.

10   For example, each year, the Toronto Board of Education sponsors a workshop for Grade 7 and 8 girls. The annual workshop is an attempt "to break down the barriers that deflect girls from math and science in high school and beyond" (Lewington, "Maths a Plus" A6). The workshop provides those girls with positive

role models of women who have succeeded in non-traditional, technical careers. Recognizing that "math anxiety" usually erupts in Grade 9, this workshop is an attempt to inoculate the younger girls against it. The emphasis during the workshop is on the practical applications of math, and a recognition of the girls' need for self-esteem and assurance of success. In the words of Deb Harvey, one of the role models, it shows "why it's really important to know math" (Lewington, "Maths a Plus" A6).

11   The co-chair of this workshop, Myra Novogrodsky, also runs a program for the parents of girls in Grade 7 and 8. In educating the parents about the deleterious effects of "math anxiety," there is a hope that the parents can be positive role models and provide support for their daughters. The program attempts to remedy the stereotypes that "can seriously undermine the confidence of girls who may have an interest in technical subjects or non-traditional work" (Finlayson, 4).

12   Workshops and programs like these in Toronto are given across Canada. A real effort is being made to change the ways the girls in high school and their parents view math and sciences. However, what is being done about the teachers of math? As the data quoted by Susan Estrich suggests, part of the problem girls in high school encounter is a direct result of the teaching style. Finlayson also refers to this when she quotes John Clark, coordinator of mathematics at the Toronto Board of Education:

> Math is usually presented as a search for the right answer rather than as a process of enquiry. Some sociologists believe that females have a more collaborative style. They want to work by consensus and talk with other people. (Finlayson 8)

13   An Ontario Math Forum, organized by the Ministry of Education and Training on May 6, 1994, "to make math more relevant, rigorous and fun" (Lewington, "Math Myths" A1), included the recommendation that teachers "develop different teaching strategies to improve the appeal and significance of math." (Lewington, "Math Myths" A1); in addition, clarification and standardization of the provincial curriculum and improvement of the math background for elementary school teachers were recommended. This forum was a response to a recognition that math standards in Canada as a whole are not high enough. However, the discussion and recommendations have definite implications for women. Any changes in curriculum and its presentation will have to consider the "turn-off" factor of "math anxiety."

14   The answer to "math anxiety" may not be in the single-sex schools that Susan Estrich discusses. For now, until the new curriculum is in place, there may be merit in "girls only" math courses as Estrich recommends, since, as she puts it, "the problems of gender bias stubbornly persist" (39). Certainly the contagious idea that math is a "male" subject has got to be wiped out, and there are many initiatives involving the students, parents, and teachers that are attempting to do that. More "hands on" and interactive methods of learning math are recommended by the education experts consulted by Judith Finlayson. Finlayson concludes that

hands-on learning validates the children's own observations about the world. It also reinforces their sense of themselves as autonomous problem solvers, a skill linked with success in math. (10)

15 Relating math concepts to everyday life makes knowledge of math an obvious necessity. Apart from stressing the practical applications of math, individual problem solving builds the self-esteem and need for success all students, and especially girls, have. The idea that girls "can do" has to be made a reality. Without a background in math, women are cut off from the better-paying professions; they are even precluding themselves from many entry-level jobs. When women are not educated to their full potential, the social implications are great. Good math skills add up to a better future for all.

Works Consulted

Estrich, Susan. "Separate Is Better." *New York Times Magazine* 22 May 1994: 39–41.

Finlayson, Judith. "Math's Multiple Choices." *Homemaker's Magazine* Jan./Feb. 1988: 4–10.

Jacoby, Susan. "When Bright Girls Decide That Math Is 'a Waste of Time.'" *New York Times* 2 June 1983: 2.

Lewington, Jennifer. "Math Myths Have Got to Go, Forum Told." *Globe and Mail* 7 May 1994: A1.

Lewington, Jennifer "Maths a Plus, Schoolgirls Assured." *Globe and Mail* 8 February 1992: A6.

Documentation

The last page of Dean's essay includes a list of the five articles she used to write her research paper. Dean has written her list following the rules of the *MLA Handbook for Writers of Research Papers*, one of two standard handbooks available on formats for recording works consulted. **Documentation** is the final step in preparing a research paper for your readers. It consists of two activities: making in-text references and compiling a source list to be placed at the end of the paper.

Exactly why and how must you document? Well, you must provide your sources to avoid the charge of plagiarism. You must follow standard methods of recording information based on reputable handbooks. You need to show readers that your data are valid. In the text of Cecile Dean's paper, you will have noted the use of parentheses, which enclosed references to page numbers and authors of certain works. This form of documentation is the first readers encounter. It is *in-text* documentation. At one time, it was written in the form of footnotes, numbered references at the bottom of a printed page of text. The footnote has been replaced by the *parenthetical reference*. Two formats are commonly used in education and government. The first of these formats is from the Modern Language Association and is known as the MLA style. There are numerous editions of this stylesheet and it is best to check with your resource centre or library for the latest. The examples we are using in this unit are based on the third edition, which was published in 1988.

The second format is from the American Psychological Association, and is known as the APA style. The examples shown in this unit are based on the third edition, published in 1983.

You will note that we have included only a selected number of examples. These examples were most common in student research papers. For a complete listing of all types of references, you must consult a standard style sheet.

Parenthetical Reference: Documentation within the Text of the Paper

A parenthetical reference is information about a source placed between parentheses and located within the body of the research paper.

Once you have determined the content of your parenthetical reference, place the reference at the end of a sentence and place any punctuation marks—period, semicolon—*after* the second parenthesis. When your reference refers to a direct quotation, place it *after* the last quotation mark and *before* the punctuation. Try to fit your reference smoothly into the text to avoid disruption.

MLA Style

Here are three common examples of paranthetical references written in the MLA style. They can be used for both print (books, articles, essays) and non-print (CD-ROM, WWW, Internet) sources.

Author and page   Put the author's name and page number in the article of the quoted material inside the parentheses. No comma is needed to separate the two.

> With math and women, "Things have changed since then, but not as much as one would hope" (Estrich 39).

Author directly named in text   In this case, when the author of the article appears in your sentence, simply put the page number of the quoted material from the article in the parentheses.

> Susan Estrich has asked, "If schools shortchange girls, why is it surprising when the tests show that they're doing less well?" (39)

Author of more than one reference   If you include two or more articles by the same author in your paper, tell readers which one you are referring to in parentheses by including the author's last name and adding a comma, a short form of the specific article you are referring to, and the page number.

> Is anything being done to relieve math anxiety? "The forum, organized by the Ministry of Education and Training ... called for changes in math content, teaching methods and testing" (Lewington, "Math Myths" A1).

APA Style

Here are three common examples of paranthetical references students use, written in the APA style. Like the MLA style examples above, they can refer to both print and non-print sources.

Author and date   Include the author's name and publication date, separated by a comma.

> With math and women, "Things have changed since then, but not as much as one would hope" (Estrich, 1994).

Author directly named in text   In this case, if you name the author in your article, put the date in parentheses right after the author's last name.

> Susan Estrich (1994) has asked, "If schools shortchange girls, why is it surprising when the tests show that they're doing less well?"

Author of more than one reference   If you refer to more than one work by an author, put the date of the specific reference of your quotation right after the author's name, as above. If you refer to more than one work by an author in the *same, single* reference, record the author's last name and include the dates of the works you have used, separated by commas.

> There have been several essays in the past few years that claim math myths must be re-examined and that young girls must be assured math is a suitable subject to study (Lewington, 1992, 1994).

You can choose in the above case to refer to the author and the dates of the articles directly in your text, and eliminate the parenthetical reference:

> As Lewington has pointed out in 1992 and 1994, math myths must be re-examined and young girls must be assured math is a suitable subject to study.

The above examples of in-text documentation remind readers as they read your paper where you found your data. The source list at the end of the paper gives readers the exact location of the complete source by referring to the books and articles you selected.

Works Consulted/References: Documentation at the End of the Paper

The MLA style and the APA style are similar in many ways when it comes to listing the works used in the preparation of your research paper. Students are usually requested to include only works that were directly quoted from or summarized in the data of the paper. Often students add long lists of titles to impress readers, but none of those titles refers to any data in the text. This will be seen as a form of "padding," since readers may wonder why so much material was read but not cited.

In any case, it is necessary to tell readers precisely what sources you used to write your paragraphs. Compare and contrast the following MLA and APA styles of presenting source lists.

MLA Style

The MLA style calls this separate sheet of paper at the end of the research paper the *Works Cited* or *Works Consulted*. If your sources list contains only the works referred to in your essay, it is called *Works Cited;* if it contains all the items you found useful in researching your essay, it is called *Works Consulted.*

In your list you would present your sources *alphabetically* by authors' last names. If your list has sources with no authors' names, list the titles. Put the title *Works Consulted* at the top and centre of your separate sheet, without underlining or quotation marks. Begin each entry of your list at the *left* margin but indent each of the next lines (five spaces) so that the authors' names are prominent. Double-space each line, but do not number the entries.

Each entry contains *author's name,* the *title* (and *subtitle*) of the work, and *publication information.* Underline titles of books and periodicals. Put titles of articles and short fiction (a short story or poem) in quotation marks. Capitalize all major words in titles and subtitles. Place subtitles after a colon and one space. For an article, do not state the place of publication, only the magazine in which the article appears, volume number, year of publication, and the inclusive page numbers.

APA Style

The APA style calls the source page *References;* this page appears at the end of the paper but before any appendices (notes on experiments, for example). List sources by authors' names, *alphabetically,* and include only those sources referred to in your work. If a work has no author named, list title but exclude *the, an,* and *a.* If you cite more than one work by the same author, list the works *chronologically* under the author's last name.

As with the MLA style, this list of sources is placed on a separate page with the word *References* centred at the top, without underlining or quotation marks. Begin each entry at the *left* margin; indent the lines that follow three spaces. Double-space each line.

Each entry contains the *author's name* (unlike the MLA, write out just the *initials of the author's first names*), the *publication date,* the *title and subtitle,* and *publication information.* Underline titles of books and periodicals, but unlike the MLA style do *not* underline or put into quotation marks the titles of articles. For books and article titles, capitalize only the *first* word of the title and subtitle and any proper noun. For a magazine or periodical, name the title only (not the place of publication), the volume or issue underlined, and the inclusive page numbers.

Keeping in mind the differences between the two formats, examine the following. Here are several examples, commonly used by students, of source entries. Contrast the ways each style—the MLA and the APA—records the vital information. For further details on source entries not mentioned here, consult the outline of your own school's handbook, or the style sheets of the MLA and APA in the resource centre or library.

A book written by one author
MLA: Faulkner, William. *The Sound and the Fury.* New York: Vintage Books, 1987.
APA: Faulkner, W. (1987). *The sound and the fury.* New York: Vintage Books.

A book written by two authors
MLA: Breuer, Michael, and Rosemary Neering. *Historic Alberta.* Toronto: Oxford University Press, 1986.
APA: Breuer, M., & Neering, R. (1986). *Historic Alberta.* Toronto: Oxford University Press.

An article in an encyclopedia
MLA: "Gas, Natural." *Oxford Junior Encyclopaedia.* 1st ed. 1949.
APA: Gas, natural. (1949). *Oxford Junior Encyclopaedia.* 1st ed.

A government publication
MLA: Alberta. Dept. of Agriculture. *Services and Programs 1980–81.* Edmonton, 1981.
APA: Alberta Department of Agriculture. (1981). Services and Programs 1980–81. Edmonton.

An article in a monthly magazine
MLA: Price, Reynolds. "Full Day." *Harper's* Jan. 1991: 56–61.
APA: Price, R. (1991, Jan.). Full day. *Harper's,* pp. 56–61.

An article in a newspaper
MLA: Lewington, Jennifer. "Maths a Plus, Schoolgirls Assured." *Globe and Mail* 8 Feb. 1992, sec. B:1.
APA: Lewington, J. (1992, Feb. 8). Maths a plus, schoolgirls assured. *Globe and Mail,* p. B1.

Documentation based on non-print sources (electronic sources such as e-mail, the Internet, CD-ROM) is similar to that based on print sources (articles, books, government publications). Much on-line material does not have page numbers or formal publication dates and names of publishing houses. On-line electronic information changes quickly and so the *access date* is one of the most important pieces of information you can give. Both the MLA and APA style manuals now available include rules and examples on how to document material generated by electronic sources.

An article on CD-ROM
MLA: "Gas, Natural." *Oxford Junior Encyclopaedia.* CD-ROM. Oxford. New Media, Inc. 1992.

APA: Gas, Natural. (1992). *Oxford Junior Encyclopaedia*. CD-ROM. Oxford. New Media, Inc.

An article from a computer service

MLA: Price, Reynolds. "Full Day." *Harper's Magazine*. Jan. 1991: 56–61. *Magazine Database*. Online. CompuServe. 12 Dec. 1996.

APA: Price, R. (1991, Jan.). Full Day. *Harper's Magazine,* pp. 56–61. *Magazine Database*. Online. CompuServe. 12 Dec. 1996.

An article taken from microfilm

MLA: Alberta. Dept. of Agriculture. *Services and Programs 1980–81*. Edmonton, 1981. Microfiche: ER Document Service ED90 (1981).

APA: Alberta Department of Agriculture. (1981). Services and Programs 1980–81. Edmonton. Microfiche: ER Document Service ED90 (1981).

An article from the World Wide Web

MLA: National Par Service. "Waterton Lakes Eco-System Renewal." *National Parks Home Page*. http://www.prk.nat/~19endsp/programs. (15 August 1996).

APA: National Park Service. (1996) Waterton Lakes Eco-System Renewal. (Online). http://www.prk.nat/~19endsp/programs.

Whichever style you choose, check your work to be sure you have been consistent and accurate.

Articles

For her research paper, one of Dean's sources was the article "Maths a Plus," by Jennifer Lewington, which is reprinted earlier in this unit. Dean also referred to the following four articles: "Separate Is Better," by Susan Estrich, "Math's Multiple Choices," by Judith Finlayson, "When Bright Girls Decide That Math Is 'A Waste of Time,'" by Susan Jacoby, and "Math Myths Have Got To Go, Forum Told," by Jennifer Lewington.

Read these articles carefully and see how Dean has used the information in them to write the research paper you have read. Compare her two outlines to her final version, and then compare how her research paper relates to her sources. Once you have done cross-reference reading between Dean's final version and her sources, read and answer the questions that follow the articles.

Separate Is Better

Susan Estrich

1   Twenty years ago, when I attended Wellesley College, an all-women's college, coeducation fever was gripping America. Yale and Princeton had just "gone"; Dartmouth "went" next. My freshman year, we were polled on whether we

thought Wellesley should join the stampede. What did I know? I said yes. But now I know I was wrong, and I'm glad my vote didn't change anything.

2   This year, 60 percent of the National Merit Scholarship finalists are boys, because boys outscored on the Preliminary Scholastic Assessment Test (P.S.A.T.), which determines eligibility for the scholarships. The test doesn't ask about sports; it does ask about math and science, though, and that's where the differences between boys and girls are most pronounced. The American Civil Liberties Union and the National Center for Fair and Open Testing filed a Federal civil rights suit in February charging that the test discriminates against women. The plaintiffs want more girls to get National Merit Scholarships. So do I. But I want to see the girls earn them, in schools that give them a fair chance.

3   I didn't win a Merit Scholarship either, although if the Fair Test people had their way, I might have. My grades were near perfect. But I didn't take the tough math and science courses. I had different priorities. I started junior high as the only girl on the math team. By high school, I'd long since quit. Instead, I learned to twirl a baton, toss it in the air and catch it while doing a split in the mud or the ice. The problem wasn't the P.S.A.T., but me, and my school.

4   Things have changed since then, but not as much as one would hope. The American Association of University Women did a major study in 1992 about how schools shortchange girls and concluded that even though girls get better grades (except in math), they get less from school. Teachers pay less attention to girls and give them less encouragement. Two American University researchers, Myra and David Sadker, reached a similar conclusion after 20 years of study. Girls are the invisible students; boys get the bulk of the teachers' time. Boys call out eight times as often as girls do. When the boys call out, they get answers; when the girls do, they're often admonished for speaking out. And that's true whether the teacher is a man or a woman. Even the new history textbooks devote only about 2 percent of their pages to women. What is happening, says Elisabeth Griffith, a historian and headmistress of the Madeira School in McLean, Va., is that "boys learn competence, girls lose it."

5   If schools shortchange girls, why is it surprising when the tests show that they're doing less well? It isn't just P.S.A.T.'s, where 18,000 boys generally reach the top categories and only 8,000 girls do. While the gap has narrowed, boys also outscore girls on 11 of the 14 College Board Achievement tests, and on the A.C.T. exams and on the S.A.T.'s. It is possible to jimmy selection standards to make sure girls win more scholarships, but equal results don't count for much if those results are forced. Instead of declaring equality, society should be advancing it. The challenge isn't to get more scholarships for baton twirlers but to get more baton twirlers to take up advanced mathematics.

6   One place that happens is in girls' schools and women's colleges. Sometimes separate isn't equal; it's better. Changing the way teachers teach in coed schools, changing the textbooks to make sure they talk about women as well as men, educating parents about raising daughters—all of these things make sense, since most girls will be educated in coed classrooms. But we've been talking about them for a decade, and the problems of gender bias stubbornly persist. In the meantime, for many girls, single-sex education is working.

7   In girls' schools, 80 percent of the girls take four years of science and math, compared with the national average of two years in a coed environment. Elizabeth Tidball, a George Washington University researcher, found that graduates of women's colleges did better than female graduates of coed colleges in terms of test scores, graduate school admissions, number of earned doctorates, salaries and personal satisfaction. One-third of the female board members of Fortune 1,000 companies are graduates of women's colleges, even though those colleges contribute less than 4 percent of total graduates. Forty-three percent of the math doctorates and 50 percent of engineering doctorates earned by female liberal-arts college students go to graduates of Barnard, Bryn Mawr, Mount Holyoke, Smith or Wellesley—all women's colleges. Graduates of women's colleges outnumber all other female entries in *Who's Who.*

8   I stopped twirling my baton when I got to Wellesley. I'd like to say that I knew I needed a women's college after all those years in the mud at football games, but it doesn't always work that way. I went to Wellesley because they gave me a generous scholarship, and because Radcliffe rejected me (the test scores, maybe). I was actually miserable a good deal of the time I was there, particularly during the long winters when the janitor was the only man around. But what I learned was worth it. I spent the better part of four years in a world in which women could do anything, because no one told us we couldn't. I even took some math courses. By senior year, somehow I'd become an accomplished test-taker. When I got to Harvard Law School, where men vastly outnumbered women and sexism was the rule, a professor told me on the first day that women didn't do very well. I laughed and decided to prove he was wrong. That's a Wellesley education.

9   I'm not proposing that coed public schools be replaced with a network of single-sex academies. But if the problem is that women don't do well in math or science, then single-sex classes, and single-sex schools, may be part of the answer.

10   The evidence, though scant, is promising. In Ventura, Calif., the public high school has begun offering an all-girls Algebra II course. The girls, one teacher says, think so little of their ability that the teacher spends her time not only teaching math but also building self-confidence, repeatedly telling the girls that they're smart and that they can do it. The Illinois Math and Science Academy in Aurora is experimenting with a girls-only calculus-based physics class for the first semester, with the girls joining the coed class at midyear. In the girls-only class, the students report that they are jumping up to ask and answer questions instead of sitting back, hoping that the teacher doesn't call on them. One student said she was worried about the transition to a coed classroom: "We need to make sure we don't lose our newfound physics freedom." "Physics freedom" for girls—what a wonderful concept.

11   The biggest obstacles to such classes, or even to all-girls public schools, are erected by lawyers bent on enforcing legal equality. In the 1954 case of Brown v. Board of Education, the Supreme Court declared that "separate but equal" was inherently unequal. That was certainly true in Topeka, Kan.; whose school system was challenged. It was true of the black-only law school established to keep blacks

out of the University of Texas law school. It is not necessarily true of the Ventura High School math class for girls or the Aurora Academy calculus-based physics class, whose futures are in jeopardy because of the knee-jerk application of Brown.

12   Classes like those in Ventura County or Aurora, Ill., survive constitutional challenge by formally opening their doors to men, with a wink and a nod to keep them from coming in. Otherwise, the schools could be stripped of Federal support, and even enjoined under the Constitution by Federal court order, because they are "discriminating." Private schools may open their doors only to boys or girls under an exemption from Federal laws mandating "equality." But public schools enjoy no such freedom. The reality is that if you need a Wellesley education in America, you have to pay for it. That's the price of committing to formal equality instead of committing to real opportunity.

13   Boys may pay the price as well. Some educators in the African-American community believe that all-boys classes may be part of the solution to the dismal failure and dropout rates of African-American boys in school. But the courts prevented the Detroit school district from establishing three public all-boys schools, effectively stopping similar projects planned in other cities. Nonetheless, all-boys classes are being held quietly in as many as two dozen schools around the country, mostly in inner cities.

14   Such programs may or may not succeed in the long run. Research and careful study are plainly needed. But research and careful study are difficult when classes are held in near secrecy for fear of discovery by lawyers and Government officials intent on shutting them down in the name of equality.

15   If girls don't want to go to all-girls schools, or if parents don't want to send them, that's their choice. If the experiments with girls-only math classes or boys-only classes should fail, then educators can be trusted to abandon them. But short of that, let the educators and the parents and the students decide, and leave the lawyers and judges out of it.

Math's Multiple Choices

Judith Finlayson

1   The world has been transformed in the past twenty years. Geared to microchips, floppy disks, and video display terminals, today's society demands a higher degree of mathematical skill than ever before. But, sadly and even dangerously misinformed about the realities of the world, many teenaged girls across the country are repeating their mothers' mistake, a mistake that has propelled the majority of Canadian working women into low-paying, dead-end jobs. In high school, they are dropping out of science and math.

2   Today, a background in math is required for most high-paying technical jobs in fields such as computer technology and microelectronics, as well as for many apparently unrelated professions such as law, interior design, and urban planning. Some companies require Grade 12 math for all entry-level positions, even for caretaking jobs.

3   The need for mathematical competence has been heightened not only by the extraordinary technological change of the past two decades, but by social change as well. Women have entered the work force in unprecedented numbers. They can also expect to stay there—from 25 to 45 years, even if they choose to marry and have children as well as a job outside the home. And they should anticipate changing careers at least twice during that time.

4   As Donna Stewart, educational co-ordinator for WomenSkills, a Vancouver organization devoted to education and research on women's work, warns: "Whole fields of work are shrinking or disappearing entirely. We export enormous amounts of work to countries where labour is cheap, or we give it to machines. One result is that greater levels of competence are required, even for low-level jobs."

5   It's not surprising that a research report published in 1987 by the Economic Council of Canada stressed the value of flexibility in today's workplace. Not only are better-educated and highly skilled women more likely to benefit from technical change, but the report also concluded that their adjustment may be dependent upon how successfully they enter nontraditional occupations. It is important to note, however, that both higher education and nontraditional work are increasingly linked with competence in math.

6   Consider, for instance, that a minimum of high-school math is often required for entrance to university courses such as nursing, teaching, and law. It is also mandatory for many social-science courses such as psychology and sociology, as well as for admission to a substantial number of community college courses. The problem is, female students tend to drop math and sciences as they progress through high school. This fact has led educators to conclude that math is an "invisible filter" denying females entry into the growth-related industries of the future.

7   Math and science avoidance in females is generally acknowledged as a serious issue, but unfortunately there are no national statistics that document the full extent of the problem. Research by the Toronto Board of Education, however, shows that even at the introductory level, the ratio of students in computer science courses is two-thirds male to one-third female. By Grade 13, approximately two-thirds of girls in Toronto schools have dropped out of maths and sciences.

8   "I'm still seeing the Cinderella myth at work," says Arlene Day, a resource teacher for equality in education with the Manitoba Teachers' Society. "Even though they see their mothers working outside the home because the family needs the money, girls are refusing to believe that the same thing will happen to them. They're still aiming for clerical jobs. Most are not even acquiring the computer skills that are necessary to be successful at office work." And her view is echoed in *What Will Tomorrow Bring?,* a 1985 Canadian Advisory Council on the Status of Women report that concluded, "adolescent girls still see their lives in very traditional and romanticized terms."

9   Statistics confirm that the majority of women (almost 60 percent) hold clerical and service-sector jobs, which are generally low paid, offer little potential for advancement, and may be in danger of becoming obsolete. Although women have made serious inroads into some male-dominated professions, such as business, medicine, and law, they are still segregated outside the more scientific fields, such

as engineering and computer science. According to Statistics Canada, at the university level, the majority of women remain concentrated in the traditional fields of study, such as education, nursing, and the humanities. The pattern also holds true for community colleges, where most women continue to study secretarial science, community and social services, nursing, education, and the arts.

10   "To some extent, women have succumbed to the myths about women's work," comments Donna Stewart. "They want to be helpers and to work with people. They may be avoiding nontraditional jobs and careers that require a sound basis in math because they haven't seen the human context to these jobs. Social service agencies need to balance their books. And no one builds bridges alone. You're part of a team."

11   Women who avoid math may be ignoring more than the human context of working with numbers. Mathematical training has been linked with high salaries and job security in fields that have been targeted for future growth. Engineering technology, a profession that is 92 percent male, is one example of this trend. Two years after graduating from community college, an engineering student can expect to earn $20 000 a year. Perhaps more importantly, engineering technologists who reach the senior level will likely make more than $30 000 and, if they rise in management, they can earn up to $50 000 annually.

12   Compare these salaries to those in a female-dominated field. Ninety-nine percent of secretaries are female. Not only is their average salary just $14 100 two years after graduation from community college, but according to a 1983 Labour Canada report, even those who reach senior levels earn on average under $20 000.

13   This kind of wage discrepancy alarms educators who see girls avoiding math. "Nowadays, a math and science background is necessary for most of the higher-paying jobs," says Linda McClelland, a science teacher at Crescent Heights High School in Calgary. "And girls are losing out on these credentials at the same time that more and more women are entering the work force. In addition, there is a rising number of women supporting families on their own who really need to earn a decent wage."

14   Tasoula Berggren, an instructor of calculus and linear algebra at Simon Fraser University in Burnaby, British Columbia, points to at least 82 careers for which math education is a prerequisite. Last November, she organized what she hopes will become an annual conference, Women Do Math, for girls in Grades 9 and 10 and their parents. Four students from each of 85 Vancouver schools were invited. "I thought we would get 100 people," Berggren recalls, "and 300 registered, with many more schools asking to bring more students."

15   Berggren designed the conference not only to introduce girls to women professionals but to provide an introduction to basic mathematical concepts. "Once they see the application of calculus—how a formula can give them the volume of a lake—they find it exciting. They say, 'This is great, I'm enjoying math!'"

16   She stresses the necessity of constant parental encouragement, something that Myra Novogrodsky, co-ordinator of women's labour studies at the Toronto Board of Education, observes does not come naturally. She is conducting a new program designed to make parents of Grade 7 and 8 girls aware of the importance of math and science education to their daughters' futures.

17   "I usually begin the workshops with a true-or-false quiz designed to test awareness," she says. "I've discovered that a lot of people haven't thought much about the implications of social change. They still think that most girls will live in a nuclear family and be secondary wage earners, if they work outside the home at all."

18   One result of this misconception is that many parents have lower career expectations for their daughters than for their sons. Their attitude is reinforced by negative role modelling, which can include apparently innocuous statements such as "Women don't have a head for figures" or "Her mother can't balance a cheque-book." These stereotypes can seriously undermine the confidence of girls who may have an interest in technical subjects or nontraditional work.

19   "By Grade 10, I knew I was mechanically oriented, but people said that physics was too hard for me and I believed them," recalls Heather Bears, who is currently studying electronics technology at Red River Community College in Winnipeg. As a result, after graduating from high school, she spent two unsatisfactory years in the work force doing odd clerical or child-care jobs. Career counselling finally revealed her scientific aptitude and motivated her to return to high school as an adult student. Not only did she make up her physics courses, but she earned straight A's.

20   Today, as a second-year electronics student, she still feels the negative effects of gender roles. "When I entered the course there were only two other girls and approximately 100 guys. There was a real sense that we were bucking the system and it was scary. At its most basic, I'm only five-foot-two and most of the male students are in the six-foot range."

21   Although Bears admits that it is difficult being a pioneer—"some teachers pick on us and others favour us"—the satisfaction of doing what she finds fulfilling is worth the price. "If I had one piece of advice for girls in high school, it would be, 'Don't be afraid to enter a man's world.' I believed people who said I couldn't do it because I was a girl, and that's what held me back."

22   Mary Elizabeth Morris, a math teacher at Castle Frank High School in Toronto, believes that the "my mother/my self syndrome" can also influence a girl's career expectations. "A woman who does low-level work could undermine her daughter's success because she might not convey the sense that work can be a rewarding experience," she says. "If her mother is a poor role model in terms of job satisfaction, a girl may cling to the Cinderella myth because she doesn't see work outside the home as desirable."

23   Studies such as *What Will Tomorrow Bring?* show that professional mothers tend to be positive role models for their daughters. But mothers who don't work outside the home can also encourage their daughters to develop an interest in traditionally male domains by organizing scientifically oriented excursions, such as a visit to a science museum, or by doing traditionally masculine tasks.

24   "We live on a farm, so my mother is a real handyman," says Robin Chant, a Grade 12 student at MacGregor Collegiate Institute in MacGregor, Manitoba, who excels at maths and sciences. "I think one of the reasons I do well in math is because, like her, I enjoy figuring things out."

25   Chant was the only girl in her physics class last year and there is only one other girl in this year's math class, compared to nine boys. "Most of my girlfriends

have dropped math because they think it's too hard," she says. "They all want traditional jobs as secretaries and day-care workers. They plan to get married and have kids. I'm different because I really want to have a career."

26   Myra Novogrodsky believes that if mothers are to help their daughters overcome their negative outlook toward math, they must become aware of and overcome their own negative feelings. If parents "suffered" through math class themselves, they may convey their anxiety and inadvertently undermine their children's performance. Equally important are the role models that girls receive outside the home.

27   "It's hard for girls to accept the message that they can have high career aspirations and study maths and sciences if they don't see any other women doing it," says Linda McClelland. "We need more female math and science teachers as role models, as well as more women in nontraditional careers."

28   All the women math and science teachers interviewed for this article strongly agreed. Moreover, those who kept statistics on the ratio of males to females in their class reported that the fact that a woman was teaching the subjects had a positive effect on girls.

29   "In the past there was usually only one female student in senior-level physics," recalls Shelagh Pryke, who teaches physics classes at Kwalikum Secondary School in Qualicum Beach, B.C. "Now as many as 42 percent of my students are girls, and I know the fact that I'm a woman who is married with a family has played a role in this change. The girls see that it's socially acceptable to be a woman who is interested in science."

30   Lydia Picucha, a math and science teacher at Mount Elizabeth Junior and Senior Secondary School in Kitimat, B.C., shares this point of view. "I've been teaching here for seven years and I know my female students relate to the idea of a woman who enjoys her work and takes her career seriously. As a result, most of my female students—about 70 percent—have continued with science into Grade 11, when girls normally start dropping out."

31   The lack of female teachers as role models is complicated by the way maths and sciences are taught in schools. Mathematics, for example, may alienate girls because it is typically taught in a masculine style. John Clark, co-ordinator of mathematics at the Toronto Board of Education, says, "Math is usually presented as a search for the right answer rather than as a process of enquiry. Some sociologists believe that females have a more collaborative style. They want to work by consensus and talk with other people."

32   Whether or not there is any inherent difference between the male and female aptitude for mathematics remains a hotly debated issue. However, there is no doubt that the way girls are socialized undermines whatever natural ability they might have. For example, the kinds of throwing, jumping, and mechanically oriented play that boys engage in actually prepare them for an understanding of maths and sciences.

33   Consider the game of baseball. Most boys catch balls better than most girls simply because by constantly playing ball sports that they have learned how to estimate where the ball will land and, therefore, how to position their hands. What is less obvious is that this skill requires an understanding of the relationships

between distance, force, and velocity that serves them well once they begin to study physics.

34   At the Institute of Child Study, a school that operates in conjunction with the University of Toronto's Faculty of Education, teacher Robin Ethier confirms that there is a division of play along gender lines by the time the children arrive at kindergarten. "The boys choose blocks and sand to build larger spaces, whereas the girls prefer small paper projects," she says. "The few girls who prefer large motor-skill projects really stand out. They are identified as tomboys."

35   Even so, Anne Cassidy, the Grade 5 teacher at the school, says she is not aware of a gender difference in her students' approach to maths and sciences. To some extent, she believes the school's emphasis on intuitive and personalized learning has helped minimize the difference. Classes are small and teachers strongly encourage children to learn through their own activities. For example, to teach the laws of averages, she might ask her class to count up the pennies all seven grades collected for UNICEF over Hallowe'en. When she asks her students to work out approximately how many each grade collected, they soon realize that to get an average they must divide the total number of pennies by the number of classes. In the end, they discover the mathematical formula all on their own.

36   This kind of hands-on learning validates the children's own observations about the world. It also reinforces their sense of themselves as autonomous problem solvers, a skill linked with success in math. Parents can play an important role in helping their children develop this problem-solving ability by transforming daily activities into informal lessons in maths and sciences. Children should be encouraged to play mathematically oriented games such as backgammon and chess. Cooking is an excellent activity for teaching fractions as well as the principles of chemistry. Similarly, carpentry teaches measurement and spatial concepts, and comparing sizes and prices at the supermarket can turn even shopping into a learning experience.

37   "People make the mistake of trying to introduce new math concepts with paper and pencil," according to Dr. Ada Schermann, principal of the Institute of Child Study. "Start with a game or a fun activity such as cooking, gardening, or playing a mathematically based card game like 21. Then children don't think they're being taught, and the learning comes naturally."

38   Girls' poor problem-solving abilities have been linked to the fact that they are not usually encouraged to assert themselves as individuals. So perhaps it's not surprising that they begin to retreat from maths and sciences during their teenage years. During this period their willingness to consider a nontraditional career also wanes.

39   It must be the responsibility of parents and teachers to erase the myth that an interest in math makes a girl "different" or "unfeminine." From preschool to high school, maths and sciences should be as natural and nonthreatening subjects of study as English or history. Without a solid grounding in these subjects, the doors of opportunity will slam shut for yet another generation of young women—and, unfortunately, unemployment figures are the numbers *everyone* understands.

When Bright Girls Decide That Math Is "A Waste of Time"

Susan Jacoby

1   Susannah, a 16-year-old who has always been an A student in every subject from algebra to English, recently informed her parents that she intended to drop physics and calculus in her senior year of high school and replace them with a drama seminar and a work-study program. She expects a major in art or history in college, she explained, and "any more science or math will just be a waste of my time."

2   Her parents were neither concerned by nor opposed to her decision. "Fine, dear," they said. Their daughter is, after all, an outstanding student. What does it matter if, at age 16, she has taken a step that may limit her understanding of both machines and the natural world for the rest of her life?

3   This kind of decision, in which girls turn away from studies that would give them a sure footing in the world of science and technology, is a self-inflicted female disability that is, regrettably, almost as common today as it was when I was in high school. If Susannah had announced that she had decided to stop taking English in her senior year, her mother and father would have been horrified. I also think they would have been a good deal less sanguine about her decision if she were a boy.

4   In saying that scientific and mathematical ignorance is a self-inflicted female wound, I do not, obviously, mean that cultural expectations play no role in the process. But the world does not conspire to deprive modern women of access to science as it did in the 1930s, when Rosalyn S. Yalow, the Nobel Prize-winning physicist, graduated from Hunter College and was advised to go to work as a secretary because no graduate school would admit her to its physics department. The current generation of adolescent girls—and their parents, bred on old expectations about women's interests—are active conspirators in limiting their own intellectual development.

5   It is true that the proportion of young women in science-related graduate and professional schools, most notably medical schools, has increased significantly in the past decade. It is also true that so few women were studying advanced science and mathematics before the early 1970s that the percentage increase in female enrollment does not yet translate into large numbers of women actually working in science.

6   The real problem is that so many girls eliminate themselves from any serious possibility of studying science as a result of decisions made during the vulnerable period of mid-adolescence, when they are most likely to be influenced—on both conscious and subconscious levels—by the traditional belief that math and science are "masculine" subjects.

7   During the teen-age years the well-documented phenomenon of "math anxiety" strikes girls who never had any problem handling numbers during earlier schooling. Some men, too, experience this syndrome—a form of panic, akin to a phobia, at any task involving numbers—but women constitute the overwhelming

majority of sufferers. The onset of acute math anxiety during the teen-age years is, as Stalin was fond of saying, "not by accident."

8   In adolescence girls begin to fear that they will be unattractive to boys if they are typed as "brains." Science and math epitomize unfeminine braininess in a way that, say, foreign languages do not. High-school girls who pursue an advanced interest in science and math (unless they are students at special institutions like the Bronx High School of Science where everyone is a brain) usually find that they are greatly outnumbered by boys in their classes. They are, therefore, intruding on male turf at a time when their sexual confidence, as well as that of the boys, is most fragile.

9   A 1981 assessment of female achievement in mathematics, based on research conducted under a National Institute for Education grant, found significant differences in the mathematical achievements of 9th and 12th graders. At age 13 girls were equal to or slightly better than boys in tests involving algebra, problem solving and spatial ability; four years later the boys had outstripped the girls.

10   It is not mysterious that some very bright high-school girls suddenly decide that math is "too hard" and "a waste of time." In my experience, self-sabotage of mathematical and scientific ability is often a conscious process. I remember deliberately pretending to be puzzled by geometry problems in my sophomore year in high school. A male teacher called me in after class and said, in a baffled tone, "I don't see how you can be having so much trouble when you got straight A's last year in my algebra class."

11   The decision to avoid advanced biology, chemistry, physics and calculus in high school automatically restricts academic and professional choices that ought to be wide open to anyone beginning college. At all coeducational universities women are overwhelmingly concentrated in the fine arts, social sciences and traditionally female departments like education. Courses leading to degrees in science- and technology-related fields are filled mainly by men.

12   In my generation, the practical consequences of mathematical and scientific illiteracy are visible in the large number of special programs to help professional women overcome the anxiety they feel when they are promoted into jobs that require them to handle statistics.

13   The consequences of this syndrome should not, however, be viewed in narrowly professional terms. Competence in science and math does not mean one is going to become a scientist or mathematician any more than competence in writing English means one is going to become a professional writer. Scientific and mathematical illiteracy—which has been cited in several recent critiques by panels studying American education from kindergarten through college—produces an incalculably impoverished vision of human experience.

14   Scientific illiteracy is not, of course, the exclusive province of women. In certain intellectual circles it has become fashionable to proclaim a willed, aggressive ignorance about science and technology. Some female writers specialize in ominous, uninformed diatribes against genetic research as a plot to remove control of childbearing from women, while some well-known men of letters proudly announce that they understand absolutely nothing about computers, or, for that

matter, about electricity. This lack of understanding is nothing in which women or men ought to take pride.

15   Failure to comprehend either computers or chromosomes leads to a terrible sense of helplessness, because the profound impact of science on everyday life is evident even to those who insist they don't, won't, can't understand why the changes are taking place. At this stage of history women are more prone to such feelings of helplessness than men because the culture judges their ignorance less harshly and because women themselves acquiesce in that indulgence.

16   Since there is ample evidence of such feelings in adolescence, it is up to parents to see that their daughters do not accede to the old stereotypes about "masculine" and "feminine" knowledge. Unless we want our daughters to share our intellectual handicaps, we had better tell them no, they can't stop taking mathematics and sciences at the ripe old age of 16.

Math Myths Have Got to Go, Forum Told

Jennifer Lewington

1   Math education in Ontario must become more relevant, rigorous and fun, to shatter the myth "that it's okay not to be good at it," delegates to a conference on the subject were told yesterday.

2   The forum, organized by the Ministry of Education and Training after Ontario's poor showing on the first-ever national mathematics test last year, called for change in math content, teaching methods and testing.

3   The one-day event drew about 400 math teachers, parents, students, trustees and representatives of business who offered scores of recommendations. These include measures to:

- Clarify provincial math standards and reduce repetition in the curriculum;
- Diversify teaching strategies to make math more relevant and appealing to students than at present;
- Raise the math education requirements for elementary school teachers;
- Involve parents in the math education of their children.

4   "The system is not as strong as its parts," forum co-chairman Wayne Samuelson told delegates at the close of the session. He said there is "a need for building connections between students and teachers, between school and the community, between the education system and society."

5   Next week, Education Minister David Cooke is expected to respond to the recommendations—even before the Royal Commission on Learning tables its report on education reforms later this year.

6   The Ontario forum signals a growing national interest in the improvement of math education, said Roger Palmer, a senior Alberta education official who helped develop the national math test sponsored by the provinces last year.

7   "It's part of a general movement across the country," he said of the Ontario meeting.

8   For example, the four western provinces and two territories are members of a consortium developing a math curriculum that sets clear, more specific outcomes. Elsewhere, the Maritime provinces have embarked on their own project to share in the development of curriculum.

9   In a speech to the Ontario forum yesterday, York University math professor Patricia Rogers said some myths about math must be shattered to ensure lasting reform.

10   In her view, too many people believe math is bound by strict rules—those usually set by the teacher. Another false view, she contends, is that math is open only to those with innate ability, making it easier for students and their parents to give up on the subject.

11   Finally, she said, too many people believe "it's okay" if they are inept at mathematics.

12   "We don't mind being called readers. If we can't read and write it's a matter of personal shame. People who can't do mathematics to a certain level are proud of it."

13   Like others at the meeting, she called for teacher education reforms. For example, she suggests that all student teachers take a mandatory mathematics course in preparation for teaching elementary school. The course should be specially designed to teach math concepts to those without a strong math background.

14   At York, she teaches such a program, but it is not a requirement for all students.

15   In Ontario, students currently do not have to take math after Grade 10. In other provinces the subject is required through Grade 11.

16   In Quebec, which outperformed other provinces on the national math test, senior elementary teachers are required to have some subject expertise in math.

RESPONDING TO THE READING

Analysis

1. Why does Dean include the anecdote about Rosalyn Yalow taken from the Jacoby article? Does she use it in a different way than Jacoby?
2. How relevant do you think the information in the two American articles is to the Canadian experience? Why do you think Dean chose to use American data?
3. Why do you think Dean chose not to endorse fully Estrich's conclusions concerning single-sex schools with reference to "math anxiety"? In answering this question, look at how Estrich has structured her article. It contains much personal anecdote which she uses in place of objective data. Why do you think she did this?
4. Two articles refer to Myra Novogrodsky as an expert. Who is she? How does Dean conflate the information about Novogrodsky in her research paper?
5. What are the four main problems Dean identifies that give rise to and per-

petuate "math anxiety"? What are her sources for each of the problems?

6. Dean makes use of paraphrase, summary, and quotation. Find an example of each in her paper and trace it back to its source.

7. The issue of gender bias underlies the symptom of "math anxiety." Which of the sources led Dean to the realization of this fact?

8. How viable are the solutions Dean presents in terms of the problems?

9. What patterns of organization can you identify in Dean's research paper? How are these patterns developed from those of her sources?

10. How clear is Dean's own point of view? At what points in her research paper does she clearly take a stand of her own?

Reading Your Writing

Before you submit any piece of writing, whether to a teacher, a supervisor, or a boss, you must take the time to ensure there are no errors in spelling, grammar, facts, or meaning. The following article, by Patty Martino Alspaugh, is taken from a professional journal called, *The Secretary*. It contains sound advice on reading your own writing.

Win the War against Typos

Patty Martino Alspaugh

1   "I can't proof my own work; I'm too close to it … I always find someone else's mistakes more easily than my own."

2   These are the familiar laments of nearly everyone who writes, even professional writers and editors. And, unfortunately, most people *do* spot others' typos more easily than their own. It's as if the typos are camouflaged—until they get into someone else's hands, that is.

3   Secretaries often are the ones on the frontlines of the typo battle—whether it's proofreading their executives' correspondence, departmental reports, or corporate publications. They're also the people who may have input the text of the communication in the first place, making it far more difficult to catch every typo—despite those handy spell-check programs, which are *not* foolproof in catching every type of error.

4   To make sure you're proofreading thoroughly and accurately, here are some tried-and-true guidelines.

Basic Training

Here are the basics for every office professional whose aim is flawless proofing:

Read through the material you are proofing twice. It's easy to overlook something in the first reading. By reading it twice you are, in effect, doubling your odds of finding all the typos.

Place a check mark next to executed edits. Checking off each edit on the marked-up version as you proof it against the cleaned-up version is about as foolproof as you can get.

If in doubt, look it up. If you have any doubt about the use of a word—grammar, syntax, etc.—consult the appropriate source.

Use the standard proofreading marks. Just as nations have universal languages, editors have standard editing marks. And just like languages, these marks are necessary for effective communication. You can find these standard proofreading marks in style manuals and in some dictionaries.

Make all edits in a *contrasting* color. This will help ensure the edits are seen. It's also a good idea to put an "x" or to repeat the proofreading mark in the right-hand margin, as well. Circle the edit if it's easily overlooked, like a comma or a hyphen—especially if you are planning to fax the edits. And, if you're making lengthy edits, use an erasable pen—you'll appreciate being able to rethink (erase) your own edits.

Take pride in your work. If you care about your work, you'll do a better job. It takes a dedicated and somewhat compulsive individual who strives for uniformity and perfection to be an editor.

Always, always use a spell-check program. This applies to anyone using a word-processing program. Never leave a file without spell-checking it—even if you are only making a few edits. But, remember, spell-check programs will not catch improper word uses, grammar errors, punctuation, and so forth.

Read good writers. Over time, you'll assimilate some of the writers' styles and more easily recognize awkward or ineffective language use when you're proofing.

Enlarge your vocabulary. Increasing your vocabulary increases your understanding of the things around you. And, the more well-rounded your thinking is, the more help you can be to the writer. If you don't understand what's being said, how can you know if it's being said *properly*? When reading, don't ignore unknown words—look them up, write them down, and refer back to them. Buy vocabulary books. Listen to vocabulary-building cassette tapes. You'll find the challenge will not only improve your depth of understanding, but will improve your verbal and written skills, too.

Use a systematic approach. For instance, if you are executing someone else's edits, first make all the edits without really paying attention to anything else. Next, check to make sure you made all the edits. Finally, read through the document to check for errors not picked up by the other proofreader(s).

First Aid

Keep these supplies on hand for every proofreading job:

A dictionary—preferably a comprehensive one. Become familiar with how your particular dictionary works, because they aren't all alike. The front of the dictionary explains how you should interpret it.

At least one style manual—This is a must—especially if your are proofreading something for publication in the print media. Style books answer such questions as: Do I put a colon before or after the quotation marks? Is *north* capitalized when it's used as a region?

Grammar books—As a reference book, a good college handbook is great. A comprehensive index makes looking up anything easy. A good grammar review book is also useful giving you a *simple* way to figure out the proper way.

A secretarial handbook—The indexes generally are laid out well, the material is up-to-date, and they include a wide variety of information geared specifically to the office person. Professional Secretaries International® (PSI®) is among publishers of secretarial handbooks.

Condensed encyclopedia-type books—These books don't cover the breadth that encyclopedias do, but they're a handy and compact source you can keep nearby. They reference everything from people to events to historical data. There are many to choose from....

Additionally, don't forget these resources:

Your local library—The literary sections of most libraries are great sources for grammar questions. Most grammar hotlines are located at libraries.

Seminars—Many offer great one-day refresher courses. There are seminars specifically on editing and proofreading, including those often conducted at the PSI International Convention. Most cost around $100.

Anticipation wins the war

Here are common—yet frequently missed—writing errors that you should anticipate every time you proof:

Watch out for job jargon. Many of your industry's bywords probably aren't known to the general public. If addressing an audience outside of your own, explain (in parentheses) the first use of industry vernacular if the universality of a word or expression is in doubt.

Be on the lookout for domino-type changes. For example, figure changes that affect cumulative figures elsewhere; changed headings that require changes in the table of contents; noun number changes that will affect verb tenses.

Make sure the dates on letters are current. Sometimes letters sit for a few days because of rewrites or routing. Take an extra second to double-check the date before sending out any letters.

Verify names. This is critical it it's an important piece of correspondence. No one likes to see her name, or even her company's name, spelled wrong.

Don't get sidetracked. Sometimes the same sentence will have two typos, but you get so caught up in finding the solution to one, that you bypass the other. Read the sentence over again after fixing a typo.

Make it attractive. How it looks—the layout is an important aspect of making the final text presentable. It might be typo-free, but if it looks shoddy (correction fluid globs, jagged edges), it's not presentable. Even the spacing between words—and lines—is important. Because, in the editing world, looks *do* count.

Be on the alert for double meanings. One classic example is the Chevrolet Nova automobile. When the company tried to market the car in Mexico, they discovered that the name means "no go" in Spanish.

Slow down. More mistakes are made because someone is in a big hurry to get something done and doesn't double-check the work. To paraphrase an old proofing expression: They can have it now, or they can have it right.

Don't assume. If, when making edits, you have any contextual questions, flag those areas on the hard copy; don't assume if you're not sure. If it's a grammatical or spelling edit, go for it; but if it's a matter of making sense, always verify changes with the writer.

Make sure the punctuation is correct. Punctuation marks are there to help guide the reader's comprehension. Missing and misused punctuation only confuses the reader. Keep an especially vigilant eye out for missing question marks and quotation marks, and misplaced commas.

Proof in pairs if it's really important. If you are proofing something *really* important—for instance, a brochure that is ready to go to the printer and will ultimately become a printed piece sent to thousands—get someone to proof with you. One method of proofing in pairs involves having one proofer read every word aloud, indicating spaces, punctuation, capitalization, and so forth, while the other proofer follows with original copy. This is particularly effective when proofing names or figures that have been entered onto a computer from another source.

Proof the printout. If proofing a file on a computer, print it out and proof it again. Mistakes are easier to spot on a hard copy.

Double-check all math. Not only should you double-check the math, but you should attach an adding machine tape for verification (if you use the computer's math program to do your calculation, put a check mark next to the totals to let the writer know).

Be consistent. Whatever you do, however you do it, do it consistently; for instance, parallel construction. If you list things beginning with verbs, don't change midway to nouns. And watch out for inconsistent bullet-point styles, i.e., beginning some bullet points with capitals and others without; ending some bullet points with periods and others without.

But remember, a typo may escape even your most thorough proofreading; they elude even the most experienced editors. So next time you find one after the fact, don't be too upset; just put yourself through the drills and prepare for your next battle.

Grammar Review

A college handbook on grammar is useful: The following *basic* grammatical rules will help you recognize and learn the more common errors in writing.

Consistency of Tense

You need to be consistent in your use of tenses. If you begin writing a piece in the past tense, don't suddenly jump to the present tense, unless the meaning requires you to do so. Notice the verb tenses in the following passage:

> *I learned respect for preparation when I helped my mother make my wedding dress. My mother was precise about measuring and allowing for alterations in the future. Before she cut out the material, we discussed whether the dress would have another life after my wedding. I decided I wanted a dress that I could use on other occasions. With this in mind, my mother made "two dresses in one." The dress she made for my wedding was altered afterwards and I wore it to formal functions like my sister's wedding and my aunt and uncle's fiftieth anniversary party. All my mother does to make my wedding dress new again is add a bit of lace or shorten the hem and sleeves. I will wear the dress to my office's first formal Christmas party.*

The shifts in tense in the above passage are correct. The author moves from the past to the present to the future, changing tense logically.

Agreement between Subject and Verb

1. In sentences beginning with *here* or *there*, the real subject of a sentence is neither *here* nor *there*, but is the noun following the form of the verb *to be* used in the sentence.

    There *are* three *trees* in my yard.
    There *will be* a big *parade* today.
    Here *are* plenty of *books* for you to read.
    There *are* in this country many *players* who cheat.
    There *are* lots of students in the cafeteria.

2. When the following words are used as subjects, they are always plural in meaning, but they always require singular verbs.

everyone	someone	anyone	no one	each
everybody	somebody	anybody	nobody	either
everything	something	anything	nothing	neither

    Everyone is happy to see you.

    Neither of the twins likes ice cream.

3. When *each* or *every* comes before singular subjects joined by *and*, a singular verb is required.

    Every man and woman has the right to vote.
    Each student and teacher has a book.

4. The introductory *it* is singular and always followed by a singular verb.

    It was the noisy children who disturbed me.

    It is his final exams that worry him.

5. Words that come between a subject and its verb do not change the number of the subject. Prepositional phrases often have this position.

   A woman, along with her thirty-seven cats, lives on that farm.
   Everyone except Sheila has a book.
   Daniel, together with his family, is visiting Ottawa.
   The teacher, along with her students, is viewing a film.
   One of the most enjoyable books published this year was written by Margaret Atwood.

6. Subjects joined by *and* or *both* take a plural verb (but see rule 2).

   A loud and sudden bang are enough to startle anyone.
   A red Honda and a blue Ford are parked outside.
   Both Jane and Michelle are coming to the party.

7. *Several, many, both,* and *few* are plural words and always take a plural verb.

   Both are going to Halifax next week.
   Only a few have failed the test.

8. Some nouns are always plural in form and always take plural verbs.

   clothing: jeans, pants, sunglasses, trousers
   tools: scissors, pliers, tweezers

   However, some of them are followed by a singular verb when used in expressions such as a *pair of*.

   Her jeans are very tight.
   That pair of jeans is old.

9. When subjects are joined by the following structures, the verb must agree with the closer subject.

   Neither the students nor the teacher likes the classroom.
   Either the teacher or the children are making the sets.
   Not only the mother but also the children are coming soon.

10. Some words may be singular or plural depending on what they refer to: *lots, all, some, any, most, half,* etc. When these words are followed by a prepositional phrase, the noun in the phrase will determine whether the verb is singular or plural.

    All of the books have been destroyed.
    All of the book has been damaged.

    Lots of the books were torn
    Lots of the book was torn

11. The expression *a number of* is plural, and the expression *the number of* is singular.

    A number of cars were stolen from the lot.
    The number of children at home is amazing.

12. Expressions stating an amount of time, money, weight, and volume, are plural in form but take a singular verb.

    Three weeks is not enough time for a visit to Italy.
    Six hundred dollars is needed as a deposit.
    Thirty extra pounds is too much to lose in a week.
    Four gallons of gasoline costs over thirty pesos.

13. Some words are always plural in form but singular in meaning. These words require singular verbs.

    mathematics, physics, economics, statistics ...
    measles, mumps, herpes ...
    news, ethics, politics ...

    Mathematics is an easy subject.

    The news was always depressing.

14. Titles of books and movies, even if plural in form, take singular verbs.

    The New York Times is a fine newspaper.
    Star Wars is an action-packed adventure.

15. Collective nouns are usually singular, but may be plural if the members are functioning independently. Watch the pronouns for clues to the singular or plural nature of the subject. Some of these words are *class, team, police, committee, audience, family, faculty,* and so on.

    The class takes its final exam next Wednesday.
    The class are finishing their spring projects.

16. Some nouns use the same form for both singular and plural meanings. The pronouns and modifiers with these words will indicate whether they are singular or plural in meaning.

    s: species, series

    That species is extinct. Those species are unusual.

    no s: sheep, deer, fish

    That deer is graceful. Those deer are young.

17. Nouns for nationality that end in *ese, ch,* or *sh* may be singular or plural depending on their meaning. Some of these words are *Chinese, French,* and *English.* When the word refers to the *people of the country,* it takes a plural verb and is preceded by the article *the.*

    Spanish is spoken in Chile.   Italians cook very well.
    English is spoken at that school.   The English adore sweet puddings.

Sentence Completion

Fragments   A sentence has a subject and a verb, and conveys a complete thought. **A sentence fragment** looks like a sentence, in that it starts with a capital letter and ends with a period, but the reader knows something is missing. There are six types of **fragments**.

1. **Prepositional phrase fragment:** A prepositional phrase has no subject or verb, and begins with a preposition. Correct the fragment by joining it to the rest of the sentence.
    a. I love skiing. *In the mountains.*
        I love skiing in the mountains.
    b. Luke read that it was cheaper to lease than to buy a new car. *In spite of the low bank rate.* He decided, nevertheless, to buy.
        Luke read that it was cheaper to lease than to buy a new car in spite of the low bank rate. He decided, nevertheless, to buy.

2. **Missing verb fragment:** There is no main verb. Correct by adding an appropriate verb.
    a. The annual George Wicken Award given by the college for teaching excellence.
        The annual George Wicken Award *is given* by the college for teaching excellence.
    b. The moon seen to have a pitted surface of craters and volcanoes.
        The moon *can be seen* to have a pitted surface of craters and volcanoes.

3. **Infinitive fragment:** The infinitive is used incorrectly as a complete verb in the sentence. Correct by combining the infinitive phrase with the sentence it belongs to or by changing the infinitive to a complete verb.

    a. You should always proofread your work carefully. *To be sure you have completed the requirements and to feel you've produced a piece you can be proud of.*

    b. You should always proofread your work carefully to be sure you have completed the requirements and to feel you've produced a piece you can be proud of.

        You should always proofread your work carefully. Then you can be sure you have completed the requirements and feel you've produced a piece you can be proud of.

4. **Participle fragment:** The *ing* participle is used alone as a complete verb, without the helping verb. Correct by adding a subject and a correct form of the verb, or by joining the participle fragment to the sentence it belongs to.
    a. He enjoyed travelling to school on the bus each day. *It being his only opportunity to daydream.*
        He enjoyed travelling to school on the bus each day. It was his only opportunity to daydream.

He enjoyed travelling to school on the bus each day, it being his only opportunity to daydream.

b. *Growing up in a vociferous family.* He became a great debater.
Growing up in a vociferous family, he became a great debater.

5. **Missing subject fragment:** There is no subject. Correct by adding a subject, often a pronoun standing in for the subject in the preceding sentence, to create a new sentence, or attach fragment to the appropriate sentence.

a. Many teachers offer help outside of the classroom. *Also assign extra work for the better students.*
Many teachers offer help outside of the classroom. They also assign extra work for the better students.
Many teachers offer help outside of the classroom and also assign extra work for the better students.

b. Even in Grade 10 I had a crush on Matthew. *Looking as vulnerable and pale as he did in those days.*
Even in Grade 10 I had a crush on Matthew. He looked so pale and vulnerable in those days.
Even in Grade 10 I had a crush on Matthew because he looked so pale and vulnerable in those days.

6. **Dependent clause fragment:** A dependent clause cannot stand alone. It is easily recognized by the conjunction that introduces it. Correct by joining the dependent clause to an independent clause, or by removing the conjunction and creating a new independent clause. You may need to replace the conjunction (if the conjunction is *who, which,* or *that*) with a subject. Common conjunctions: *although, after, because, if, as, until, since, before, so that, that, when, even, even though, who, which, where.*

a. I decided to jog home. *After I had finished my workout.*
I decided to jog home after I had finished my workout.

b. As a boy he enjoyed pulling the legs off spiders. *Which may account for why he is a serial murderer today.*
As a boy he enjoyed pulling the legs off spiders. This many account for why he is a mass murderer today.

Run-On Sentences Run-on sentences contain too much. There are three basic types: the comma splice, the fused sentence, and the cluttered sentence.

1. The comma splice: In this error two independent clauses are united with only a comma between them.
Roses are red, violets are blue.

Correct by writing the comma splice as two distinct sentences.
Roses are red. Violets are blue.
Or, correct by replacing comma with a semi-colon.
Roses are red; violets are blue.

Or, correct by following the comma with a coordinating conjunction (*and, but, so, for, or, nor, or yet*).

Roses are red, but violets are blue.

Or, correct by making one of the two clauses dependent.

Although roses are red, violets are blue.

Roses are red while violets are blue.

2. The fused sentences: This error, like the comma splice, unites two independent clauses; however, no punctuation is used.

> *I am glad March break has finally arrived I certainly need a chance to relax.*

Correct by recognizing the two independent clauses and then apply the same techniques as for the comma splice.

I am glad March break has finally arrived. I certainly need a chance to relax.

I am glad March break has finally arrived; I certainly need a chance to relax.

I am glad March break has finally arrived, and I certainly need a chance to relax.

I am glad March break has finally arrived because I certainly need a chance to relax.

Since I certainly need a chance to relax, I am glad March break has finally arrived.

3. The cluttered sentence: The cluttered sentence may be grammatically correct, but it is difficult for the reader to understand. One kind of cluttered sentence contains too many ideas and clauses.

> *The Raptors have quickly become a fixture on Toronto's sports scene, but they are not yet a top-rate team because they lose more games than they win even though Damon Stoudamire was the NBA Rookie of the Year for the 1995–96 season which may account for the team's popularity.*

Correct this type of cluttered sentence by separating the main ideas into individual sentences.

The Raptors have quickly become a fixture on Toronto's sports scene. They are as yet not a top-rate team because they lose more games than they win. Damon Stoudamire was the NBA Rookie of the Year for the 1995–96 season. This fact alone may account for the team's popularity.

Another kind of cluttered sentence contains incongruous ideas, or the relationship between ideas is not clearly stated for readers.

> *Even with OSAP, students find the financial demands of college difficult to manage and having a social life is something a lot of students don't have time for because they have to work part-time and complete their college assignments.*

Correct by making the ideas clearer and separating one from the other.

Even with OSAP, students find the financial demands of college difficult to manage. In addition, having a social life is something a lot of students don't have time for because they have to work part-time and complete their college assignments.

Correct Use of Pronouns

Agreement

1. **In number:** Pronouns agree in number with the nouns they replace (their antecedents). If the antecedent is singular, the pronoun is also singular; if the antecedent is plural, so is the pronoun. One common problem that occurs relates to the use of *each, every, any, some, no, either,* and *neither.* (See pages 219–21 on "Agreement between Subject and Verb".) These words often appear to have a plural meaning, but they are always singular. Many of the rules of agreement dealing with pronouns are the same as those that deal with verbs.

   Every student has to bring their own lunch.

   Correct by making the pronoun agree with its antecedent noun (here the noun is *student*).

   Every student has to bring his or her own lunch.
   All students have to bring their own lunches.
   (*Note:* if you change to the plural, you must make all other parts of the sentence agree.)
   Every student has to bring a lunch.

   Collective nouns and their pronouns also create problems for writers. (See page 221.) When members of a group act independently, the pronoun is plural; when members act as a unit, the pronoun is singular.

   a. The committee are researching the causes of the company's bankruptcy and will produce their reports in two weeks. (Here each member has an individual task.)
   b. The committee reached its unanimous decision to suspend trading yesterday. (Here the committee acts as a unit.)

2. **In person:** Pronouns agree in person with their antecedents. *Person* refers to the one speaking (first person—*I, me, my, mine; we, us, our, ours*), the one spoken to (second person—*you, your, yours*), and the one spoken about (third person—*he, him, his; she, her, hers; it, its; they, them, their, theirs*). Mistakes occur when point of view is changed or when writers begin in the singular and move to the plural.

a. *The prospective employee must have their résumé when they go to an interview.*

Correct by making all singular or plural.

The prospective employee must have a résumé when he or she goes to an interview.
Prospective employees must have their résumés when they go to an interview.

b. *I know how to write a good paragraph; you have to have a topic sentence.*
I know how to write a good paragraph; I have to have a topic sentence.
You know how to write a good paragraph; you have to have a topic sentence.

c. *The person who repaired my VCR did a good job and they didn't charge me much.*
The person who repaired my VCR did a good job and didn't charge me much.
The person who repaired my VCR did a good job and she didn't charge me much.

Pronouns and Antecedents

Pronouns depend upon antecedents to give them meaning. If an antecedent is not supplied or is unclear, the sentence is confusing for readers.

Kieran loves to play soccer, baseball, and hockey and he would like to be a professional one when he grows up.

The problem is with the pronoun *one*. A professional what?

Kieran loves to play soccer, baseball, and hockey and he would like to be a professional athlete when he grows up.
Lucy won so many local swimming meets that she decided to do it at the national level.

The problem is with the pronoun *it*. What did she decide to do?

Lucy won so many local swimming meets that she decided to compete at the national level.

Zazu's hobbies are reading and collecting rocks. Doing it makes her happy.

The problem is with *it*. There are two antecedents *it* could refer to (reading and collecting).

Zazu's hobbies are reading and collecting rocks. Both of them make her happy.

Parallel Structure

Whenever you write a series of items in a sentence, you should present them in a parallel structure. Parallel structure means all the items in the list have the same grammatical form. As a technique, parallel structure is worthwhile because it shows a clear connection between ideas and adds coherence.

1. Single words:
A successful student must be intelligent, diligent, and solvent.

2. Phrases:

> A first date can either be a romantic adventure or a horrendous bore, but it is always a nerve-wracking experience.

> If you want to be a good photographer, you need quality equipment, artistic vision, and suitable subjects.

3. Clauses:

> There are some things my parents did that I will never do: they married too young, they created a large family, and they scrimped every penny.

> The prime minister claimed that he would reduce the deficit, that he would increase job prospects, and that he would get tough on crime.

Placement of Modifiers

There are two problems associated with modifiers: **misplaced modifiers** and **dangling modifiers**. A modifier adds detailed information about a component of a sentence. Adjectives *modify* nouns. Adverbs *modify* verbs and adjectives and other adverbs. Modifiers can be single words, phrases, and clauses.

1. Misplaced modifiers: A misplaced modifier is placed too far away from the word to which it applies. To correct a misplaced modifier, determine the word the modifier relates to and then move the modifier accordingly.
   a. The publishing company needed someone to type *badly*.
      The publishing company badly needed someone to type.
   b. He chased the thief out of the locker room *wearing only a towel*.
      Wearing only a towel, he chased the thief out of the locker room.
   c. Barry ate a donut at the shop *that was full of Boston cream filling*.
      At the shop, Barry ate a donut that was full of Boston cream filling.
   d. Sarah fed a fresh mango to Ed *dipped in cream*.
      Sarah fed to Ed a fresh mango dipped in cream.

2. Dangling modifier: A dangling modifier has no word to relate to in the sentence. As a result, the modifier "dangles" and accidentally modifies an unintended word, often with ludicrous consequences. To correct this error, add information so that the meaning is clear.

> *Rollerblading down the hill at dusk,* the raccoon streaked in front of me.

> As I was rollerblading down the hill at dusk, the raccoon streaked in front of me.

> Rollerblading down the hill at dusk, I saw the raccoon streak in front of me.

Russell Baker in the following article treats the subject of punctuation in a light-hearted manner.

How To Punctuate

Russell Baker

1　When you write, you make a sound in the reader's head. It can be a dull mumble—that's why so much government prose makes you sleepy—or it can be a joyful noise, a sly whisper, a throb of passion.

2　　Listen to a voice trembling in a haunted room:

3　　"And the silken, sad, uncertain rustling of each purple curtain thrilled me—filled me with fantastic terrors never felt before ..."

4　　That's Edgar Allan Poe, a master. Few of us can make paper speak as vividly as Poe could, but even beginners will write better once they start listening to the sound their writing makes.

5　　One of the most important tools for making paper speak in your own voice is punctuation.

6　　When speaking aloud, you punctuate constantly—with body language. Your listener hears commas, dashes, question marks, exclamation points, quotation marks as you shout, whisper, pause, wave your arms, roll your eyes, wrinkle your brow.

7　　In writing, punctuation plays the role of body language. It helps readers hear you the way you want to be heard.

"Gee, Dad, Have I Got to Learn All Them Rules?"

8　Don't let the rules scare you. For they aren't hard and fast. Think of them as guidelines.

9　　Am I saying, "Go ahead and punctuate as you please"? Absolutely not. Use your own common sense, remembering that you can't expect readers to work to decipher what you're trying to say.

10　　There are two basic systems of punctuation:

1. The loose or open system, which tries to capture the way body language punctuates talk.
2. The tight, closed structural system, which hews closely to the sentence's grammatical structure.

11　　Most writers use a little of both. In any case, we use much less punctuation than they used 200 or even 50 years ago. (Glance into Edward Gibbon's "Decline and Fall of the Roman Empire," first published in 1776, for an example of the tight structural system at its most elegant.)

12　　No matter which system you prefer, be warned: punctuation marks cannot save a sentence that is badly put together. If you have to struggle over commas, semicolons and dashes, you've probably built a sentence that's never going to fly, no matter how you tinker with it. Throw it away and build a new one to a simpler design. The better your sentence, the easier it is to punctuate.

Choosing the right tool

13　There are 30 main punctuation marks, but you'll need fewer than a dozen for most writing.

14   I can't show you in this small space how they all work, so I'll stick to the ten most important—and even then can only hit highlights. For more details, check your dictionary or a good grammar.

Comma [,]

15   This is the most widely used mark of all. It's also the toughest and most controversial. I've seen aging editors almost come to blows over the comma. If you can handle it without sweating, the others will be easy. Here's my policy:

1. Use a comma after a long introductory phrase or clause: *After stealing the crown jewels from the Tower of London, I went home for tea.*
2. If the introductory material is short, forget the comma: *After the theft I went home for tea.*
3. But use it if the sentence would be confusing without it, like this: *The day before I'd robbed the Bank of England.*
4. Use a comma to separate elements in a series: *I robbed the Denver Mint, the Bank of England, the Tower of London and my piggy bank.*
   Notice there is no comma before *and* in the series. This is common style nowadays, but some publishers use a comma there, too.
5. Use a comma to separate independent clauses that are joined by a conjunction like *and, but, for, or, nor, because,* or *so: I shall return the crown jewels, for they are too heavy to wear.*
6. Use a comma to set off a mildly parenthetical word grouping that isn't essential to the sentence: *Girls, who have always interested me, usually differ from boys.*
   Do not use commas if the word grouping is essential to the sentence's meaning: *Girls who interest me know how to tango.*
7. Use a comma in direct address: *Your majesty, please hand over the crown.*
8. And between proper names and titles: *Montague Sneed, Director of Scotland Yard, was assigned to the case.*
9. And to separate elements of geographical address: *Director Sneed comes from Chicago, Illinois, and now lives in London, England.*

16   Generally speaking, use a comma where you'd pause briefly in speech. For a long pause or completion of thought, use a period.

17   If you confuse the comma with the period, you'll get a run-on sentence: *The Bank of England is located in London, I rushed over to rob it.*

Semicolon [;]

18   A more sophisticated mark than the comma, the semicolon separates two main clauses, but it keeps those two thoughts more tightly linked than a period can: *I steal crown jewels; she steals hearts.*

Dash [—] and Parentheses [()]

19   Warning! Use sparingly. The dash SHOUTS. Parentheses whisper. Shout too often, people stop listening; whisper too much, people become suspicious of you. The dash creates a dramatic pause to prepare for an expression needing strong emphasis: *I'll marry you—if you'll rob Topkapi with me.*

20 Parentheses help you pause quietly to drop in some chatty information not vital to your story: *Despite Betty's daring spirit ("I love robbing your piggy bank," she often said), she was a terrible dancer.*

Quotation marks [" "]

21 These tell the reader you're reciting the exact words someone said or wrote: *Betty said, "I can't tango." Or: "I can't tango," Betty said.*

22 Notice the comma comes before the quote marks in the first example, but comes inside then in the second. Not logical? Never mind. Do it that way anyhow.

Colon [:]

23 A colon is a tip-off to get ready for what's next: a list, a long quotation or an explanation. This article is riddled with colons. Too many, maybe, but the message is: "Stay on your toes; it's coming at you."

Apostrophe [']

24 The big headache is with possessive nouns. If the noun is singular, add 's: *I hated Betty's tango.*

25 If the noun is plural, simply add an apostrophe after the s: *Those are the girls' coats.*

26 The same applies for singular nouns ending in s, like Dickens: *This is Dickens's best book.*

27 And in plural: *This is the Dickenses' cottage.*

28 The possessive pronouns *hers* and *its* have no apostrophe.

29 If you write *it's,* you are saying *it is.*

Keep Cool

30 You know about ending a sentence with a period (.) or a question mark (?). Do it. Sure, you can also end with an exclamation point (!), but must you? Usually it just makes you sound breathless and silly. Make your writing generate its own excitement. Filling the paper with !!!! won't make up for what your writing has failed to do.

31 Too many exclamation points make me think the writer is talking about the panic in his own head.

32 Don't sound panicky. End with a period. I am serious. A period. Understand?

33 Well … sometimes a question mark is okay.

Short Stories

Gary Anderson was born in Jamaica and emigrated to Canada when he was six. He was educated at Ryerson Polytechnic University and at the University of Toronto.

JACK

Gary Anderson

My grandfather tells me there are good and bad insects. "Like people," he says, "there is good and bad." While I think about this he pours me hot chocolate from a pot, his face so close to mine I can feel its warmth.

"Dance fly, dragon fly, bark beetle, rove beetle, ladybug. Sometimes not a whole lot separates one from the other. Like people," he says. Then, "How's this for chocolate?"

"Okay."

"Would you like to sit in the living room? Would that make it better?"

I shrug. "Okay." The dog appears from under the table and follows me—too close to my heels. I stumble and spill some chocolate on my hand. It burns at first, but it cools quickly. Soon it's like a strange cold spot on my hand. I wipe it off on my jeans when my grandfather's not looking.

"We can watch TV," he says. He sits on the couch. I sit in the big chair. The dog sits next to him and he pushes it to the floor. It settles by his feet, its soft jaw on his slippered foot.

"How's your mother?" he asks. "Is she all right?"

"I guess so. I don't know."

"Things like that always sound worse than they are."

I nod, then stare at the window as the sun comes through the white curtains. Specks of dust float around in wide circles, like insects, thousands of them. I sip the chocolate and it goes down warm. I think about my mother and the bandage around her shoulder and under her arm. There was a stain on the first one—dark, dark red, almost black. My stepfather said it was blood but I know blood isn't that colour. I have seen blood before. Once, when I was younger, blood came pouring out of my nose for no reason. The stain on my mother's bandage was something else. Something very different from blood.

"Would you like to see a book with pictures?" my grandfather asks. I nod and he goes to the bookshelf. The dog follows him. The book is large and green. He opens it on the coffee table and the dog barks. There is a picture of a large insect with a smaller insect in its jaws. The larger insect is very powerful-looking. The smaller insect is already half-crushed.

"Praying mantis," my grandfather says and smiles. He encourages me to look at more pictures. I flip through a few pages. The dog turns around once and sits right on my foot.

"Yo Yo!" my grandfather yells. Yo Yo flinches, then quivers and farts on my shoe. My grandfather gets up, grabs him by the collar, and leads him through the kitchen, outside. "Bad dog." I can hear Yo Yo barking as my grandfather comes back into the living room.

"Stupid dog," he says as he sniffs the air. He walks back into the kitchen for a can of Lysol and returns spraying. The Lysol mist falls all around me. Lysol gets into the hot chocolate and I push the cup away.

"That's better," he says. "Now we can talk. How's your mother?"

"Fine," I say.

By the second visit to the hospital I was able to find my mother's room all by myself. She shares room 224 with this other woman behind a curtain. When I got there my stepfather was standing at the window, looking out. I put the card I had on the table and sat on my mother's bed. She was sleeping. At least she looked as if she was sleeping, but I couldn't tell for sure. I leaned real close to her to see if she was still breathing. She was breathing all right, but the sound was so faint I had to hold my own breath to hear it. She was fine, I guess. Still, her face looked funny. It looked yellow. And the longer I stared at it the yellower it got. I touched her nose to see if the yellow would come off on my finger and my stepfather grabbed me by the arm and yanked me away. He hit me once on the back of the head.

"Can't you see she's resting? What are you, mental?"

Every page has a different insect: some are flying, others are building nests in the sand, some are fighting with other insects, some have taken other insects apart. There's a ladybug on a leaf, small and perfect like a jewel. A wasp is angry. Its stinger is curled, set to sting. Small insects lay eggs in the body of a dead rat. The babies are born and eat the rat down to the bones. An African boy has a locust in his mouth. He is looking at another boy who has already crunched down on his. The hind legs of the locust stick out between the boy's white teeth. The book says this is a game African children play. The one who can make the hind legs of the locust stick out the furthest, wins.

Yo Yo trots back into the room. My grandfather asks how he got back in. Yo Yo just looks at him and pretends he doesn't understand. My grandfather is too tired to take him out again so he lets him stay. Yo Yo sits by my feet and watches the dust move around the room. He snorts.

"I know what you want to do," my grandfather says. "You want to watch TV, don't you." I nod. The TV is turned on by remote control. Yo Yo barks at it and walks around in a circle.

"Look," my grandfather says. "Championship Wrestling." Two big men in gym suits circle each other. One has a mask on, the other is dressed like an Indian. The Indian gets the Masked Man in a headlock. The Masked Man reaches back, grabs the Indian's long hair, and flips him over his shoulder. The Indian is slammed to the ground. The Masked Man stomps on his face a couple of times.

"I used to be a wrestler," my grandfather says. "Did you know that?" I shake my head. I didn't know. "That was a long time ago. I was very young." He smiles and the dust floats around him. He's very old now, not weak, but big and with soft bones. I like him but sometimes he forgets my name. He calls me Jack. Jack was my brother's name. My brother died exactly one month after he was born. My grandfather said it was the overwhelming grief of the world that killed him.

"I have to go to the bathroom."

"Of course you do," he says. "After all that chocolate."

I smile and leave. All the way up the stairs there are pictures of insects: dragonfly, scorpion fly, assassin fly. They sound bad but they're the good guys. In the bathroom there are real insects, dead ones. Butterflies held down with small pins. It reminds me of my mother and how the metal spike went through her shoulder. My stepfather said it wasn't anybody's fault but I don't believe him. It's always somebody's fault. Like when something breaks in our house. It's always my fault.

After two weeks I found out that everyone in the hospital looks yellow—everyone that's sick. And there's a room for kids where they have tons of video games and you don't even need a quarter to play. There's a place to eat and there's a place to watch television. Then there's a place you can go to and watch the new babies. The woman who shares the room with my mother goes there a lot. She just sits there all teary-eyed and watches them wriggle.

When my brother Jack died he was just a baby, but that's not how I remember him. When I think about him, when I dream about him, he's older than me, just like he would be if he'd have lived. Sometimes when I think about Jack, we're playing at Edgar Park maybe, or in the hydro field where we're not supposed to. Jack isn't afraid of anything. He's smarter and stronger than I am. Sometimes when we're tired, Jack and I sit and talk about our stepfather. We talk about our secret plans to rub him out. We invent traps with swinging hammers and break-away floors. On little pieces of paper we show how hidden knives will pop out of walls and cut him to ribbons.

Steven Heighton was born in 1961 and graduated from Queen's University. He has won many awards for his writing and for a number of years was editor of the literary journal *QUARRY*.

Magi

Steven Heighton

It wasn't like the falling star that crosses the night in a split second, catching your eye as it vanishes. The light was brighter than any meteor, brighter than the other stars, and like a signal flare it fell slowly, pulsing, from a point high above the sky-line.

We watched for a while in silence before Richard, the oldest of us, decided it was an airplane. And that it was going to crash.

There's nothing else it could be, he told us.

And after he'd said it we began to notice the faint glimmering tail following the light as it descended. Accelerating, little by little.

None of us spoke. The others may have been listening, like me, for the cinematic sounds we'd come to expect: a long subsiding wail, a baritone roar as the falling craft met earth in a bubbling orange fireball.

But there were no explosions, no fearful screams. Around us the fields hummed with a dull, hypnotic rhythm, cicadas chanted in foliage by the path. A drone of cars on the highway a mile off through the wood, and our anxious, unsteady breathing.

Maybe he can still pull out of it.

Murmurs of agreement. *He's still not dropping too fast.*

He is—can't you see he's speeding up?

Come on. Pull out of it.

He's really going to crash.

We've got to do something—come on.

But Richard told us it was too far.

Even if we run?

Too far. A hundred miles, maybe. A thousand.

A cluster of fireflies rose from the field beside us and drifted across the path. The falling speck was glowing brighter as it neared the skyline.

I wonder if the pilot's afraid.

Of course he's afraid. Wouldn't you be afraid?

And someone added, *He's all alone.*

Which was a strange thing for any of us to say, because the light could have been a thousand things for all we could tell, a jetliner from Asia with hundreds aboard, a returning satellite or approaching warhead. But no one objected. The light was solitary and small and we knew whoever it carried must be alone.

And now the ghostly tail trailing the light began to change, to fan out and pulsate with a prismatic glow. Soon the light would touch the skyline.

He'll never pull out now.

Maybe he can jump—maybe he's got a parachute.

We'd never see it from here.

And in the watchful silence that followed, like the vapour trail behind the falling light, there was agreement. We knew the pilot would not get out.

Something told us. Perhaps the brittle, expectant stillness of the fall air—or did we sense something in the light's resemblance to a star, its timeless arc across the night-sky compressed to a few seconds?

But we were only children.

For a moment more we froze in that constellation, David behind me, Richard to my right; the others had slipped away. The light reached the dense blackness of earth and we waited for the explosion. Some day we would trace our scattered, solitary orbits to this place.

Richard raised his hand for silence; we waited intently. But the light was too far off and crashed behind the skyline or into deep forest, or was swallowed by a lake, for it vanished suddenly and left the sky infinitely darker. The air had turned cool. From far off the almost-human shriek of some bird.

The stars themselves were clearer now that the sharper light was gone; the Milky Way pulsed and blazed and to the east Mars glistened like the eye of a reptile. The Magi might have seen the heavens with the same transfigured wonder when the star of Bethlehem finally fell, and the rough desert track they were following home to their kingdoms vanished into the dark... .

I craned my head back to see Orion and count the Pleiades, but before I was done I lost my balance and stumbled.

Alistair MacLeod was born in Saskatchewan in 1936, but his family returned to their farm in Cape Breton when he was ten. Cape Breton is the setting of many of his short stories.

To Everything There Is a Season

Alistair MacLeod

I am speaking here of a time when I was eleven and lived with my family on our small farm on the west coast of Cape Breton. My family had been there for a long, long time and so it seemed had I. And much of that time seems like the proverbial yesterday. Yet when I speak on this Christmas 1977, I am not sure how much I speak with the voice of that time or how much in the voice of what I have since become. And I am not sure how many liberties I may be taking with the boy I think I was. For Christmas is a time of both past and present and often the two are imperfectly blended. As we step into its nowness we often look behind.

We have been waiting now, it seems, forever. Actually, it has been most intense since Halloween when the first snow fell upon us as we moved like muffled mummers upon darkened country roads. The large flakes were soft and new then and almost generous and the earth to which they fell was still warm and as yet unfrozen. They fell in silence into the puddles and into the sea where they disappeared at the moment of contact. They disappeared, too, upon touching the heated redness of our necks and hands or the faces of those who did not wear masks. We carried our pillowcases from house to house, knocking on doors to become silhouettes in the light thrown out from kitchens (white pillowcases held out by whitened forms). The snow fell between us and the doors and was transformed in shimmering golden beams. When we turned to leave, it fell upon our footprints and as the night wore on obliterated them and all the records of our movements. In the morning everything was soft and still and November had come upon us.

My brother Kenneth, who is two and a half, is unsure of his last Christmas. It is Halloween that looms largest in his memory as an exceptional time of being up late in magic darkness and falling snow. "Who are you going to dress up as at Christmas?" he asks. "I think I'll be a snowman." All of us laugh at that and tell him Santa Claus will find him if he is good and that he need not dress up at all. We go about our appointed tasks waiting for it to happen.

I am troubled myself about the nature of Santa Claus and I am trying to hang on to him in any way that I can. It is true that at my age I no longer *really* believe in him yet I have hoped in all his possibilities as fiercely as I can; much in the same way, I think, that the drowning man waves desperately to the lights of the passing ship on the high sea's darkness. For without him, as without the man's ship, it seems our fragile lives would be so much more desperate.

My mother has been fairly tolerant of my attempted perpetuation. Perhaps because she has encountered it before. Once I overheard her speaking about my sister Anne to one of her neighbours. "I thought Anne would *believe* forever," she said. "I practically had to tell her." I have somehow always wished I had not heard her say that as I seek sanctuary and reinforcement even in an ignorance I know I dare not trust.

Kenneth, however, believes with an unadulterated fervour, and so do Bruce and Barry who are six-year-old twins. Beyond me there is Anne who is thirteen and Mary who is fifteen, both of whom seem to be leaving childhood at an alarming rate. My mother has told us that she was already married when she was seventeen, which is only two years older than Mary is now. That too seems strange to contemplate and perhaps childhood is shorter for some than it is for others. I think of this sometimes in the evenings when we have finished our chores and the supper dishes have been cleared away and we are supposed to be doing our homework. I glance sideways at my mother, who is always knitting or mending, and at my father, who mostly sits by the stove coughing quietly with his handkerchief at his mouth. He has "not been well" for over two years and has difficulty breathing whenever he moves at more than the slowest pace. He is most sympathetic of all concerning my extended hopes and says we should hang on to the good things in our lives as long as we are able. As I look at him out of the corner of my eye, it does not seem that he has many of them left. He is old, we think, at forty-two.

Yet Christmas, in spite of all the doubts of our different ages, is a fine and splendid time, and now as we pass the midpoint of December our expectations are heightened by the increasing coldness that has settled down upon us. The ocean is flat and calm and along the coast, in the scooped-out coves, has turned to an icy slush. The brook that flows past our house is almost totally frozen and there is only a small channel of rushing water that flows openly at its very centre. When we let the cattle out to drink, we chop holes with the axe at the brook's edge so that they can drink without venturing onto the ice.

The sheep move in and out of their lean-to shelter restlessly stamping their feet or huddling together in tightly packed groups. A conspiracy of wool against the cold. The hens perch high on their roosts with their feathers fluffed out about them, hardly feeling it worthwhile to descend to the floor for their few scant kernels of grain. The pig, who has little time before his butchering, squeals his displeasure to the cold and with his snout tosses his wooden trough high in the icy air. The splendid young horse paws the planking of his stall and gnaws the wooden cribwork of his manger.

We have put a protective barricade of spruce boughs about our kitchen door and banked our house with additional boughs and billows of eel grass. Still, the pail of water we leave standing in the porch is solid in the morning and has to be broken with a hammer. The clothes my mother hangs on the line are frozen almost instantly and sway and creak from their suspending clothespins like sections of dismantled robots: the stiff-legged rasping trousers and the shirts and sweaters with unyielding arms outstretched. In the morning we race from our frigid upstairs bedrooms to finish dressing around the kitchen stove.

We would extend our coldness half a continent away to the Great Lakes of Ontario so that it might hasten the Christmas coming of my oldest brother, Neil. He is nineteen and employed on the "lake boats," the long flat carriers of grain and iron ore whose season ends any day after December 10, depending on the ice conditions. We wish it to be cold, cold on the Great Lakes of Ontario, so that he may come home to us as soon as possible. Already his cartons have arrived. They come from different places: Cobourg, Toronto, St. Catharines, Welland, Windsor, Sarnia, Sault Ste. Marie. Places that we, with the exception of my father, have never been. We locate them excitedly on the map, tracing their outlines with eager fingers. The cartons bear the lettering of Canada Steamship Lines, and are bound with rope knotted intricately in the fashion of sailors. My mother says they contain his "clothes" and we are not allowed to open them.

For us it is impossible to know the time or manner of his coming. If the lakes freeze early, he may come by train because it is cheaper. If the lakes stay open until December 20, he will have to fly because his time will be more precious than his money. He will hitchhike the last sixty or hundred miles from either station or airport. On our part, we can do nothing but listen with straining ears to radio reports of distant ice formations. His coming seems to depend on so many factors which are out there far beyond us and over which we lack control.

The days go by in fevered slowness until finally on the morning of December 23 the strange car rolls into our yard. My mother touches her hand to her lips and whispers "Thank God." My father gets up unsteadily from his chair to look through the window. Their longed-for son and our golden older brother is here at last. He is here with his reddish hair and beard and we can hear his hearty laugh. He will be happy and strong and confident for us all.

There are three other young men with him who look much the same as he. They too are from the boats and are trying to get home to Newfoundland. They must still drive a hundred miles to reach the ferry at North Sydney. The car seems very old. They purchased it in Thorold for two hundred dollars because they were too late to make any reservations, and they have driven steadily since they began. In northern New Brunswick their windshield wipers failed but instead of stopping they tied lengths of cord to the wipers' arms and passed them through the front window vents. Since that time, in whatever precipitation, one of them has pulled the cords back and forth to make the wipers function. This information falls tiredly but excitedly from their lips and we greedily gather it in. My father pours them drinks of rum and my mother takes out her mincemeat and the fruitcakes she has been carefully hoarding. We lean on the furniture or look from the safety of sheltered doorways. We would like to hug our brother but are too shy with strangers present. In the kitchen's warmth, the young men begin to nod and doze, their heads dropping suddenly to their chests. They nudge each other with their feet in an attempt to keep awake. They will not stay and rest because they have come so far and tomorrow is Christmas Eve and stretches of mountains and water still lie between them and those they love. After they leave we pounce upon our brother physically and verbally. He laughs and shouts and lifts us over his head and swings us in his muscular arms. Yet in spite of his happiness he seems surprised at the appearance of his father whom he has not seen since March. My father merely smiles at him while my mother bites her lip.

Now that he is here there is a great flurry of activity. We have left everything we could until the time he might be with us. Eagerly I show him the fir tree on the hill which I have been watching for months and marvel at how easily he fells it and carries it down the hill. We fall over one another in the excitement of decoration.

He promises that on Christmas Eve he will take us to church in the sleigh behind the splendid horse that until his coming we are all afraid to handle. And on the afternoon of Christmas Eve he shoes the horse, lifting each hoof and rasping it fine and hammering the cherry-red horseshoes into shape upon the anvil. Later he drops them hissingly into the steaming tub of water. My father sits beside him on an overturned pail and tells him what to do. Sometimes we argue with our father, but our brother does everything he says.

That night, bundled in hay and voluminous coats, and with heated stones at our feet, we start upon our journey. Our parents and Kenneth remain at home but all the rest of us go. Before we leave we feed the cattle and sheep and even the pig all that they can possibly eat so that they will be contented on Christmas Eve. Our parents wave to us from the doorway. We go four miles across the mountain road. It is a primitive logging trail and there will be no cars or other vehicles upon it. At first the horse is wild with excitement and lack of exercise and my brother has to stand at the front of the sleigh and lean backwards on the reins. Later he settles down to a trot and still later to a walk as the mountain rises before him. We sing all the Christmas songs we know and watch for the rabbits and foxes scudding across the open patches of snow and listen to the drumming of partridge wings. We are never cold.

When we descend to the country church we tie the horse in a grove of trees where he will be sheltered and not frightened by the many cars. We put a blanket over him and give him oats. At the church door the neighbours shake hands with my brother. "Hello, Neil," they say. "How is your father?"

"Oh," he says, just "Oh."

The church is very beautiful at night with its festooned branches and glowing candles and the booming, joyous sounds that come from the choir loft. We go through the service as if we are mesmerized.

On the way home, although the stones have cooled, we remain happy and warm. We listen to the creak of the leather harness and the hiss of runners on the snow and begin to think of the potentiality of presents. When we are about a mile from home the horse senses his destination and breaks into a trot and then into a confident lope. My brother lets him go and we move across the winter landscape like figures freed from a Christmas card. The snow from the horse's hooves falls about our heads like the whiteness of the stars.

After we have stabled the horse we talk with our parents and eat the meal our mother has prepared. And then I am sleepy and it is time for the younger children to be in bed. But tonight my father says to me, "We would like you to stay up with us a while," and so I stay quietly with the older members of my family.

When all is silent upstairs Neil brings in the cartons that contain his "clothes" and begins to open them. He unties the intricate knots quickly, their whorls falling away before his agile fingers. The boxes are filled with gifts neatly wrapped and bearing tags. The ones for my younger brothers say "from Santa Claus" but mine are not among them anymore, as I know with certainty they will never be again. Yet I am not so much surprised as touched by a pang of loss at being here on the adult side of the world. It is as if I have suddenly moved into another room and heard a door click lastingly behind me. I am jabbed by my own small wound.

But then I look at those before me. I look at my parents drawn together before the Christmas tree. My mother has her hand upon my father's shoulder and he is holding his ever-present handkerchief. I look at my sisters who have crossed this threshold ahead of me and now each day journey farther from the lives they knew as girls. I look at my magic older brother who has come to us this Christmas from half a continent away, bringing everything he has and is. All of them are captured in the tableau of their care.

"Every man moves on," says my father quietly, and I think he speaks of Santa Claus, "but there is no need to grieve. He leaves good things behind."

Shauna Singh Baldwin was born in Canada but raised in India. This story, which is included in a collection of her short stories, won an award from the Writers' Union of Canada.

Jassie

Shauna Singh Baldwin

I'll be sixty-five this month, and now I know I will die in a foreign land. The nurses are all very cheerful, and my daughter and her husband, who has blue eyes, come to visit me every day. At least, I think they come to visit me. My son-in-law's mother shares my room and there are times when I am not certain.

Elsie is a Christian woman, very frail, very pale. Me, I am brown and my skin is not as wrinkled. She tells me stories from her past but I have none to give her that she could understand. I only smile, and mostly we share silence and the magnolia tree outside. She calls me "Jessie," though my name is "Jassie," as all my teachers did, and she does not seem to know there is a difference. And in the evenings Ted, the big smiling black man whose talk I do not understand, comes to help us walk down the hall for the usual spiceless dinner.

On Sundays, they have mass on the loudspeaker, and I say the responses with Elsie, out of habit. "The Lord be with you. And also with you. Lift up your hearts. We lift them up to the Lord." But afterwards, I unwrap my old gutka with its handsewn cloth binding and I say the *Japji*. When I am bitter, I say it loud, as if I do not know the strange sounds bother her. Sometimes she asks me how it is I know the mass so well, and I answer that I went to a Christian school. Perhaps one day when she is forgetful, I may tell her some of my story to bring it into words.

We have little in common, Elsie and I. Only that we are both mothers, and our children are married. But motherhood is a word with many meanings.

In those days, many of us had two mothers, and some had more. The more mothers you had, the more rich and powerful your father must be, for each woman—wife or concubine—was expected to be housed and clothed and jewelled. And we, their children, must be schooled in the best of schools—missionary schools, with uniforms and English lessons.

My birth mother was a full wife, married with all the rites of the Anand Karaj ceremony, at sixteen. My other mother was the wife whose failure no one ever mentioned, out of kindness. I was raised to show respect and love for both mothers, and I did so gladly, for both women loved me as their own. This was difficult for white women who had never known the love of children to understand.

Oh, they meant well. I would not have you think that I did not respect my teachers—but they wanted us to follow their ways. I remember most particularly how important was the filling in of forms. "Mother's Name" was written in one box. But for this, I had devised a fair solution. I would give my mothers turns. I had only two, so this was easy.

"Mother's Maiden Name" was more difficult, for our custom was to change a woman's first name to one of her husband's choosing. But the last name of a Sikh woman remains the same, from birth to death—Kaur, meaning princess. I knew the maiden name of my birth mother (it was tattooed midway up her forearm, and she wore a watch with its face turned inward to cover the blue smudge when in company of Europeans, out of respect for their customs and sensibilities), but I knew not the maiden name of my father's first wife, she being married too young to remember it. So when it came her turn, I would write her married name, Krishnawanti, as her maiden name and hope she would forgive the lie. I would not have anyone believe she had kept a name not of her husband's choosing.

It wasn't as if they did not know and practice our customs, for were they not the several wives of a dead and risen God? And how were they different from the thousand consorts of Krishna, the God of the Hindus? Their senior-most wife was always given most respect; she was called Mother Superior. But my senior mother could not be acknowledged. Oh, it made me angry, then and now.

But I would not say this to Elsie, for I would not have her think I am ungrateful for the teachings of these women. I wondered often if their families had cast them out or if they, realizing their sin of barrenness, had exiled themselves in shame and penance? In later years they told me they chose their exile, but I am not convinced. Widows, even widows of Gods, are not the ones who choose.

In their church on Sundays, with the chants that sounded all the same, burning foreign-smelling incense in the land of incense, they asked us to pray for the health of the Pope and all the bishops and archbishops, although these men were not their husbands. I felt these men were those who had power over my teachers, so I prayed—but not to their God—that they would be generous.

I like to watch the soap operas; they are like the *Ramayan* and the *Mahabharat*— they go on and on. There are some days when I want to be sure there are stories that never end. Elsie likes classical music and says the TV bothers her; it has too much violence.

I say, that is not the kind of violence one should fear. The kind of violence one should fear is always quiet and comes all wrapped up in words like Love until you live with it daily and you value only that which is valuable to the violator.

We were taught to speak like proper British ladies. "No sing-song," said Mother Francis, as we chorused speeches from Shakespeare and poems by Kipling. On the streets our people sang "Bande Mataram" and the truck drivers carried explosives from roadside tea stalls to the Indian National Army. "My Lord, child. Can't you learn to say 'victory,' not 'wictory'?" Mother Mary of Grace said, while in the temples the Brahmins received a family's lifelong savings as prayashchit—penance for having fought the white man's war. At assembly we would sing, "Jesus loves me, this I know, For the Bible tells me so," while the Tagore poem that was to become our national anthem was whispered by poor wretches in prison, "Janta Gana Mana." We learned we should be grateful for the telegraph and the trains and two hundred years of civilizing rule, while Shiva danced the dance of death on trains that carried Muslims one way, Hindus and Sikhs the other. We learned ballroom dancing from Mother Agatha, the red ribbons in our long heavy black braids flying out behind us, while the British packed away their brollies and shipped home rent-free.

Ted says he is not black, he is African-American. And slowly I am beginning to understand him. I have read about Martin Luther King and how he had a dream and then how he was killed, but Ted says his people are still fighting for their rights. I told him it would be easy if the only fight were against a conqueror, against history.

If you believe that everything that ever happened had to happen or you wouldn't be here, then you would believe that ballroom dancing led me to betray my husband before I met him. And then you would know that I deserve my pain and even to die in a foreign land. Mother Agatha said we should have a "social," to practice. And so I met Firoze. Blue-blazered, with his Eton-like school tie, a "proper gentleman," said Mother Agatha approvingly. When she said we came from the same background, she meant we both knew English history and none of our own, that we both expected servants to have darker skin than our own. But this is not enough, even today, with which to arrange a marriage in India. The ballroom dancing stopped when Firoze's family left for Pakistan.

The man my father chose for me instead was a good man, slight of build, quiet and kind. He was the son of Sikh landowners, had a missionary education but no connections. I thought he had no business sense, either, when he opened a shop to sell khadi cloth. I told him no one would buy cloth made in India; everyone wanted cloth made on machines in Manchester. But he believed Gandhi had been his best salesman, and he was right. Every newly elected Indian politician came to our shop to buy khadi.

My father gave my husband a house in old Delhi as my dowry, and my husband gave me first this daughter for my old age and then two sons. I named my daughter with a Muslim name, Yasmeen, in memory of Firoze. Yasmeen Kaur. My Sikh family blushed for me and ever after called her Minni.

Minni comes to visit and she has brought me gulabjamuns, those big, fat, perfectly rounded light brown sweets. But my arthritis is so painful today I cannot hold them in my hands, and she has to feed me as I used to feed her. Her husband stands at his mother's bed and jokes how he will take us both dancing next weekend. I feel pain just to think of it and Elsie smiles faintly. He reminds me of a movie star, big, white and unafraid. Minni is small and quick and dark next to him and her voice reminds me of Mother Ursula's clipped English tones. My husband, thinking to please me, sent her to England to study, but now I am irritated when I realize it is her accent my son-in-law finds *so* attractive.

Elsie was married many years but she talks very little about her husband. She says he was a policeman and she worried every day of their marriage that he would be killed. I didn't worry about my husband, only about my sons. They were both in the army when the second war with Pakistan broke out. They were the first to be sent to the front, perhaps because they were Sikhs and not Hindus. I wondered sometimes if they fought with Firoze's sons.

It doesn't matter now; they are both gone.

After we had given two sons, we sold the khadi store and came away as far as we could fly. Minnie welcomed us both, as a dutiful daughter should. But it is cold in America. A coldness of the soul that my husband never became accustomed to. I was cold to him, too—I had never been otherwise. My warmth was left in India, where I earned this pain ballroom dancing to the convent's Steinway with Firoze.

Despite my son-in-law's joking, Elsie is not going dancing next weekend. In fact, I had to strain to hear her breathing last night. Ted came in and helped the nurse to put an oxygen mask over her face, but it hurts her and she tries to do without it. I am able to sit up today and her voice is very faint. "Jessie, will you sit next to me? I think I am having an anxiety attack." I have to manoeuvre my walker over to her side of the room and then lower myself into the chair next to her bed. She is "perspiring profusely," as Mother Conrad would have put it.

"I'm glad you're here, Jessie," she says.

And then, very faintly, she says, "Jessie, will you pray with me?"

I want to say, "My name is Jassie, not Jessie. You would not understand my prayers, and you don't like to hear me speak Punjabi, and you need Christian prayers, not mine."

But this is not the time and she is not the women to whom I want to say the words. I take her rosary from the bedpost and say, "Our Father, who art in Heaven … "

I wonder, could I have learned the namaaz as easily as I learned the rosary?

Additional Essays

What Your Body Language Says about You

Gerald Astor

1   "Your lips say, 'No, no, no,' but your eyes say, 'Yes, yes, yes'" is a line from an old popular song. It may sound somewhat phony, but the author was hinting at that kind of nonverbal communication known as body language. It can reflect a person's views more accurately than any words coming from his or her mouth.

2   Body language covers the infinite range of facial and body movements, including the myriad ways to smile, to walk, to manipulate your eyes, to move your hands and arms. We draw messages from body language, whether it's the "no" that a shake of the head conveys, the "I'm not interested" that a turning away of the head can suggest, or the "Hey, I'm bad" statement Richard Pryor and Gene Wilder expected their swaggers to make in *Stir Crazy*. Sometimes, the messages are conveyed through deliberate, conscious gestures; other times, our bodies talk without our even knowing. But conscious or not, our body language helps us portray a wide range of feelings, including boredom, amusement, impatience, fatigue, concentration, interest, puzzlement, and embarrassment.

3   Some of our body-language expressions are common idioms. To most people, for example, the thumb and forefinger forming a circle means "Everything's okay." A fist with the thumb pointing up is "Good luck" or "All systems go." Desmond Morris, a behavioral scientist and the author of *The Naked Ape* (McGraw-Hill), was among those who studied the interpretations of twenty specific gestures by people in Europe, North Africa, and the Middle East. He found similarities in understanding despite the geographic and cultural differences. (The most universally recognized signal was the thumb at the tip of the nose with the fingers spread!)

4   Body language becomes more complicated when we try to translate the movements, postures, and facial expressions that a person has little or no control over—the actions that spring from the dark well within us, our unconscious. These bits of body language are often subtle, may contradict our words, and frequently involve a series of actions.

5   The eyes are one of the most revealing instruments of body language. Keith, seventeen, from Montclair, New Jersey, learned the hard way about one message the eyes can convey. "I had a teacher who graded heavily on classroom discussion," Keith says. "He seemed to have a weird ability to know just when I didn't have the answers. I couldn't figure out how he could be so sharp. Then it dawned on me. Whenever I didn't know the answer, I would avoid looking at him. When I did know what to say, I always stared straight back at him. From that moment on, I taught myself to look him in the eye, whether I knew the work or not. That trick has saved me a lot of grief."

6   Many people, including some policemen, believe eye contact is a good test of honesty. If someone can't look you dead in the eye, then he or she is not playing straight, they insist. After many experiments, however, a number of experts have concluded that good liars can fake eye contact. (If you still believe that a chap staring straight into your baby blues will never lie to you, then someday, I'd like to interest you in a share of the Grand Canyon.)

7   Eye contact, though not a sure sign of honesty, is a clear way to show interest in another person. When a person looks at you and continues to do so, you know his attention is focused on you. When he turns his head away, his mind is probably elsewhere: you are no longer "numero uno." But there are exceptions. A shy person may have trouble making and maintaining eye contact, no matter how interested he is in the other person. And certain nationalities, such as the British and the Germans, are much less oriented to eyeball-to-eyeball encounters than, say, the French and the Arabs.

8   When the eyes act in concert with other parts of the face, communication becomes increasingly explicit. In a study in which psychologists A. Thayer and W. Schiff showed a series of facial diagrams to a panel of people, there was very strong agreement on the messages (the results of their study were published in the *American Journal of Psychology* in 1969). Pleasure widens the eyes and is usually accompanied by a smile. Thus, poker players who are dealt a good hand must learn to control their body language and develop a "poker face." The "drop dead" or "if looks could kill" expression is produced by wrinkling the eyebrows, narrowing the eyes, and turning down the corners of the mouth. Surprise sends the eyebrows skyward and widens the gaze. Despair hoods the eyes, makes the mouth droop, and often causes the entire body to slump.

9   Like the eyes, the smile is remarkably varied. The genuinely happy smile flashes both upper and lower teeth and is accompanied by open eyes and relaxed brows. In the sheepish smile—you've spilled your soda pop and that nice fellow offers his help—the corners of the mouth are turned up, the eyebrows lifted. The fiendish smile consists of a wide grin and a scrunching of the eyebrows.

10   Hand movements are another area where there is common understanding of the action. Shake your fist, and everyone realizes that you're angry. Rub your palms together, and you're probably anticipating something good. Rub your palms and the backs of your hands, and you're probably just cold. Point, and you are signaling a direction. Point a finger at someone, and you're making an accusation.

11   Sometimes a person brings a hand up to his mouth while talking. That gesture could be an effort to stop others from hearing or an unconscious admission of doubt or that there's something being concealed. A hand at the throat may indicate some uncertainty about the words being spoken.

12   Politicians frequently use hand movements to hold the attention of an audience. Former President Gerald Ford, regarded as a less than spellbinding orator, was once counseled by advisers to add a number of gestures to punctuate a speech. He did so—but apparently unsuccessfully. A poll of those who listened revealed that one third agreed with Ford, one third disagreed, and one third were so distracted by his gesticulations that they didn't know what he had said. Artificial movements are the bad grammar of body language and confuse listeners (which is why some politicians and actors rely on experts to coach them in effective nonverbal communication).

13   One of the most clearly recognized expressions of body language is the handshake. (It is believed that originally a handshake was a way of showing a person that one came unarmed.) We draw information from the quality of the squeeze. A flabby grip suggests weakness or a lack of interest. Too much pressure signals a desire to dominate.

14   The position of the entire body is also important when interpreting nonverbal communication. "When I meet someone sitting with his legs or ankles crossed tightly and his arms folded over his chest, I feel that he's closed off from me and uninterested," says sixteen-year-old Julie, a Brooklyn high school senior. She has correctly interpreted a posture that translators of body language classify as "closed." If an individual feels relaxed, giving, and receptive, he's usually in an "open position": His arms are unclasped, and his legs apart.

15   Closed positions tend to discourage intruders. And as Marianne La France and Clara Mayo, the authors of *Moving Bodies* (Wadsworth) note, anyone in this posture is also far less likely to be convincing in a discussion; listeners may feel he's not revealing as much as he should. It's important, though, to keep in mind that whether or not a person assumes a closed or open position may have a lot to do with upbringing. Women, for example, because of the female tradition of wearing skirts, have customarily been taught to assume a "ladylike" position and keep their legs together (though that may be changing with the growing acceptance of women wearing pants).

16   Of course, there are other communicative postures besides the closed and open positions. For example, resting the chin upon the hand—the posture of Rodin's sculpture "The Thinker"—is an accepted sign of cogitation. But, says Ellen, an eighteen-year-old from New York, "When a person rests his cheek on his hand, it can mean, 'I'm uninterested.'"

17   Posture—indeed, all of body language—is wrapped up in a person's self-image. People uncomfortable with their bodies may adopt a round-shouldered slouch and wear baggy clothes. People who are content with their self-image are more likely to stand straight and wear form-fitting apparel.

18   Body language can also serve as a kind of dialogue between two people. For example, if two people sit on a couch with their arms and legs in similar positions, it usually means they're in agreement. A man and a woman on the same couch who have adopted widely different ways of sitting and who are not looking at one another are probably out of touch with each other. A male and female sitting on a couch, facing each other, are announcing closeness. If one leans forward, that one is trying to get even closer. If the other is not interested in more involvement, he or she may lean back.

19   But once again, cultural differences play a role. Wendy, a high school junior from Scarsdale whose parents are Korean and who spent her first years of life in Korea, says, "I don't like showing signs of closeness in public. I feel uncomfortable greeting people at a party with a hug or kiss. I wasn't brought up that way." Those unaware of the cultural differences might mistakenly read her body language as a sign of aloofness or coldness.

20   Other mistakes are common when trying to translate body language. Says Kathy, a seventeen-year-old from New York, "When someone just spreads himself out, I can't tell whether he's terribly relaxed or just a slob." When an adolescent slouches in front of an adult, it may be a rebellious statement (parents are always demanding that one stand up straight), or it may be that the person is very much at ease.

21   But although you can never fully understand another's body language—or fully control your own—you can be aware that nonverbal cues are as important to communication as words. Increase your knowledge of body language, and you'll be a little less confused in a world of many different messages.

In the Market for a Mate? Shop Around

H.J. Barrie

1   If you are going on 60 and it is five years since your wife died, and you are tired of living alone, or if you would like a little romance in your life, or if you just want someone to play Scrabble with on Sunday night, forget the singles bars, church basements, agony column and Fred Astaire's dancing classes. Think supermarkets.

2   There is no other place where you can study the fair sex in its natural habitat so closely and few places where you can so easily strike up a conversation without causing offence. A great tide of women flows through the aisles all day long, and with very little trouble, you can find out a lot about a prospective partner before you even try to strike up an acquaintance. For any lonely male who would like to take advantage of this suggestion, here are a few tips.

3   The day of the week is important. You will be looking for a woman with time on her hands, and you won't find her pushing through the crowds on the week-

ends. Her presence on Monday may mean that she is incapable of catering for more than a few days at a time and does not know that the vegetables will not be very fresh. Tuesday is a very good day.

4   You are not hoping for a raving beauty; you just want someone with a face and figure you can live with, and you may have to wait some time. Buy a paper and find a seat at the entrance where people pick up their shopping carts. When a likely prospect comes through the swinging doors, look for an easy move, a woman who has a quarter handy and does not have to spend two minutes rummaging through an untidy bag. Watch to see if she gets hysterical when she puts in her quarter and the carts remain jammed together, but remember that many good women wait for male aid when there is any sort of a mechanical problem, so you should respond accordingly.

5   Now you follow her discreetly down the aisles. You will soon find out if she lives alone. If she buys a seven-pound bag of potatoes, you will know that she either has company at home or is oblivious to the smell of rotting potatoes in the cupboard under the sink. Look for someone who buys a handful of French beans, two Spanish onions, two avocados and an aubergine. If she buys lobok, nappa or escarole, she is probably well travelled and maybe an inventive cook or a good conversationalist. Buying raspberries and asparagus in December will indicate a woman expensive to feed, and this will be confirmed by asking for 150 grams of rainbow trout without asking the price.

6   Watch her at the cheese counter. Extra old cheddar is good; spiced cheeses are bad. In every aisle you will find out more about her character and tastes. If she buys potatoes in a tin, go back to the entrance and try again. Do not follow her down the aisle reserved for women's concerns. It is none of your business, and you can always take a peek into her basket at the checkout counter. She may have a daughter at college.

7   The meat section is important. If she buys two big filet mignon steaks, her Sunday evenings are probably spoken for. Oxtails are good; a big family pack of chicken wings is bad. Does she go up and down the aisles methodically or does she reach the yogurt and then have to dash back to the peanut butter?

8   Bread is important, not for any theoretical reasons but to determine how much your tastes lie in common. Does she buy a French stick or dark rye? Too much unground cereal is a warning sign, big bags of chips a no-no.

9   Watch her as she passes the paperback rack. If she slips a bodice-ripper into her cart, it is not a good sign unless you have similar proclivities.

10   When she approaches the checkout counter, watch to see if she is sufficiently alert to choose the one with the most efficient cashier. Now is the time to make up your mind. Do not wait until you discover whether she can find the opening in the plastic bags. It will be too late then.

11   Do not expect perfection. Such a thing is not possible. Just add up the pros and cons and come to a decision. It is always reversible. If you give yourself the go-ahead, arrange a slight collision and after the apology say, "We seem to have similar tastes." One look at your cart will send her the message, and if she is looking for someone to play Scrabble with, the conversation may continue.

12   If you get an unmistakeable brushoff, go back to the entrance for another try, replacing on the shelves as you go the handful of French beans, two Spanish onions, five potatoes and the big pack of chicken wings.

Lingophobia ... Anxiety of Choice

Arthur Black

1   Do you have trouble with languages—other than the one we're using right now, I mean? Lingophobia seems to be the anxiety of choice these days. I hear people muttering about the French on the back of the cereal box. I run across other folks gnashing their dentures over the unreadability of "Japanified" assembly instructions that come with their "so-easy-a-child-could-put-it-together" barbecues.

2   Well, pas de probleme, ami. I'm here to convince you that you are a linguistic whiz. Bilingual? You're multilingual—polylingual even. Before you leave this page I'll have you nattering in Japanese, Mandarin, Ojibway, Malaysian, Iroquoiian, German, and Spanish. Best of all, I won't be teaching you—you already know this stuff.

3   Let's start by examining the status quo. I don't want to feed your ego but the fact is you're no ignoramus. Without going into the pros and cons, conducting a referendum, or issuing an ultimatum, it's safe to say that you have already mastered a substantial chunk of foreign language you may never have studied in school.

4   You understood that last paragraph, didn't you? It contained eight unadulterated Latin words—which is but a fraction of the Latin words you use every day. Each time you enter an "arena" or a "stadium," try to shoot under "par" on the golf course, read "propaganda" about a "moratorium" or shake your head about the number of "major" and "minor" penalties called in a match that featured one team "versus" another ... you might as well be having a chat with Cicero.

5   You speak French too—and not just the obvious imports like chaise lounge, filet mignon, and bouquet but also words like envelope, hotel, and prairie.

6   You speak Greek of course (everything from asbestos to zoology) and Dutch (cookies, coleslaw, waffles). You know German (sauerkraut, noodles, pretzels, hamburgers). You have a little Swedish (smorgasbord), a good deal of Indian patter (papoose, toboggan, moccasin, wigwam, raccoon)—why you even have a smattering of Arabic (zero, algebra, assassin). Why, it's enough to make a guy run amok (Malaysian) or even go berserk (Old Norse).

7   Anyway, I think you get my point. If you're bad at language, then Wayne Gretzky wears tube skates. You're a regular walking Tower of Babel, chum. But here's a couple of tips that will make your command of languages even more impressive.

8   Some foreign linguistic trivia first: Know what the Hawaiians call an itsy-bitsy reef-dwelling fish about as long as your thumb?

9   They call him (or her) "humohumokunokuapuaa."

10   Know what those same Hawaiians call another fish—a boxcar-sized denizen of the deep that's big enough to swallow your surfboard sideways?

11   They call him "O."

12 Foreign linguistic trivia, subsection: traffic signs. Did I mention that your command of Jamaican patois would leave Harry Belafonte gaping in amazement? Of course it would. What would you realize if you were driving into Kingston and saw a road sign warning: "No uovatek naar pass"—that it was against the law to overtake or pass, naturally. Say, you've really got a gift for this sort of thing, haven't you?

13 But enough bantering. I promised you some helpful language tips and it's time to deliver. Here's one: In Spanish there is an endlessly useful phrase that wins friends, melts hearts, and may even get the other hombre to buy the next round of Fundador. The phrase means "That's right" or "You've got it!" People—Spanish or otherwise—love to be told that they're brilliant. In Spanish the phrase is: "Eso si qeue es!" But forget that. All you have to remember is what you wear between your shoes and your bare bunions—socks—and spell it out. S-O-C-K-S.

14 Perfectamente.

15 Japanese? A snap. Want to say "You're welcome"? It's "dooitashimaskite." You'll get by if you say "Don't touch my moustache"—real fast. Similarly you should remember that when you say "hi" in Japanese you are really saying "yes" (hai); when you want to say "Good Morning" just think of the state of Ohio (okayo)—and remember too that the word "Mother" in Japanese is "ha-ha."

16 That shouldn't be hard to remember—just think of your mother-in-law.

17 Ooops. My Olivetti is registering Plus Nine on the Richter Scale—I forgot the Old Coot was staying with us. Have to run. For my life. Sayonara, muchachos.

Don't You Think It's Time to Start Thinking?

Northrop Frye

1 A student often leaves high school today without any sense of language as a structure.

2 He may also have the idea that reading and writing are elementary skills that he mastered in childhood, never having grasped the fact that there are differences in levels of reading and writing as there are in mathematics between short division and integral calculus.

3 Yet, in spite of his limited verbal skills, he firmly believes that he can think, that he has ideas, and that if he is just given the opportunity to express them he will be all right. Of course, when you look at what he's written you find it doesn't make any sense. When you tell him this he is devastated.

4 Part of his confusion here stems from the fact that we use the word "think" in so many bad, punning ways. Remember James Thurber's Walter Mitty who was always dreaming great dreams of glory. When his wife asked him what he was doing he would say, "Has it ever occurred to you that I might be thinking?"

5 But, of course, he wasn't thinking at all. Because we use it for everything our minds do, worrying, remembering, day-dreaming, we imagine that thinking is something that can be achieved without any training. But again it's a matter of practice. How well we can think depends on how much of it we have already done. Most students need to be taught, very carefully and patiently, that there is no such thing as an inarticulate idea waiting to have the right words wrapped around it.

6   They have to learn that ideas do not exist until they have been incorporated into words. Until that point you don't know whether you are pregnant or just have gas on the stomach.

7   The operation of thinking is the practice of articulating ideas until they are in the right words. And we can't think at random either. We can only add one more idea to the body of something we have already thought about. Most of us spend very little time doing this, and that is why there are so few people whom we regard as having any power to articulate at all. When such a person appears in public life, like Mr. Trudeau, we tend to regard him as possessing a gigantic intellect.

8   A society like ours doesn't have very much interest in literacy. It is compulsory to read and write because society must have docile and obedient citizens. We are taught to read so that we can obey the traffic signs and to cipher so that we can make out our income tax, but development of verbal competency is very much left to the individual.

9   And when we look at our day-to-day existence we can see that there are strong currents at work against the development of powers of articulateness. Young adolescents today often betray a curious sense of shame about speaking articulately, of framing a sentence with a period at the end of it.

10   Part of the reason for this is the powerful anti-intellectual drive which is constantly present in our society. Articulate speech marks you out as an individual, and in some settings this can be rather dangerous because people are often suspicious and frightened of articulateness. So if you say as little as possible and use only stereotyped, ready-made phrases you can hide yourself in the mass.

11   Then there are various epidemics sweeping over society which use unintelligibility as a weapon to preserve the present power structure. By making things as unintelligible as possible, to as many people as possible, you can hold the present power structure together. Understanding and articulateness lead to its destruction. This is the kind of thing that George Orwell was talking about, not just in *Nineteen Eighty-Four*, but in all his work on language. The kernel of everything reactionary and tyrannical in society is the impoverishment of the means of verbal communication.

12   The vast majority of things that we hear today are prejudices and clichés, simply verbal formulas that have no thought behind them but are put up as a pretence of thinking. It is not until we realize these things conceal meaning, rather than reveal it, that we can begin to develop our own powers of articulateness.

13   The teaching of humanities is, therefore, a militant job. Teachers are faced not simply with a mass of misconceptions and unexamined assumptions. They must engage in a fight to help the student confront and reject the verbal formulas and stock responses, to convert passive acceptance into active, constructive power. It is a fight against illiteracy and for the maturation of the mental process, for the development of skills which once acquired will never become obsolete.

Back to the Land? No Way—Big Cities Are Here to Stay

John Kettle

1 Although Canada has grown steadily more urban throughout its history, people still think Canadians really want to live in the country.

2 Canada once was undeniably rural, if not downright wild. Yet ever since the first census we have known that Canadians have been leaving the land and heading for city pleasures.

3 Recently, demographers believed the trend was reversing: Former city dwellers were thought to be discovering the delights of rural simplicity.

4 Nothing of the kind occurred.

5 It is not just that urban life has proved to be more appealing than rural—the biggest cities have grown the fastest, making clear that what Canadians like is city life as full and complex as it can be.

6 Take just the nine largest cities in Canada: Vancouver, Edmonton, Calgary, Winnipeg, Hamilton, Toronto, Ottawa–Hull, Montreal and Quebec City. In 1931, they had less than one-third of the population. Now they house about half of it.

7 But there is more to it than that. At a certain point a city advances to a higher status, not just home to a lot of people but a magnet that draws touring players, resident symphony orchestras, art galleries, architecture, great restaurants, and the visitors who would never venture to a big town that was simply big. The city becomes a metropolis.

8 At least a third of a million people, probably as many as half a million today, are needed to support the kind of metropolitan arts, shops and shows that attract tourists. Once a metropolis gets to that point, it is close to being self-sustaining— famous for being famous. It is visited because it has so many visitors. It also becomes an exciting place to live.

9 In 1931, only 18 per cent of the population lived in cities with populations of half a million or more. In fact, only Montreal and Toronto were in that giant category. Now all nine top cities have at least half a million people and can plausibly claim to be successful and glittering metropolises rather than just places inhabited by a lot of people.

10 So what of all the talk in the big metropolises about people driven out of town by high real-estate prices, rising crime rates and pollution?

11 Well, the truth is that when people say such things, they don't quit Vancouver and move to Prince Rupert, or pull up stakes in Montreal and head for Trois Pistoles. They move just as far as it takes to find less-expensive housing, and certainly not beyond commuting distance. They like to stay in the local phone-call area. They want cable TV and the metropolitan newspaper, the chance to go into town for an afternoon's shopping, or the major-league ball game, or dinner and an evening at the theatre. If they want to be less intensely urban, they certainly don't want to be rural.

12   The fastest-growing areas of the country are those that ring the main cities. The boundaries of Greater Vancouver and the Montreal Urban Community are not surrounded by fields but by more urbanization. With a population of 3.8 million, the urbanized area that surrounds downtown Toronto (what Statistics Canada defines as the Toronto metropolitan area) stretches farther afield than the political entity of Metropolitan Toronto and much farther than the City of Toronto. It houses 1.5 million more people than Metro, and three million more than the city—where almost all the metropolitan glamour is located. These millions may be people who don't want to live in Toronto, but they don't want to get too far away from it, either.

13   The Canadian metropolises continue to attract immigrants and the young, and for much the same reason as always. Because these are world-renowned cities. Because they are still where the jobs are. Where young people have the best chance of meeting other young people. Where the fun is, and the rarer and more elegant things to buy, and the more exciting things to do.

14   The big metropolises—Montreal, Toronto and Vancouver—house the national media, too. The media, reflecting the interests and values of the people they know, produce programming and content that are essentially metropolitan. And this becomes the national norm. How're you going to keep 'em down on the farm after they've seen TV?

15   With all that going for them, you can expect the nine metropolises to go on spreading. It wouldn't be surprising if in another 20 years they were home to two-thirds of the population. The metropolitan way of life has arrived.

A Modest Proposal

For Preventing the Children of Poor People in Ireland from Being a Burden
to Their Parents or Country, and for Making Them Beneficial to the Public

Jonathan Swift

1   It is a melancholy object to those who walk through this great town or travel in the country, when they see the streets, the roads, and cabin doors, crowded with beggars of the female sex, followed by three, four, or six children, all in rags and importuning every passenger for an alms. These mothers, instead of being able to work for their honest livelihood, are forced to employ all their time in strolling to beg sustenance for their helpless infants, who, as they grow up, either turn thieves for want of work, or leave their dear native country to fight for the Pretender in Spain, or sell themselves to the Barbadoes.

2   I think it is agreed by all parties that this prodigious number of children in the arms, or on the backs, or at the heels of their mothers, and frequently of their fathers, is in the present deplorable state of the kingdom a very great additional grievance; and therefore whoever could find out a fair, cheap, and easy method of making these children sound, useful members of the commonwealth would deserve so well of the public as to have his statue set up for a preserver of the nation.

3   But my intention is very far from being confined to provide only for the children of professed beggars; it is of a much greater extent, and shall take in the whole number of infants at a certain age who are born of parents in effect as little able to support them as those who demand our charity in the streets.

4   As to my own part, having turned my thoughts for many years upon this important subject, and maturely weighed the several schemes of other projectors, I have always found them grossly mistaken in their computation. It is true, a child just dropped from its dam may be supported by her milk for a solar year, with little other nourishment; at most not above the value of two shillings, which the mother may certainly get, or the value in scraps, by her lawful occupation of begging; and it is exactly at one year old that I propose to provide for them in such a manner as instead of being a charge upon their parents or the parish, or wanting food and raiment for the rest of their lives, they shall on the contrary contribute to the feeding, and partly to the clothing, of many thousands.

5   There is likewise another great advantage in my scheme, that it will prevent those voluntary abortions, and that horrid practice of women murdering their bastard children, alas, too frequent among us, sacrificing the poor innocent babes, I doubt, more to avoid the expense than the shame, which would move tears and pity in the most savage and inhuman breast.

6   The number of souls in this kingdom being usually reckoned one million and a half, of these I calculate there may be about two hundred thousand couples whose wives are breeders; from which number I subtract thirty thousand couples who are able to maintain their own children, although I apprehend there cannot be so many under the present distresses of the kingdom; but this being granted, there will remain an hundred and seventy thousand breeders. I again subtract fifty thousand for those women who miscarry, or whose children die by accident or disease within the year. There only remain an hundred and twenty thousand children of poor parents annually born. The question therefore is, how this number shall be reared and provided for, which, as I have already said, under the present situation of affairs, is utterly impossible by all the methods hitherto proposed. For we can neither employ them in handicraft or agriculture; we neither build houses (I mean in the country) nor cultivate land. They can very seldom pick up a livelihood by stealing till they arrive at six years old, except where they are of towardly parts; although I confess they learn the rudiments much earlier, during which time they can however be looked upon only as probationers, as I have been informed by a principal gentlemen in the county of Cavan, who protested to me that he never knew above one or two instances under the age of six, even in a part of the kingdom so renowned for the quickest proficiency in that art.

7   I am assured by our merchants that a boy or girl before twelve years old is no salable commodity; and even when they come to this age they will not yield above three pounds, or three pounds and half a crown at most on the Exchange; which cannot turn to account either to the parents or the kingdom, the charge of nutriment and rags having been at least four times that value.

8   I shall now therefore humbly propose my own thoughts, which I hope will not be liable to the least objection.

9   I have been assured by a very knowing American of my acquaintance in London, that a young healthy child well nursed is at a year old a most delicious, nourishing, and wholesome food, whether stewed, roasted, baked or boiled; and I make no doubt that it will equally serve in a fricassee or a ragout.

10   I do therefore humbly offer it to public consideration that of the hundred and twenty thousand children, already computed, twenty thousand may be reserved for breed, whereof only one fourth part to be males, which is more than we allow to sheep, black cattle, or swine; and my reason is that these children are seldom the fruits of marriage, a circumstance not much regarded by our savages, therefore one male will be sufficient to serve four females. That the remaining hundred thousand may at a year old be offered in sale to the persons of quality and fortune through the kingdom, always advising the mother to let them suck plentifully in the last month, so as to render them plump and fat for a good table. A child will make two dishes at an entertainment for friends; and when the family dines alone, the fore or hind quarter will make a reasonable dish, and seasoned with a little pepper or salt will be very good boiled on the fourth day, especially in winter.

11   I have reckoned upon a medium that a child just born will weigh twelve pounds, and in a solar year if tolerably nursed increaseth to twenty-eight pounds.

12   I grant this food will be somewhat dear, and therefore very proper for landlords, who, as they have already devoured most of the parents, seem to have the best title to the children.

13   Infant's flesh will be in season throughout the year, but more plentiful in March, and a little before and after. For we are told by a grave author, an eminent French physician, that fish being a prolific diet, there are more children born in Roman Catholic countries about nine months after Lent than at any other season: therefore, reckoning a year after Lent, the markets will be more glutted than usual, because the number of popish infants is at least three to one in this kingdom; and therefore it will have one other collateral advantage, by lessening the number of Papists among us.

14   I have already computed the charge of nursing a beggar's child (in which list I reckon all cottagers, labourers, and four fifths of the farmers) to be about two shillings per annum, rags included: and I believe no gentleman would repine to give ten shillings for the carcass of a good fat child, which, as I have said, will make four dishes of excellent nutritive meat, when he hath only some particular friend or his own family to dine with him. Thus the squire will learn to be a good landlord, and grow popular among the tenants; the mother will have eight shillings net profit, and be fit for work till she produces another child.

15   Those who are more thrifty (as I must confess the times require) may flay the carcass; the skin of which artificially dressed will make admirable gloves for ladies, and summer boots for fine gentlemen.

16   As to our city of Dublin, shambles may be appointed for this purpose in the most convenient parts of it, and butchers we may be assured will not be wanting; although I rather recommend buying the children alive, and dressing them hot from the knife as we do roasting pigs.

17   A very worthy person, a true lover of his country, and whose virtues I highly esteem, was lately pleased in discoursing on this matter to offer a refinement upon my scheme. He said that many gentlemen of this kingdom, having of late destroyed their deer, he conceived that the want of venison might be well supplied by the bodies of young lads and maidens, not exceeding fourteen years of age nor under twelve, so great a number of both sexes in every county being now ready to starve for want of work and service; and these to be disposed of by their parents, if alive, or otherwise by their nearest relations. But with due deference to so excellent a friend and so deserving a patriot, I cannot be altogether in his sentiments; for as to the males, my American acquaintance assured me from frequent experience that their flesh was generally tough and lean, like that of our schoolboys, by continual exercise, and their taste disagreeable; and to fatten them would not answer the charge. Then as to the females, it would, I think with humble submission, be a loss to the public, because they soon would become breeders themselves: and besides, it is not improbable that some scrupulous people might be apt to censure such a practice (although indeed very unjustly) as a little bordering upon cruelty; which, I confess, hath always been with me the strongest objection against any project, how well soever intended.

18   But in order to justify my friend, he confessed that this expedient was put into his head by the famous Psalmanazar, a native of the island Formosa, who came from thence to London above twenty years ago, and in conversation told my friend that in his country when any young person happened to be put to death, the executioner sold the carcass to persons of quality as a prime dainty; and that in his time the body of a plump girl of fifteen, who was crucified for an attempt to poison the emperor, was sold to his Imperial Majesty's prime minister of state, and other great mandarins of the court, in joints from the gibbet, at four hundred crowns. Neither indeed can I deny that if the same use were made of several plump young girls in this town, who without one single groat to their fortunes cannot stir abroad without a chair, and appear at the playhouse and assemblies in foreign fineries which they never will pay for, the kingdom would not be the worse.

19   Some persons of a desponding spirit are in great concern about that vast number of poor people who are aged, diseased, or maimed, and I have been desired to employ my thoughts what course may be taken to ease the nation of so grievous an encumbrance. But I am not in the least pain upon that matter, because it is very well known that they are every day dying and rotting by cold and famine, and filth and vermin, as fast as can be reasonably expected. And as to the younger labourers, they are now in almost as hopeful a condition. They cannot get work, and consequently pine away from want of nourishment to a degree that if at any time they are accidentally hired to common labour, they have not strength to perform it; and thus the country and themselves are happily delivered from the evils to come.

20   I have too long digressed, and therefore shall return to my subject. I think the advantages by the proposal which I have made are obvious and many, as well as of the highest importance.

21   For first, as I have already observed, it would greatly lessen the number of Papists, with whom we are yearly overrun, being the principal breeders of the nation as well as our most dangerous enemies; and who stay at home on purpose

to deliver the kingdom to the Pretender, hoping to take their advantage by the absence of so many good Protestants, who have chosen rather to leave their country than to stay at home and pay tithes against their conscience to an Episcopal curate.

22 Secondly, the poorer tenants will have something valuable of their own, which by law may be made liable to distress, and help to pay their landlord's rent, their corn and cattle being already seized and money a thing unknown.

23 Thirdly, whereas the maintenance of an hundred thousand children, from two years old and upwards, cannot be computed at less than ten shillings a piece per annum, the nation's stock will be thereby increased fifty thousand pounds per annum, besides the profit of a new dish introduced to the tables of all gentlemen of fortune in the kingdom who have any refinement in taste. And the money will circulate among ourselves, the goods being entirely of our own growth and manufacture.

24 Fourthly, the constant breeders, besides the gain of eight shillings sterling per annum by the sale of their children, will be rid of the charge of maintaining them after the first year.

25 Fifthly, the food would likewise bring great custom to taverns, where the vintners will certainly be so prudent as to procure the best receipts for dressing it to perfection, and consequently have their houses frequented by all the fine gentlemen, who justly value themselves upon their knowledge in good eating; and a skillful cook, who understands how to oblige his guests, will contrive to make it as expensive as they please.

26 Sixthly, this would be a great inducement to marriage, which all wise nations have either encouraged by rewards or enforced by laws and penalties. It would increase the care and tenderness of mothers toward their children, when they were sure of a settlement for life to the poor babes, provided in some sort by the public, to their annual profit instead of expense. We should see an honest emulation among the married women, which of them could bring the fattest child to the market. Men would become as fond of their wives during the time of their pregnancy as they are now of their mares in foal, their cows in calf, or sows when they are ready to farrow; nor offer to beat or kick them (as is too frequent a practice) for fear of a miscarriage.

27 Many other advantages might be enumerated. For instance, the addition of some thousand carcasses in our exportation of barreled beef, the propagation of swine's flesh, and improvement in the art of making good bacon, so much wanted among us by the great destruction of pigs, too frequent at our tables, which are no way comparable in taste or magnificence to a well-grown, fat yearling child, which roasted whole will make a considerable figure at a lord mayor's feast or any other public entertainment. But this and many others I omit, being studious of brevity.

28 Supposing that one thousand families in this city would be constant customers for infants' flesh, besides others who might have it at merry meetings, particularly weddings and christenings, I compute that Dublin would take off annually about twenty thousand carcasses, and the rest of the kingdom (where probably they will be sold somewhat cheaper) the remaining eighty thousand.

29   I can think of no one objection that will possibly be raised against this proposal, unless it should be urged that the number of people will be thereby much lessened in the kingdom. This I freely own, and it was indeed one principal design in offering it to the world. I desire the reader will observe, that I calculate my remedy for this one individual kingdom of Ireland and for no other that ever was, is, or I think ever can be upon earth. Therefore let no man talk to me of other expedients: of taxing our absentees at five shillings a pound: of using neither clothes nor household furniture except what is of our own growth and manufacture: of utterly rejecting the materials and instruments that promote foreign luxury: of curing the expensiveness of pride, vanity, idleness, and gaming in our women: of introducing a vein of parsimony, prudence, and temperance: of learning to love our country, in the want of which we differ even from Laplanders and the inhabitants of Topinamboo: of quitting our animosities and factions, nor acting any longer like the Jews, who were murdering one another at the very moment their city was taken: of being a little cautious not to sell our country and conscience for nothing: of teaching landlords to have at least one degree of mercy toward their tenants: lastly, of putting a spirit of honesty, industry, and skill into our shopkeepers; who, if a resolution could be now taken to buy only our native goods, would immediately unite to cheat and exact upon us in the price, the measure and the goodness, nor could ever yet be brought to make one fair proposal of just dealing, though often and earnestly invited to it.

30   Therefore I repeat, let no man talk to me of these and the like expedients, till he hath at least some glimpse of hope that there will ever be some hearty and sincere attempt to put them in practice.

31   But as to myself, having been wearied out for many years with offering vain, idle, visionary thoughts, and at length utterly despairing of success, I fortunately fell upon this proposal, which, as it is wholly new, so it hath something solid and real, of no expense and little trouble, full in our own power, and whereby we can incur no danger in disobliging England. For this kind of commodity will not bear exportation, the flesh being of too tender a consistence to admit a long continuance in salt, although perhaps I could name a country which would be glad to eat up our whole nation without it.

32   After all, I am not so violently bent upon my own opinion as to reject any offer proposed by wise men, which shall be found equally innocent, cheap, easy, and effectual. But before something of that kind shall be advanced in contradiction to my scheme, and offering a better, I desire the author or authors will be pleased maturely to consider two points. First, as things now stand, how they will be able to find food and raiment for an hundred thousand useless mouths and backs. And secondly, there being a round million of creatures in human figure throughout this kingdom, whose sole subsistence put into a common stock would leave them in debt two millions of pounds sterling, adding those who are beggars by profession to the bulk of farmers, cottagers, and labourers, with their wives and children who are beggars in effect; I desire those politicians who dislike my overture, and may perhaps be so bold to attempt an answer, that they will first ask the parents of these mortals whether they would not at this day think it a great happiness to have been sold for food at a year old in the manner I prescribe, and thereby have avoided such a perpetual scene of misfortunes as they have since gone through by the oppression of landlords, the impossibility of paying rent without money or trade, the want of common sustenance, with neither house nor clothes to cover them from the inclemencies of the weather, and the most inevitable prospect of entailing the like or greater miseries upon their breed forever.

33   I profess, in the sincerity of my heart, that I have not the least personal interest in endeavouring to promote this necessary work, having no other motive than the public good of my country, by advancing our trade, providing for infants, relieving the poor, and giving some pleasure to the rich. I have no children by which I can propose to get a single penny; the youngest being nine years old, and my wife past childbearing.

Hand Over Hand

Margaret Visser

1   The human body is less symmetrical than it looks. Internally, our organs are not divided neatly down the middle—the heart, for example, being both inclined and on the left—and externally our hands are almost invariably quite unequal, although they apparently mirror each other. About ninety per cent of people are right-handed; the other ten per cent have a strong preference for the left. This is one of our differences from animals, among whom fifty per cent prefer the right front leg, fifty per cent prefer the left, and ambidextrous behaviour is far more common than in human beings.

2   Body images are among the most powerful metaphors we have; "culture" seizes upon the body and uses it to express moral ideas, social structures, prejudices, preferences, fears, and ideals. Often the metaphor squeezes the facts into its own mould: the "heart" of anything is its middle, even though our hearts are definitely off-centre. We have always emphasized the difference in efficiency between our two hands; we have then meditated on the weakness of the left, and used it to confirm our worst suspicions.

3   The right hand, in almost every language and culture on earth, means permanence, reliability ("a right-hand man"), power, truth, and rectitude. Dexterity, acceptability, immediacy, and correctness are "right-handed" in English; "sinister" means "left," a word that itself derives from Anglo-Saxon *lyft*: "weak" or "worthless." *Droit* in French is "straight" and also "just," while someone *gauche* ("gawky" in English) is maladroit. An Italian who is *mancino* is left-handed—or treacherous. In many cultures dealings with the dead are carried out with the left hand, since its connotations are with the dark, the inept, the polluted, the obstinately unknowable. Leftness is commonly used to express whatever is outside the official life of the group.

4   Women have tended everywhere to be classified as "left." The feeling behind this is that they are irrational, lower, dark, marginal, fluid, cold, deceitful, and generally sinister. Men (on the other hand) are high, dry, straightforward, lucid, bright—and right.

5   On the continent of Europe, couples when marrying give each other rings, a custom that is spreading as equality strengthens between the sexes. Among post-Reformation Anglo-Saxons, only the woman has traditionally worn the ring, on the fourth finger of the left or "female" hand. The "ring" or "gold" finger was believed to have a direct arterial connection with the left-leaning, passionate, irrational, but—one hoped—faithful heart.

6   Left-handed people have always been pressured by the majority to conform. Even when not forced by anxious parents and misguided educators to use the less capable hand, they have had for example to shake hands with the right because other people do it, or to use tools constructed for right-handers. More men than women are in fact left-handed; in the ancient world they had worse difficulties than we, because it mattered desperately in battle that your shield arm covered your heart, while the other did the fighting.

7   In many societies where eating is done with the hands, the left hand is disqualified as profane, and kept for polluting and unpleasant tasks deemed beneath the dignity of the right. Roman diners put left hands out of commission by leaning on their left elbows as they reclined at meals, and eating with the right; a left-hander attempting to use his more capable hand would find himself lying down the wrong way round.

8   Modern science has shown us that the right hand has usually been governed by the *left* side of the brain all along—and vice versa. Speech, even in most left-handers, is a function mainly of the left brain. The right half of the brain has become the subject recently of much attention and speculation: it is as large, as complex, as the left half, but we are far less certain what it does, apart from its evident governance over perceptions of space, including the ability to recognize faces.

9   "Left" and "right" have lost some of their force as metaphors, as the strength ebbs from the prejudice against women which they used to express. But left- and right-handedness have acquired a powerful new fascination: they are now recognized as clues, the full significance of which remains mysterious, to the workings of the human brain.

Copyright Acknowledgments

Permission to reprint copyrighted material is gratefully acknowledged. Information that will enable the publisher to rectify any error or omission will be welcome.

The authors are grateful to the following students for permission to reprint their essays: Cecile Dean ("Math Anxiety: The Real Social Disease"), Jeff Haas ("The Common Stone"), Stuart Johns ("How to Use Less Communication"), Marcelo Olenewa ("Effective Driving"), Mayra Perea ("Canadian and American: Is There a Difference?"), and Sandra Stewart ("*Aladdin* and *Beauty and the Beast*").

John Allemang. "Bedtime Stories," from *The Globe and Mail*, 7 February 1991. Reprinted by permission.

Gary Anderson. "Jack," from *The Third Macmillan Anthology* (1990). Macmillan Publishing Canada.

Maya Angelou. "The Fight," from *I Know Why the Caged Bird Sings,* by Maya Angelou. Copyright © 1969 and renewed 1997 by Maya Angelou. Reprinted by permission of Random House, Inc.

Charlie Angus. "Deliberate Strangers," originally published in *Compass.* Reprinted by permission of the author.

Gerald Astor. "What Your Body Language Says about You," from *Seventeen®️ Magazine,* 1981. Reprinted by permission of the author.

Margaret Atwood. "The Great Communicator," from *The Globe and Mail*, 24 January 1991, p. C1. Reprinted by permission.

Russell Baker. "How to Punctuate," from *The Power of the Printed Word* series. Reprinted by permission of International Paper. "The Plot against People," from *The New York Times*, 18 June 1968. Copyright © 1968 by The New York Times Company. Reprinted by permission.

H.J. Barrie. "In the Market for a Mate? Shop Around," from *The Globe and Mail*, 21 March 1994. Reprinted by permission of the author.

Shauna Singh Baldwin. "Jassie," from *English Lessons and Other Stories* by Shauna Singh Baldwin. Copyright © Shauna Singh Baldwin, 1996. Reprinted by permission of Goose Lane Editions.

Neil Bissoondath. "I'm Not a Racist But ...," from *Between Worlds,* by Neil Bissoondath. Copyright © 1989 by Neil Bissoondath. Reprinted with the permission of the author.

Arthur Black. "Lingophobia ... Anxiety of Choice," from *The Globe and Mail.* Reprinted by permission of the author.

Nicola Bleasby. "How Can You Mend a Broken Heart?" from *The Globe and Mail,* 14 February 1996. Reprinted by permission of the author.

Rachel Carson. "A Fable for Tomorrow," from *Silent Spring,* by Rachel Carson. Copyright © 1962 by Rachel L. Carson, renewed 1990 by Roger Christie. Reprinted by permission of Houghton Mifflin Co. All rights reserved.

Austin Clarke. "A Stranger in a Strange Land," from *The Globe and Mail*, 15 August 1990. Reprinted by permission of the author.

Michael Cobden. "Why Can't a Man Be More Like a Woman?" from *The Globe and Mail,* 22 November 1996. Reprinted by permission of the author.

Pat Deiter-McArthur. From "Saskatchewan's Indian People—Five Generations," from *Writing the Circle: Native Women of Western Canada.* Edmonton: NeWest Press, 1990.

Michael Dorris. "The Minnie Mouse Kitchen," from *Parents* Magazine, December 1990. Copyright © 1990 Gruner + Jahr USA Publishing. Reprinted by permission.

Joseph Epstein. "The Virtues of Ambition," from *Ambition: The Secret Passion,* by Joseph Epstein. Copyright © 1980 by Joseph Epstein. Reprinted by permission of Georges Borchardt, Inc., for the author.

Susan Estrich. "Separate is Better," from *The New York Times Magazine,* 22 May 1994. Copyright © 1994 by The New York Times Company. Reprinted by permission.

Judith Finlayson. "Math's Multiple Choices," from *Homemaker's Magazine,* May 1994. Reprinted by permission of the author.

Northrop Frye. "Don't You Think It's Time to Start Thinking?" from *The Toronto Star,* 25 January 1986. Reprinted by permission of the Estate of Northrop Frye.

George Galt. "Creative Non-Fiction," from *Event* 25(3), Winter 1996/97. Reprinted by permission of the author.

Catherine George. "Curtain Up," from *The Toronto Star,* 7 September 1991. Reprinted with permission—The Toronto Star Syndicate.

David Ginsburg. "Smoking is Good for My Business," from *The Globe and Mail.* Reprinted by permission of the author.

Steven Heighton. "Magi," from *Flight Paths of the Emperor* (1992). Reprinted by permission of The Porcupine's Quill Press.

Susan Jacoby. "When Bright Girls Decide That Math Is 'A Waste of Time.'" Copyright © 1983 by Susan Jacoby. Reprinted by permission of Georges Borchardt, Inc., for the author.

Terry E. Johnson. "Slang: Language That's Out of Date," from *The Toronto Star,* 23 March 1985. Reprinted with permission of Knight-Ridder/Tribune Information Services.

John Kettle. "Back to the Land? No Way—Big Cities Are Here to Stay," originally published in the "Trends" segment of Fifth Column section, *The Globe and Mail,* 16 September 1992. Reprinted by permission of the author.

Stephen King. "The Man Who Loved Flowers," from *Night Shift,* by Stephen King. Copyright © 1976, 1977, 1978 by Stephen King. Used by permission of Doubleday, a division of Bantam Doubleday Dell Publishing Group, Inc.

Mark Kingwell. "Babes in Toyland," from *Saturday Night,* February 1997. Reprinted by permission of the author.

Michele Landsberg. "Let's Just Shamble Back to the Cave for Some Bone Gnawing," from *The Globe and Mail,* 11 April 1987. Reprinted by permission.

Index

To the owner of this book

We hope that you have enjoyed *Reading Writing,* Second Edition, and we would like to know as much about your experiences with this text as you would care to offer. Only through your comments and those of others can we learn how to make this a better text for future readers.

School _____ Your instructor's name _____

Course _____ Was the text required? _____ Recommended? _____

1. What did you like the most about *Reading Writing?*

_____

_____

_____

2. How useful was this text for your course?

_____

_____

_____

3. Do you have any recommendations for ways to improve the next edition of this text?

_____

_____

_____

4. In the space below or in a separate letter, please write any other comments you have about the book. (For example, please feel free to comment on reading level, writing style, terminology, design features, and learning aids.)

_____

_____

_____

Optional

Your name _____ Date _____

May ITP Nelson quote you, either in promotion for *Reading Writing* or in future publishing ventures?

Yes _____ No _____

Thanks!

You can also send your comments to us via e-mail at
college_arts_hum@nelson.com

MAIL ✈ POSTE
Canada Post Corporation
Société canadienne des postes

Postage paid   Port payé
if mailed in Canada si posté au Canada
Business Reply   Réponse d'affaires

0066102399   01

Nelson

0066102399-M1K5G4-BR01

ITP NELSON
MARKET AND PRODUCT DEVELOPMENT
PO BOX 60225 STN BRM B
TORONTO ON M7Y 2H1